GURDJIEFF: THE KEY CONCEPTS

This unique book offers clear definitions of Gurdjieff's teaching terms, placing him within the political, geographical and cultural context of his time. Entries look at diverse aspects of his work, including:

- possible sources in religious, Theosophical, occult, esoteric and literary traditions
- the integral relationships between different aspects of the teaching
- its internal contradictions and subversive aspects
- the derivation of Gurdjieff's cosmological laws and enneagrams
- the receptive form of New Work teaching introduced by Jeanne de Salzmann

An accessible and fully cross-referenced A–Z guidebook, this is an invaluable companion for both the newcomer and those more versed in Gurdjieff's thought and teachings.

Sophia Wellbeloved is the author of *Gurdjieff, Astrology and Beelzebub's Tales* and is a former member of the London Gurdjieff Society.

ROUTLEDGE KEY GUIDES

Routledge Key Guides are accessible, informative and lucid handbooks, which define and discuss the central concepts, thinkers and debates in a broad range of academic disciplines. All are written by noted experts in their respective subjects. Clear, concise exposition of complex and stimulating issues and ideas make *Routledge Key Guides* the ultimate reference resources for students, teachers, researchers and the interested lay person.

GURDJIEFF

The Key Concepts

Sophia Wellbeloved

Routledge
Taylor & Francis Group

LONDON AND NEW YORK

For David Head

First published 2003
by Routledge
11 New Fetter Lane, London EC4P 4EE

Simultaneously published in the USA and Canada
by Routledge
29 West 35th Street, New York, NY 10001

Routledge is an imprint of the Taylor & Francis Group

© 2003 Sophia Wellbeloved

The right of Sophia Wellbeloved to be identified as the Author of this Work has been
asserted by her in accordance with the Copyright, Designs and Patents Act 1988

Typeset in Times by Taylor & Francis Books Ltd
Printed and bound in Great Britain by St Edmundsbury Press, Bury St Edmunds,
Suffolk

British Library Cataloguing in Publication Data
A catalogue record for this book is available from the British Library

Library of Congress Cataloging in Publication Data
A catalog record for this book has been requested

ISBN 0–415–24897–3 (hbk)
ISBN 0–415–24898–1 (pbk)

CONTENTS

ACKNOWLEDGEMENTS

I offer grateful thanks to all those who have helped me so generously towards the completion of this text: to Professor Paul Beekman Taylor of Geneva University for his kindness in writing the Foreword and giving me access to his knowledge and understanding of matters Gurdjieffian; to David Head for his discernment as editor and proofreader; to Jeremy Cranswick for suggestions as to further reading; to Professor Charles Burnett of the Warburg Institute and Chris Thompson for their interest in the text; to Ed Coffield and David Copland for a major contribution in computer and technical help. I am grateful for information and contributions towards bibliographical notes (Appendix 1) from Marlena O'Hagan Buzzell, Professor Roger Friedland of the University of California, Santa Barbara, and Harold Zellman.

For their moral, financial and intellectual support and encouragement I am most grateful to Machiko Kitamura, Seymour Ginsburg and Dorothy Usiskin, Sibylle Moller, Balloo and David Scholfield, Ann Seymour, Chris Thompson, Dr Katerina Korinlaki, John Robert Colombo, Dr Irene Steinbrecher, Dr Daren Kemp, Michael Dorey, the Anglican community of St James Piccadilly, and those who attended the All & Everything Conferences from 1996–2000, especially Pat Bennett, Harry Bennett, Dr Keith Buzzell, Marlena O'Hagen Buzzell, Bonnie Phillips and John Scullion. From 1962–75 I was a member of the Gurdjieff Society in London and am grateful to all those who taught and studied there. I thank the British Library team in Humanities Two for being consistently kind and helpful. The responsibility for errors remains mine.

I would like to offer thanks to the following for permission to quote from works: to Triangle for Gurdjieff's writings and to Triangle and William Patrick Patterson for the material from Gurdjieff's group meetings in *Voices in the Dark* and *Ladies of the Rope*; to James Moore for *Gurdjieff: The Anatomy of a Myth* and other writings; to Abintra for *Gurdjieff, Astrology and Beelzebub's Tales*; to Paul Beekman Taylor for

Shadows of Heaven: Gurdjieff and Toomer and *Gurdjieff and Orage: Brothers in Elysium*; to Adam Nott for C.S. Nott's *Teachings of Gurdjieff* and *Journey Through This World*; and to George Bennett for J.G. Bennett's writings.

ABBREVIATIONS

G.I. Gurdjieff

Herald
> *The Herald of Coming Good*. Edmunds, WA: Sure Fire Press, 1988; reprint 1st pub., Paris: privately published, 1933.

Tales
> *An Objectively Impartial Criticism of the Life of Man or Beelzebub's Tales to His Grandson*. London: Routledge & Kegan Paul, 1950.

Meetings
> *Meetings with Remarkable Men*. Trans. A. R. Orage, London: Picador, 1978; 1st pub., London: Routledge & Kegan Paul, 1963.

Life
> *Life is Real Only Then, When 'I Am'*. London: Viking Arkana, 1991; 1st pub., New York: Duton for Triangle Editions, 1975.

Views
> *Views from the Real World: Early Talks of Gurdjieff*. London: Routledge & Kegan Paul, 1976; 1st pub., 1973.

C.S. Nott

Journey
> *Journey Through This World*. London: Routledge & Kegan Paul, 1969.

Teachings
> *Teachings of Gurdjieff: A Pupil's Journal*. London: Arkana, 1990.

P.D. Ouspensky

Search
> *In Search of the Miraculous: Fragments of an Unknown Teaching*. London: Arkana, 1987; 1st pub., 1949.

William Patrick Patterson

Voices
> *Voices in the Dark*. Fairfax: Arete Communications, 2000.

LIST OF CONCEPTS

bodies
brains
breath/breathing
buffers
'C' influences *see* INFLUENCES
'carbon'
carriage, horse, driver and master
centres
centre of gravity
chief feature
circles of humanity
civilisation
conscience
conscious circle of humanity
conscious labour and intentional/voluntary suffering
conscious shock
consciousness
considering
corns
cosmology
cosmoses
crystallisation
dances/dancing
daydreaming
death/rebirth
denying force *see* FORCES; LAW OF THREE
deputy steward *see* 'I'/IDENTITY; STEWARD/DEPUTY STEWARD
dervishes *see* DANCE; MUSIC; SUFI/SUFISM
descending octave *see* LAW OF OCTAVES
destruction
Diagram of Everything Living *see* LAW OF RECIPROCAL MAINTENANCE/
RECIPROCAL FEEDING
difficulties
dimensions
disappointment
dog
doing
dreams
drugs *see* NARCOTICS
duty/striving
education
egoism/egoist

elements
emanations
emotional centre/emotions; feelings
energy
enneagram
entity
escape
esoteric/esotericism
essence
eternal, the *see* TIME/THE ETERNAL
evil *see* GOOD AND EVIL
evolution/involution
exercises
experiments
factory *see* THREE-STOREY FACTORY/DIGESTION OF THREE FOODS
faith
Fall
false personality *see* PERSONALITY
fasts/fasting
fate
fear
food diagram *see* THREE-STOREY FACTORY/DIGESTION OF THREE
FOODS
food/eating
forces
formatory apparatus
Foundations *see* APPENDIX 2
Fourth Way *see* WAYS/FOURTH WAY
friction
gender
Gnosticism
good and evil
good householder *see* OBYVATEL
grace
groups
group meetings during World War II (1940–4)
Gurdjieff Society, The *see* APPENDIX 2
habit
Hanbledzoin; Sacred-Hanbledzoin *see* GRACE; MAGNETISM/ANIMAL
MAGNETISM
Hasnamuss
harmony/harmonious/harmonic

head
Herald of Coming Good
Hermeticism
hope
horse, carriage and driver *see* CARRIAGE, HORSE, DRIVER AND MASTER
humanity
humour
'hydrogen'
hydrogens, table of
hypnosis/hypnotism
'I am' *see* EXERCISES; 'I'/IDENTITY
ideal
'I'/identity
identification
idiotism, toasts of the idiots *see* TOAST OF/TO THE IDIOTS, IDIOTISM
imagination
immortality *see* BODIES; MORTALITY
impressions
influences
initiates/initiation
inner animal
inner/internal considering *see* CONSIDERING
instinctive centre *see* MOVING/INSTINCTIVE CENTRE
Institutes
intellectual/thinking centre; intelligence
intentional suffering *see* CONSCIENCE; SUFFERING/PLEASURE
intervals
involution *see* EVOLUTION/INVOLUTION
justice
knowledge
kundabuffer
kundalini
language
Law of Accident
Law of Duality/Two
Law of Octaves
Law of Reciprocal Maintenance/Reciprocal Feeding
Law of Seven
Law of Solioonensius
Law of Three
Laws: An overview
legomonism

secrecy/silence
Seekers of/after Truth
self-observation
self-remembering
sensation/sensing
Seven, Law of *see* LAW OF SEVEN
sex
sex centre
shocks
sin
sincerity
sitting *see* NEW WORK TERMINOLOGY
slavery/slaves
sleep
'sly' man
Solioonensius, Law of *see* LAW OF SOLIOONENSIUS
soul
stairway
state *see* CONSCIOUSNESS
step diagram *see* LAW OF RECIPROCAL MAINTENANCE/RECIPROCAL
FEEDING
steward/deputy steward
stop exercise
strivings
Struggle of the Magicians
subconscious
suffering/pleasure
Sufi/Sufism
Sun Absolute, the
Suns, All *see* RAY OF CREATION
super-effort
symbols/symbolism
System/the System
table of hydrogens *see* HYDROGENS, TABLE OF
talking
teacher
telepathy
terror of the situation, the
theory/practice
Theosophical addition
Theosophy
thinking/thoughts

ILLUSTRATIONS

FOREWORD

Gurdjieff's *All and Everything* has been recognised as one of the most influential works written, and yet it remains agonisingly difficult to read. More than one Gurdjieff instructor has told pupils that the work is to be 'appreciated', not analysed. This is not the intent of Gurdjieff, who prepared instructors 'to put into the lives of people what I had already learned' (*Life*, p.28). The learning Gurdjieff displays, Well-beloved argues appropriately, is not set out in a systematic exposition along philosophical lines, but in the form of a story. He resolved to write in order that the authority for his teaching, his vast learning 'might be accessible to the understanding of everyone' (*Life*, p.5). *Gurdjieff: The Key Concepts* does just this by its careful scan of all of Gurdjieff's writings, syntheses of his 'system' by others, and records of his talks and lectures. This text will prove very soon to be of inestimable value to both the first-time reader of Gurdjieff and the experienced pupil who is teaching, as well as those who would study the breadth and complexity of Fourth Way thought.

For Gurdjieff the purpose of art in general and his own books in particular is to preserve and transmit knowledge that has been forgotten, obscured or ignored. To his pupils he announced that the stories he tells are invaluable, but pupils must learn to read and understand them. Understanding of his enigmatic and deceptive writings can come only from careful guidance, from 'alarm clocks', as he was wont to call teachers dedicated to waking others to their personal essence, their real 'I'. Gurdjieff's works define and exemplify 'objective' art that conveys meaning in proportion to the capacity of his audience to understand, rather than transmitting the subjective views of its author. Objective art is reflected in all three major works, or 'series', although each has its own distinct style. The first, *Beelzebub's Tales to His Grandson*, is written in a dense style, replete with neologisms and arcane lore distant from modern literary forms. The story is in the genre of science fiction, explaining the laws governing the anatomy and physiology of the universe, spanning the history and character of the civilisations of the earth in terms that challenge stereotypical cultural conceptions. The second, *Meetings with Remarkable Men*, a fictionalised account of Gurdjieff's formative years, displays the prose clarity of an autobiographical narrative as it characterises the search for esoteric lore so typical to late nineteenth-century intellectuals. The third, *Life is Real Only Then, When 'I Am'*, considered the most esoteric work in the trilogy, situates its story in New York City between 6 November 1934 and 10 April 1935 to report on a number of *kairoi* (propitious moments for action) in Gurdjieff's life.

These 'Three Series' display narrative surfaces that cover deep meaning, for Gurdjieff expressed truth best, as he said, in the form of a 'lie'. Deep thoughts lie beneath the surface of words (*Life*, pp.122–3). His stories, as Wellbeloved points out in her Introduction, are threads of a myth and – like the Greek epics of Homer, Hesiod's genealogies of the gods and the Babylonian epic of Gilgamesh that Gurdjieff as a young boy heard his father sing – are encyclopedic. They are not to be taken literally, she warns, for his symbols have no fixed meanings. Nonetheless, there has been little detailed or comprehensive explication of Gurdjieff's myths, though his early teaching in Russia was elaborated in systematic form by P.D. Ouspensky. Until now there has been no handy map to guide readers through the maze of Gurdjieffian writing. A.R. Orage, one of the finest critical minds of the twentieth century, called Gurdjieff's myth of World Creation and World Maintenance superior to the thousand books he had read on philosophy. He regretted, however, that he had not yet a key to decipher its deep structure of sense.

Sophia Wellbeloved has provided here a tool for delving beneath Gurdjieff's veil of words. Her identification and definition of crucial concepts in Gurdjieff's writings and teaching constitute a commentary on his work for both the specialised reader and the general public, and an invitation to further scholarly investigation. Her references to the writings of others that touch upon his key concepts invite further reading in the growing corpus of biographical and critical studies of Gurdjieff. Her cross-referencing brings into relief Gurdjieff's conceptual genius, and shows her reader that, despite his scientific and artistic complexity, he interlaces expressions of his ideas so that they shape an entire cosmology and cosmogony. As Plato and his philosophical heirs pointed out, the same laws that govern the universe govern the structure and function of human beings and their lives.

Wellbeloved's explanations of technical terms like intentional suffering, formatory apparatus, chief feature, centre of gravity, essence and personality will help readers to understand Gurdjieff's 'system' of thought. Her exposition of Gurdjieff's views on time, space, love, dreams, hypnosis, food, music, art, energy, war and justice brings into relief Gurdjieff's vast learning, as well as his profound concern and hope for humanity. In all, this is a work that honours Gurdjieff's gift to the moral and spiritual welfare of mankind.

Paul Beekman Taylor

INTRODUCTION

One day in Paris, during World War II, Gurdjieff showed some of his pupils an engraving of seven Oriental dancers with head-dresses 'like gigantic spherical hats surmounted by antennas'. They are striking tambourines and blowing pipes, under the direction of a man who holds a sort of pennant. Gurdjieff asks the pupils what they think it represents and, agreeing with the suggestion that these may be Tibetan dancers, tells them the following story.

He explains that the dancers make the most beautiful celestial music, not with instruments, but through vibrations that result from the extreme precision of their outer and inner movements. When a pupil points out that in the engraving the dancers do have instruments, Gurdjieff says 'that helps' but that they don't use the instruments, it is the totality of their interior experience that forms the music. This is gathered in their head-dresses and transmitted through the antennae to the 'pennant' held by their leader, and from there sent to a similar 'pennant' in the valley below. There a divine music resounds to the astonishment of all who hear it.

Gurdjieff knows about this because the music is part of an initiation ceremony that he himself had received. He had been stupefied, like a madman, wondering how the music had been made when there was no-one to make it and nothing to be seen but mountains and snow. Later he learned that the 'pennants' were a kind of radio, yet his initiation had taken place thirty-five years earlier, fifteen years before the invention of radio.

He likens the skill and dedication of these Tibetan dancers to the ones he has written about in *Meetings with Remarkable Men* and connects both of them with his own pupils' work in the 'sacred dancing' he is teaching them. He says that if the Tibetan dancers are not precise in their movements their music will be cacophonous and, although his pupils are not going to make music, yet they too must be exact in what they do and have a real feeling of 'I am', for which he has just given them one of seven exercises. Gurdjieff ends this story by wondering aloud about the pupil making notes,

> and our Mr District Attorney writes and writes. How can he understand all this when I myself do not very well understand all I have been saying?

(Voices: 166–8)

I have begun with this story because it shows us a side of Gurdjieff that may seem absent in the drier definition of terms that follows. Gurdjieff's question, which provokes uncertainty about his story, its veracity or purpose, may act, if we allow it, to soften and open the apparent rigidities and certainties of his cosmological and psychological teachings. Gurdjieff told Taylor (1998: 183): 'Story is breath, life. Without story man have no self'.

Gurdjieff's stories, those he told about himself, about humanity's past, present and future, and those told about him by his pupils and others, all these are threads of the myth that is still being woven about him, and I have tried to bear this in mind while spinning my own thread. In what follows we will look first at a brief outline of Gurdjieff's life in relation to the changing forms of his teaching and at some of the cultural contexts that influenced these changes; second, we will look at the sources for the definition of terms and the way the entries are structured, together with a note on the contents of the bibliography.

Gurdjieff, life and teaching

George Ivanovitch Gurdjieff (1866?–1949) was born on the borders of Russia and Armenia and travelled widely in the Middle and Far East. When he returned to Russia in c.1911, he taught that people are 'asleep', have no central 'I' and function mechanically. When he died he 'left behind him a school embodying a specific methodology for the development of consciousness' that, according to Gurdjieff, requires 'a harmonious blending of the distinctive energies of mind, feeling, and body' (de Salzmann 1987: vol.6, pp.139–40). These teachings, which have taken practical and theoretical, oral and written forms, have had an influence on twentieth-century thinking about consciousness in the fields of new religious movements and therapies, popular psychology and the arts: music, theatre, dance and literature (Wellbeloved 2001a: 1–2).

Gurdjieff's teaching, known as 'the Work', began to be modified during his lifetime, first by Gurdjieff himself in response to the needs of the times, and also by the pupils who taught his ideas and brought their own emphasis and abilities to the teaching. After Gurdjieff's death his pupils were led by his long-term pupil and successor Jeanne de Salzmann. In the mid- to late 1960s she instituted changes in Work practice that served to allow pupils, who no longer experienced Gurdjieff's charismatic presence, to be receptive to a helping energy analogous to grace. Short biographical notes on Gurdjieff's principal pupils are given in Appendix 1.

Appendix 2 lists the Foundations, some of which were established by Gurdjieff and are now led by his pupils. It gives brief details of the principal groups that have assimilated Gurdjieff's teaching into new forms, including that of the enneagram of personality.

The facts of Gurdjieff's early life are known only from his own mythologised autobiographical writings. He grew up in Kars, an area that suffered from the many social, economic and political changes brought about by the successive overthrow of ruling powers. Due to these circumstances Gurdjieff experienced a multiplicity of languages, religions and political ideologies. It may be that the absence of any sense of a permanent, unchanging identity, both in himself and in his surroundings, is reflected in one of the basic tenets of his teaching: that man has no central or permanent 'I', that he is formed of a multiplicity of small, ever-changing 'I's, each of whom has no relation to or contact with the others. During Gurdjieff's childhood, Kars was (and still is today) a centre for bardic poets, known as Ashokhs, and there was a strong tradition of oral story-telling in Gurdjieff's childhood. Gurdjieff accompanied his Ashokh father to song contests, and this influence can be found in the subject matter and in the form and structure of Gurdjieff's writings. The process that Gurdjieff used to write his books, which included reading chapters aloud to groups, also reflects something of the tradition of the Turkic epic story-teller, who both responds to his listeners and demands active listening from them.

Gurdjieff's wanderings in the Near and Far East, from around 1885 until 1911, are in accord with contemporary interests in archeological and anthropological explorations of ancient cultures. Interest in the East arose not only from the empire-building aspirations of both Russia and Britain, but also from the occult revival of the late nineteenth and early twentieth centuries. The subject matter of Gurdjieff's autobiographical writings reflects these interests.

The mythology of his early life-story echoes that of Helena Blavatsky, founder of Theosophy, and although he repudiated her teaching Gurdjieff was strongly influenced by Theosophy. His cosmological teachings are derived from and/or given in a form compatible with

Theosophical concepts, and he employed some Theosophical terminology. The aims that Gurdjieff gives for his own 'Three Series' of
books, *All and Everything*, echo Blavatsky's aims for her own writings.
Like Blavatsky Gurdjieff was an anti-Enlightenment, anti-establishment
synthesiser of teachings from a variety of occult and traditional sources,
and like her he seemed to court the reputation of charlatan guru. There
is, however, a profound difference between the teachings in that, while
Blavatsky included some practical teaching, Gurdjieff's teaching is
practical in essence.

Throughout his life Gurdjieff changed the form and focus of his
teaching in order to correspond with contemporary interests. Occult
studies and practice as a hypnotist in Tashkent, from around 1905,
prepared Gurdjieff well for his arrival in pre-Revolutionary Russia,
where Moscow and St Petersburg were centres of the occult revival.
Gurdjieff arrived in Russia in about 1912, and began to form and
teach his first groups of pupils in these cities. He gave his teaching in
the form of an occult-based cosmology and from this time onwards
there are pupil records of his life and teaching.

P.D. Ouspensky, who was one of Gurdjieff's early pupils, sets out an
account of the teaching he received in Russia. First published in 1949,
In Search of the Miraculous: Fragments of an Unknown Teaching is generally
regarded as the most comprehensive outline of Gurdjieff's teaching
and often forms the basis from which Gurdjieff and his teaching are
understood. However, it is worth bearing in mind that Ouspensky
writes only about the first seven years of Gurdjieff's teaching (that is,
until 1922), while Gurdjieff continued to teach for another twenty-
seven years.

Ouspensky's text provides a thorough and wonderfully comprehensive expression of Gurdjieff's ideas, yet Ouspensky's approach to
the Work is more intellectual and rigid than Gurdjieff's. For example,
Ouspensky writes of the precise classification afforded by Gurdjieff's
system of ideas: 'everything anomalous, unexpected, and accidental
disappeared, and an immense and strictly thought-out plan of the
universe began to make its appearance' (*Search*: 140). However, a close
reading of Ouspensky's text reveals that Gurdjieff uses additional
clauses, 'generally speaking', 'in most cases', that serve to subvert the
precision of his explanations and definitions.

There are anomalies in Gurdjieff's ideas, which Ouspensky either
did not see or did not wish to see. For example, Gurdjieff taught that
an exact language is necessary for the transmission of an exact
knowledge, but he also tells his pupils not to take what he says literally
and not to regard symbols as fixed in meaning. Thus his pupils had to

make some interpretation of what he was saying. Overall, the reader of Ouspensky's writings must question his own ability to understand what he reads because, first, if he accepts Gurdjieff's premise that man is asleep, then he himself is asleep and incapable of judging, and, second, at every step of the way described, a man may lose his way, may not find the help of a teacher and school, may fall into the hands of a wrong school, or may already be so damaged that his machine cannot be repaired.

Gurdjieff left Russia because of the Revolution and the civil war that followed, finding his way through the Caucasus to Constantinople with a group of pupils and members of his own family. He took advantage of the war conditions to introduce pupils to other aspects of his Work, including manual labour and sustained physical efforts.

In 1919 Gurdjieff opened a prototype Institute for the Harmonious Development of Man at Tiflis, where he met the artist Alexandre and his wife Jeanne [de] Salzmann (b.1889), a teacher of Eurythmics. Her pupils gave the first performance of Gurdjieff's sacred dances; she was to become his successor and lead the Gurdjieff Foundations from 1949 until her death in 1990.

Gurdjieff settled in France in 1922 in Fontainbleau-sur-Avon, some forty miles from Paris, where he established his Institute for the Harmonious Development of Man. The most important source for the definition of the terms of Gurdjieff's teaching during his travels and his time at the Institute is *Views from the Real World: Early Talks of Gurdjieff*, published in 1976. These talks, which were written down by pupils, were not always given in English, so some of them must have been translated. However, there is no note of which talks were originally in English. The talks convey a more immediate teaching than that expressed by Ouspensky, but in both the Work has a Gnostic tone. It emphasises the alienation of man, lost, asleep and distant from God. Gurdjieff said that his teaching was only for those who were not happy with life. The time and places in which he taught, before and during the Russian Revolution, and just after World War I in France, provided large numbers of prospective pupils. These were people who had lost faith in the established powers of church or state and, having fully experienced their own powerlessness in the face of mass destruction and chaos, could no longer count on progressive liberalism's trust in education and science.

Gurdjieff's pupils were prepared to undertake the hard labour, fasts and frictions of life at Gurdjieff's Institute because they, like others, felt 'a longing for salvation from the times by penetrating a different world in what psychologists were now calling the unconscious' (Raschke 1980: 134).

In 1924, as a result of a near fatal car accident, Gurdjieff changed the form and focus of his teaching once more. He reduced his activities within the Institute and began to put his teaching into a written form. Gurdjieff's pupils came from groups of people who were involved in the modernist interests of the day; in addition to Theosophy and the occult, these included literature, folklore, myth and the psychology of the unconscious arising from Freudian and Jungian analytical psychology.

Gurdjieff was in Paris during the 1920s when the city was a centre of modernist writing 'drawing on Russian émigrés, Dadaists from Zurich, and a whole generation of young American writers of an experimental disposition' (Bradbury and McFarlane 1976: 96–104). Gurdjieff's teachings influenced American and British writers of the time, some of whom were his pupils (Margaret Anderson, Kathryn Hulme, A.R. Orage, Jean Toomer) and others who came across the teaching. Among the latter were T.S. Eliot, whose 'late poems and plays' are permeated by Gurdjieff's teaching theory (Webb 1980: 478), Aldous Huxley, who attended group meetings given by Gurdjieff's pupil Ouspensky in London in the 1930s (Bennett 1962: 364), and J.B. Priestley, who 'used the work of Gurdjieff and Ouspensky to expand his own consciousness' (Cooper 1970: 229). Jorge Luis Borges is said to have attended meetings in Argentina in the 1950s. By then Gurdjieff's influence was widespread in South America, with groups also held in Peru, Chile, Uruguay and Mexico (Webb 1980: 492).

Due in part to the death of the writer Katherine Mansfield at the Institute, and to the literary careers of two of Gurdjieff's pupils, Margaret Anderson and A.R. Orage, there were strong connections between the literary worlds of London, Paris and New York, and Gurdjieff's Institute. Thus the change in the way Gurdjieff chose to present his teaching once again reflected contemporary interests.

The Three Series of his complete work, *All and Everything*, were probably completed by 1935. The First Series (*An Objectively Impartial Criticism of the Life of Man or Beelzebub's Tales to His Grandson*) was published in 1950, a year after Gurdjieff's death; the Second Series (*Meetings with Remarkable Men*) was first published in 1963; the Third Series (*Life is Real Only Then, When 'I Am'*) in 1975. Gurdjieff's *Herald of Coming Good*, published in 1933 and withdrawn by him the following year, was the only text to be published during his lifetime. Gurdjieff's writings reveal the influence of his early exposure to the oral tradition, his interest in the occult and an awareness of contemporary literary modernism. These texts formed a major part of Gurdjieff's teaching. However, the ideas expressed in the Three Series and *Herald* are interrelated. They are often contradictory, and need to be understood in relation to the specific text and to Gurdjieff's aim for that text. We should be aware of this and not take statements as definitive expressions of Gurdjieff's own views. For these reasons *Search* and pupils' records of the teachings given in *Views* are the principal sources for the definition of the terms given here.

From 1924 until the outbreak of World War II, Gurdjieff made eight visits to America. He established branches of his Institute in New York and Chicago, and continued to teach pupils in both America and France.

Gurdjieff had differing attitudes to publicity. From 1922–36 the Work was a high-profile teaching; Gurdjieff was well known and he attracted other well-known people to wherever he was teaching. After 1936 he changed to a much quieter mode of living and teaching. However, had Gurdjieff not had some time in the spotlight he would not have acquired the pupils who continued to come to him in later years. The Work Foundations today follow the quiet approach to the teaching and do not advertise.

During World War II Gurdjieff remained in Paris, teaching his French pupils. When the war ended, pupils from England and America returned to visit Gurdjieff in Paris; Gurdjieff made a last visit to New York from December 1948 to February 1949.

The memoirs of pupils through each of the stages of Gurdjieff's teaching, from Russia in 1912 until post-war Paris, provide valuable primary source material; they support and expand the understanding of Gurdjieff's teaching, and are therefore listed in a separate section of the Bibliography. However, we should also be aware that not all memories are accurate: as Gurdjieff's pupils do not seem to differ from other people in this respect, accounts of events may be inexact, either unintentionally or intentionally, and so further research is needed to look at anomalies in the dates and events recalled in pupil memoirs.

Gurdjieff said that it is sometimes necessary to 'steal' knowledge, and that his teaching had come from a variety of sources, which he gives as Eastern, from Tibet, from the Sarmoung monastery and from an unnamed Sufi centre. However, as well as references to the major traditions (Hinduism, Buddhism, Judaism, Christianity and Islam), many of the concepts in his teaching can be related, as mentioned above, to Theosophy and also to Western European ideas from occult and other sources. Where there are strong similarities between these concepts and Gurdjieff's, they are mentioned within the definition of the terms as possible sources or influences upon Gurdjieff and his teaching.

The terms

The aim of this book is to provide a clear definition of the terms used in the key concepts of Gurdjieff's teaching as given from around 1912–49; to give some of the possible origins for these concepts; to show some of the political, geographical and cultural contexts in which the concepts were taught; and to provide sources and suggestions for further reading and research.

The terms include those that exist only within Gurdjieff's teaching (e.g. 'Legominism'); those that are understood by Gurdjieff in a specific way (e.g. 'bodies', 'centres'); and general terms (e.g. 'suffering', 'relativity') about which Gurdjieff held specific views or displayed specific attitudes and that significantly affect the theory and practice of his teaching. Gurdjieff used the term 'man' to mean both men and women; as this usage, and the thinking it implies, is integral to the teaching, I have followed it here, although occasionally I have referred to 'humanity' or 'people'. There are two terms ('New Work', and 'sitting') that spring from the major change of direction given in the late 1960s and 1970s to the teaching by Gurdjieff's successor Jeanne de Salzmann. It is necessary to include these terms because they help to define changes that have now been incorporated into the theory and practice of the Work, especially within the Foundations, but also in some other groups. They also give some indication of how the teaching is being restructured, so as to more closely resemble a religious tradition.

Gurdjieff's native languages were Greek and Armenian. He spoke many other languages, including Russian and English, and although he wrote or dictated his work in a mixture of Russian and Armenian it was rendered into English, under his direction, through a complex series of translations and re-edits. The most influential of these was by A.R. Orage (for the importance of Orage as teacher, editor and interpreter of Gurdjieff's ideas, see APPENDIX 1 and APPENDIX 2).

Gurdjieff saw the United States as being the most receptive place for his teaching, so the English-language version of *Tales* was of prime importance. However, versions of his texts in other languages, French, German and Russian, were also under simultaneous production. Gurdjieff's oral teaching was carried out in Russian and French, as well as in English. The terms of the Work, expressed here in English, reflect the specific shades of meaning that, in themselves, influence the understanding of terms. There is a Russian text of *Tales*, a forthcoming translation of which will be awaited with interest for the light it may throw on the English editions. Nonetheless, the English-language version was primary; Gurdjieff saw the proofs of this version a few days before his death.

As referred to above, there are many contradictions or anomalies in Gurdjieff's theory. Some may be due to differences of emphasis given during different periods of his teaching, some may be the result of misreporting and misunderstanding, and some may have occurred because Gurdjieff was teaching individuals and advised them specifically according to their needs. Nonetheless, Gurdjieff deliberately used humour, paradox, symbolism and deception within his texts and within his oral teaching of pupils in order to deliver shocks that arouse an active and questioning mode of being.

At the same time, it may be argued that some of the apparent anomalies (e.g. the conflicting demands for the pupil to have complete trust in his teacher, set against the injunction to the pupil to verify everything he hears and to believe nothing) can be understood in relation to the specific stage the pupil has reached. Initially the pupil needs to have total trust in his teacher, later on the pupil must learn to question. Similarly notions that may be incomprehensible to a pupil at the start of his Work on himself will become clear to him later as he develops his own being and thus his capacity to understand. Attention is drawn to some of the apparent and the actual contradictions within terms.

Gurdjieff's concept of relativity means that none of his concepts can be understood on their own, but only in relation to all the others. The Key Concepts form is useful here, as we can see how each term is interrelated to all the others, how the ideas of the teaching revolve around each other, how they define and are defined by each other. The circular nature of the definitions does lead inevitably to some overlaps, and sometimes information appears more than once.

The definitions of terms given here come from written records of Gurdjieff's teaching and from pupil memoirs. In some few cases the written sources have been augmented or clarified by Gurdjieff's surviving pupils. Definitions of terms are usually set out in a specific order:

1 summaries of information taken from *Search*, because these are the first records of Gurdjieff's early teaching in Russia;
2 information from *Views*;

3 information from Gurdjieff's own writings;
4 the direct experience or commentaries on the teaching from his pupils' writings;
5 any relevant political, social, economic, cultural or geographical contexts for the term; and
6 any possible or likely origins of the teachings (e.g. Theosophical or Christian origins).

This order of references will allow the reader to place the term historically within the teaching, to see whether the term became widely used during different periods of the teaching and, if so, whether these uses are consistent with earlier definitions or the term taken on new shades of meaning.

The Bibliography is divided into sections: first works by Gurdjieff; then those of his pupils; a general section that includes academic publications relating to Gurdjieff, together with some works that may serve to widen the scope of Gurdjieff studies in other relevant fields: the oral tradition, the archaic epic, Sumerian, Greek, and Turkic; the Romantic tradition; Nietzsche, Theosophy, and new religious movements; together with some literary and analytical texts related to the literary worlds of Russia and Paris, to psychology, and to the occult background of Gurdjieff's teaching and finally a section of reference works.

Appendix 1 gives brief biographical details of some of Gurdjieff's pupils who went on to become Work teachers. Appendix 2 lists the Foundations and also some Work-derived groups.

Although we will experience the terms given here without the practical methodology through which Gurdjieff taught and, as mentioned above, without his stories, I have sought within the definitions to bring an awareness of just how much remains to be explored in the field of Gurdjieff studies. More especially, I have sought to provide an impetus that may open the way for a critical appreciation of Gurdjieff's texts.

'A' INFLUENCE *see* influences

ABSOLUTE, THE

The Absolute is the name given to the incomprehensible All or One that comprises all worlds (see **world/s, all worlds**).

> It is the state of things when the All constitutes one Whole, . . . the primordial state of things, out of which, by division and differentiation arise the diversity of the phenomena observed by us.
>
> (*Search*: 76)

The three **forces**, which exist everywhere, exist in the Absolute as a whole possessing **will**, full **consciousness**, and understanding of themselves and all they do. The unity of three forces is expressed, for example, in the consubstantial and indivisible Trinity, in the Trimurti of Brahma, Vishnu and Siva. The Absolute gives birth to perhaps an infinite number of different worlds, each of which begins a new Ray of Creation. The direct **influence** of the Absolute does not reach man. (For a description of the process through which the **Law of Three** creates the diversity of worlds from the unity of the Absolute, see **ray of creation**.) The will of the Absolute can only manifest itself in our world by mechanical laws. Ouspensky provides an analogy in which even God may not beat the ace of trumps with an ordinary deuce (*Search*: 83–4, 94–5).

Gurdjieff equates the Absolute, in philosophical terms, with the Hindu term 'Brahman' as the 'ultimate principle lying beyond all worlds' (*Views*, 1924: 66). He also equates the Absolute, at the top of the Ray of Creation, with God. The Absolute alone has will and creates from Himself; all subsequent creations are mechanical. The three forces, which are manifest in the world below the Absolute, correspond to the manifestation of the one God, in the three-fold form of God the Father, God the Son and God the Holy Ghost. Our (physical) system is threefold, similar to God's.

> If we consciously receive three matters and send them out, we can construct outside what we like, this is creation. When they are received through us it is the creation of the creator. In

1

this case, all three forces manifest through us and blend outside. Every creation can be either subjective or objective.

(*Views*, 1924: 195–7)

For the 'three matters', see **air**, **food/eating**, **impressions** and **unity**.

Further reading

Lovejoy 1936 examines two conflicting Platonic notions of the Absolute or God, represented both as both serene and complete within himself, and as God reacting angrily to the created world.

ACCIDENT *see* Law of Accident

ACCUMULATOR

In each of the **centres**, there are two accumulators. These are connected to each other, to the centre next to it and to a large accumulator. Energy is drawn from the substances contained in these accumulators; when one accumulator is empty, energy can be drawn from the one next to it. In the event that all energy is drawn off and used before it can be replenished from the large accumulator, energy is drawn directly from the large accumulator. If all the energy were to be drawn from the large accumulator, a person would die. Yawning is a sign that energy is being pumped into the small accumulators. Laughter is a sign that excess energy is being pumped out of centres. The extra energy required for work on oneself (for **self-remembering**, for example) can be drawn directly from the large accumulator, but only via the emotional centre – the other centres are connected only to small accumulators (*Search*: 233–5). In relation to the mind, although the accumulator of the intellectual centre (see **intellectual/thinking centre, intelligence**) cannot be enlarged, it is possible to augment its energy through the involvement of other parts and their accumulators. If all the small accumulators work 'one after the other in a certain definite combination', it is also possible to charge the large accumulator with energy that then has a store of reserve energy 'during moments when a certain energy is not being spent' (*Views*, 1923: 234–5).

The **Moon** is also an accumulator.

See also: **organic life**

AIM

ACT/ACTOR

In *Tales* (455, 465, 478–88, 494–5), Beelzebub joins the 'Adherents' of a club where learned beings strive for self-perfection through a variety of arts, one of which was the 'mysteries' or theatre.

An ordinary actor cannot direct and change his associations, only a real man with a real 'I' can act: 'the aim of every religion, or every knowledge, is to be an actor' (*Views*, 1924: 177–8; see also **roles**).

Webb (1980: 536–40) looks at similarities between Gurdjieff and other exponents of theatrical techniques and vocabulary: the curative role-playing used in psychodrama by the Romanian psychoanalyst Jacob L. Moreno; Konstantin Stanislavsky (1863–1938), through whose 'method acting' an actor may expand his awareness to a higher consciousness; and N.N. Evreimoff (1879–1953), who developed the 'monodrama' in which the drama of inner conflict is shown on stage. Contemporary theatre directors Peter Brook and Jerzy Grotowski have been influenced by Gurdjieff's ideas.

Further reading

Brook 1988; for the theory and practice of Russian actor Mikhail Aleksandrovich Chekhov (1891–1955), see von Maydell in Rosenthal 1997: 153–67.

ACTIVE FORCE *see* **forces; Law of Three**

AIM

Ouspensky records a number of different statements by Gurdjieff about aim in relation to new pupils, to groups, to the group teacher and to the school. The **Work** itself does not have an aim, except to show people how to obtain their own aims. However, man-as-machine cannot carry out aims because he is unable to be or do (see **being**; **doing**). A man's first aim must be freedom from slavery, both within and without. He can achieve this aim only through self-knowledge gained through **self-observation**. A man must aim to perceive himself with all four **centres**. If a man seeks to change himself before he understands how his machine functions he will fail to achieve anything (*Search*: 99–100).

A **group** does have an aim, and this is to take part in Work and not to degenerate into a social group (*Search*: 225). A group may be connected with an aim of which the members are unaware, pupils must understand that this aim belongs to their teacher. The better a pupil understands his teacher's aim, the better the results of their own work (*Search*: 222). Fourth Way schools always arise for a specific purpose, and when that purpose is achieved they disappear (see **schools**). This 'purpose' seems to be in contradiction with the statement above that the Work does not have an aim.

Gurdjieff encouraged pupils to take a small aim, for example the breaking of a small habit, and to make it 'your God'. Once a small aim is accomplished, a larger one can be attempted. To find an aim, sit for an hour relaxing muscles, and allow associations to flow, but do not become identified with them (see **identification**). At the end of an hour write your aim down; keep the paper with you and read it constantly, so that your aim becomes a part of you. Through undertaking and achieving a voluntary aim, we acquire the ability to do and magnetism (see **doing**; **magnetism/animal magnetism**). Usually we do not have enough **energy** to fulfil our aims, because we waste it (*Views*, 1930: 91–2). Our aim is to develop our soul and fulfil our higher destiny (*Views*, 1924: 191–2; see also **soul**). A person who wishes to discover their aim cannot do it alone, but they can be helped: two friends can help each other, then later a teacher can help them (*Views*, 1924: 241).

Gurdjieff expresses his own aim (*Herald*: 13, 16–17) as being to understand the precise significance of the life processes on earth and of all outward forms of breathing creatures, in particular of the aim of human life. This aim penetrated the marrow of his bones; he fell under its spell and became a slave of this aim (see **slavery/slaves**), instilled in him by the Will of Fate.

The aim of Gurdjieff's **writings** is to make his readers aware of the necessity of helping one's neighbour (*Herald*: 7) and to overcome people's mass psychosis. Should he succeed in the latter, he expresses two further aims: to uproot forever an 'evil "nothing" ' in men that is connected with lack of **conscience**, and to set up the training of the spiritual instructors who are needed to establish particular psychic factors in children (*Herald*: 75–6; see also **psyche/psychic/psychology**). Addressing his past pupils, Gurdjieff confesses that they may not have learned from him as they should partly because he was inwardly pursuing an 'altogether different aim', but they should now have acquired this aim for themselves (*Herald*: 82–3). However, these aims are not further defined.

In *Life* (26–8), Gurdjieff's own two principal aims were expressed as: 'to understand the exact significance and purpose of the life of man', and to discover some means for preventing the 'mass psychosis' that leads to war.

Gurdjieff said that during his life he had 'had many aims, a different aim for each phase. Now I tell you what my aim is: to destroy all values' (letter from Jean Toomer to Edith Taylor, 1926, quoted in Taylor 1998: 99).

Jeanne de Salzmann (see **appendix 1**) writes, in terms suggesting a long-term overall aim for the Work, that Gurdjieff showed that evolution 'cannot be approached through mass influences but is the result of individual inner growth; that such an opening was the aim of all religions, of all the Ways', that the pre-eminence of Being, discovered by pupils with the help of a teacher, could later be diffused among mankind (*Views*: v–vi; see also **evolution/involution**). She also stated, around 1982, that the aim of individual work is for the service of something higher, that 'without conscious work, the Earth will be in great danger' (Ravindra 1999: 100; see also **new work**).

One current view about the aim of the Work is expressed in terms of individual development. Another view focuses on the evolution of humanity and of the planet. Peters (1976 [1964, 1965]: 39) records Gurdjieff saying that his work was not for everyone, that it was difficult and could be dangerous. Tracol (1994: 87 [1978]; 1994: 136 [1982]) writes that Gurdjieff thought that man is not on earth by accident but has a mission to awaken to himself; however, there is no prevailing doctrine in the Work regarding attitudes to political and social problems (see **politics, political ideology**).

AIR

Air is one of the three foods that sustain the human organism, the others are the food we eat and the **impressions** we receive (see **three-storey factory/digestion of three foods**). In this triad of foods, air represents the active force, physical food represents the passive second force, and impressions the reconciling third force.

Gurdjieff said that air contains many elements unknown to science (see **'hydrogen'**). Although some of these elements are absorbed into the organism by everyone, only people who already have corresponding substances in their organisms can retain the finer substances. An analysis of inhaled and exhaled air will show how the number of elements absorbed varies from person to person; he compared this with **alchemy** (*Search*: 188–9).

One of the fundamental secrets of initiates (see **initiates/ initiation**) has been the fact that air is the 'chief actualising factor' not only in human but also in external forms of life. Air is composed of two kinds of active element that are 'contradictory in their totality'. One element involves the subjective process of evolutionary striving and the other of involutionary striving. Air is formed according to 'common cosmic laws ... depending upon the position and reciprocal action [of] other large cosmic concentrations, in our case the planet [earth]'. Gurdjieff is about to define the specific particularity of air that has always been one of the 'chief secrets of initiates of all ranks of all epochs', when the text breaks off: 'this particularity is that ...' (*Life*: 129–30).

'The secret of being able to assimilate the involving part of air' is to realise the inevitability of one's own death and that of everyone else (*Views*, 1931: 194). Air functions as the blood of the astral body.

See also: **astrology; bodies**

Further reading

Blavatsky (1988 [1888]: 2, 593) equates *prana* (air), the active power, with the element 'oxygen' (see elements); see also Vivekananda on *prana* (air): 'Prana is the infinite omnipresent power of this universe' (Vivekananda 1953: 592; written in the 1890s).

ALARM CLOCKS

Alarm clocks are a mechanical means by which a man can be woken up; however, he gets used to them very quickly and so, in order for him to be woken, it is necessary to be in a group of people all working to be woken up. The rules given by a teacher to the group also function as alarm clocks. In order to serve their purpose, rules must be 'difficult, unpleasant and uncomfortable' (*Search*: 221–2, 226).

See also: **difficulties; groups; reminding factor**

ALCHEMY

Alchemy is one of the symbologies that express a synthesis of knowledge (*Search*: 281). However, we know little about 'real' alchemical schools, only the results of their work – if we are able to distinguish it from imitations (*Search*: 313).

Gurdjieff uses an alchemical analogy for the functioning and growth of the four **bodies**: physical, astral, mental and causal. In this analogy, a vessel or retort is filled with a mixture of various metallic powders that have unstable and impermanent interrelations. A fire placed under the vessel can fuse the powders, turning them into stable individual chemical compounds. This describes the formation of the second body. The 'fire' is produced by **friction**, which comes from a person's struggle with his desires. If he does not give in to desires that hinder his **aim**, a fire is created that transforms his inner world into a whole. The resulting alloy may be worked on further, giving it new properties, e.g. making it magnetised or radioactive. This process corresponds to the formation of a third body and its acquisition of new knowledge and powers. However, these are not yet permanent. The process of making them so through special work constitutes the formation of the fourth body. A man with a fourth body is immortal. The fire, which fuses all the powders in the retort, is **conscience** (*Search*: 40–3, 156; see also **bodies**; **friction**; **occult/ occult revival**).

There is a special chemistry of alchemy that functions as the **Law of Three**. All substances function as conductors of the three forces, or none if no force is manifesting through it. All substances have four different states, which are related not to the chemical elements but to the alchemical **elements** of fire, earth, air and water. In Gurdjieff's teaching these are named 'carbon', 'oxygen', 'nitrogen' and 'hydrogen' (*Search*: 89–90; see **astrology**; **theosophy**). A light of consciousness is thrown on man's inner functioning and inner processes by **self-observation**; his inner alchemy is changed in the presence of light (*Search*: 146; see **allegory/analogy**; **symbols/symbolism**). In speaking about the retention of fine substances, which are part of the **air** we breathe, Gurdjieff referred to the process as alchemy. If there is no gold, i.e. none of the finer substances, already in our bodies, we cannot retain these substances from the air. Alchemy is an allegory for the work of the body in transforming base metals or coarse substances into gold or fine substances (*Search*: 189). Gurdjieff referred to the **enneagram** as 'the philosopher's stone of the alchemists' (*Search*: 294).

Further reading

For alchemy in *Tales*, see pp.174 and 831; for alchemy and food, see pp.970–2, 1017–23; see also the alchemy entries in Hastings *et al.* (1921: vol.1, pp.287–98) and Eliade *et al.* (1987: 183–202).

ALL AND EVERYTHING

Three of Gurdjieff's texts have the overall title: *All and Everything: Ten Books in Three Series*. These consist of the First Series *An Objectively Impartial Criticism of the Life of Man or Beelzebub's Tales to His Grandson* (in three books), the Second Series *Meetings with Remarkable Men* (in three books) and the Third Series *Life is Real Only Then, When 'I Am'* (in four books).

Gurdjieff gave specific aims for each of his texts: *Tales* was intended to destroy the world-view of its readers, *Meetings* aimed to give material for the creation of a new world, and *Life* was to help the reader to perceive the 'real world'. In terms of Gurdjieff's **Law of Three**, *Tales* can be understood as functioning as a second or passive force, *Meetings* functions as a first or active force, and *Life* as a third or reconciling force. In Biblical terms the texts echo the themes of Creation, Fall and Redemption. In the order Gurdjieff presents them, they echo the Gospel reordering of Fall, New Creation and Redemption.

These three texts form one integrated whole; their themes are symbolically and mythologically interrelated. They are structurally related in numerological terms, and each focuses on a specific period of time. *Tales* focuses on the year (both solar and lunar) and *Meetings* on the month, while *Life* focuses on specific days related to the change from Gregorian to Julian calendars. Although *Herald of Coming Good* is not listed by Gurdjieff as part of *All and Everything*, it can be seen as such through its focus on periods of a week, the measure of time that comes between the month (relevant to *Meetings*) and the day (relevant to *Life*) (Wellbeloved 2001a: 73–9).

Gurdjieff saw the English language proofs of *Tales* the week before he died in 1949. It was published in 1950. He left the publication of the other two series at the discretion of his pupil and successor Jeanne de Salzmann. *Meetings* was published in 1963, and *Life* in 1975.

See also: **astrology**; *Beelzebub's Tales to His Grandson*; *Herald of Coming Good*; *Life is Real Only Then, When 'I Am'*; *Meetings with Remarkable Men*; **writings**; **zodiac**

ALLEGORY/ANALOGY

Gurdjieff gives several direct warnings not to take what he says literally. In 'Glimpses of Truth' he says to the pupil that their conversation will not be about literal meaning (*Views*, 1914: 14–15). Gurdjieff said that many naïve geocentric systems of the universe are due to a literal understanding of the **Ray of Creation**. The ancient Mysteries were theatrical productions in which the evolution of the world and of man was represented in allegorical form (*Search*: 82, 314). He also explained that the last supper in the Orthodox liturgy is taken as allegory, when in fact it should be understood more simply and psychologically; earlier, however, Gurdjieff had said that the Last Supper should be taken literally – i.e. disciples ate and drank Christ's body and blood (*Search*: 303, 96–8).

Gurdjieff wrote that he became an expert 'in the art of concealing serious thoughts in an enticing, easily grasped outer form'. These will be discernible only after a lapse of time. He extols *The Thousand and One Nights*, a book that is clearly a fantasy, 'but fantasy corresponding to the truth' (*Meetings*: 7, 18).

Eastern teachings contain allegorical pictures. The comparison of a man to a house awaiting servants is a common allegory, also to be found in the Gospels (*Search*: 60–1).

Gurdjieff describes his understanding that he was God in his own world, in terms of a 'universal analogy' (*Life*: 22–4). Later he explicitly instructs his reader to understand what he is writing in terms of an allegory that needs interpretation. He gives, as an example, his description of himself in terms of 'something [...] fishy' (*Life*: 69–71). Gurdjieff used myths and symbols as an indirect way to convey his meaning (see **atmosphere**; **myth**; **number/numerology**; **symbols/symbolism**). He changed the world-view of his pupils by rearranging their understanding of what was literal and what allegorical (see **understanding, literal**).

Further reading

For 'indirect method', see Kierkegaard 1962 [1939]: 40. For the interpretation of parables/allegory, see Dodd 1936. See also the further reading section for **lies/lying**.

ANGEL/ARCHANGEL

In *Tales* there is a bureaucratic hierarchy of angels and archangels in charge of the administration of the universe. In spite of their mistakes, which have far-reaching and catastrophic results, angels are promoted to ever higher ranks and responsibilities. The angelic hierarchy in *Tales* subverts readers' notions of 'higher beings' and puts the notion of a beneficent hierarchy in question.

Gurdjieff's pupil Orage is reported as saying that, in Gurdjieff's view, a perfected man is superior to an angel: perfected men are cells in the mind of God, while angels are God's emotions. Gurdjieff referred to 'silly angels' and said that a man who purged himself of undesirable elements by working on himself would be better than an angel because he would have more understanding and experience of the many kinds of suffering, one of which leads to the angel, one to the devil (*Teachings*: 129–30, 107, 39). Gurdjieff told Nott that angels and devils have the most vanity, but with cunning (in the old English sense: *cunnan* = to know) 'you can make them your slaves. Angel can do one thing, dabbell [devil] can do all' (*Journey*: 76, 39).

See also: **astrology; Law of Reciprocal Maintenance/Reciprocal Feeding**

Further reading

Lovejoy 1936.

APHORISMS/SAYINGS

Sayings, or verbal formulations, handed down through **schools**, serve the same function as myths and symbols (see **myth; symbols/symbolism**): they help to connect a pupil to his higher centres. 'As above so below' from the Emerald Tablets of Hermes Trismegistus and the injunction 'Know thyself' from the temple of Apollo invite man to examine the microcosmos in relation to the macrocosmos (*Search*: 280).

Aphorisms written in a script invented by Alexandre de Salzmann, and thus indecipherable for non-pupils, hung in the study room of the **Institute** (see **appendix 1**). Thirty-eight of these aphorisms are given in English in *Views* (pp.273–6). Some express aspects of the **Work** teaching (such as 'only conscious suffering has any sense' and 'remember yourself always and everywhere'), while others ('judge others by yourself and you will rarely be mistaken') seem to be closer to expressions of popular wisdom. Learning to decode the aphorism script was one of many exercises Gurdjieff gave his pupils to increase their mental agility (see Webb 1980: 238–9)

Gurdjieff's interest in popular sayings/wisdom is also revealed in references to the wise sayings of his father in *Meetings* (pp.46–7), to popular wisdom sayings that Gurdjieff said he always adhered to (*Tales*: vi, 11–12), and specifically to the sayings of Mullah Nassr Eddin. The often paradoxical sayings of the Mullah are similar to the paradoxical sayings of Sufi teachers and Christ's paradoxical sayings. Gurdjieff said that he obeyed popular sayings but, as these give conflicting advice, it is not possible to live by one without disobeying another (see also Thring 1998: 12–14).

ART

Art may be 'Subjective' or 'Objective'. 'Subjective' art is produced by a mechanical artist, that is by **man** number one, two or three, and can give only accidental **impressions**, dependent on the receiver's **associations**. In 'Objective' art there is nothing accidental; 'it is mathematics. Everything can be calculated.' The artist knows before-hand what he wishes to transmit and does so; his art is always received in the same way, although this is also according to a man's level of **being**. Art should be evaluated by its **consciousness**. Everyone who is 'sufficiently prepared' will be able to read a book on astronomy or chemistry and understand precisely what the author means; an objective work of art is 'just such a book', but it affects man emotionally as well as intellectually. Gurdjieff gives the Great Sphinx as an example of an 'Objective' work of art (*Search*: 26–7, 295–7).

The above assertion of precision can be contrasted with Gurdjieff's insistence that symbols and myths, which connect with higher emotional and intellectual centres, should never be taken literally or as having one meaning only (see **symbols/symbolism; understanding, literal**).

Gurdjieff gives Ouspensky's group the example of 'Objective' music (see **music**). The merit of art is measured by its degree of consciousness. In order to understand 'Objective' art, a person must have at least 'flashes of objective consciousness' (*Search*: 297–8). The keys to all the ancient arts were lost centuries ago, and now there is no sacred art 'embodying the laws of the Great Knowledge and so serving to influence the instincts of the multitude'. 'The contemporary priests of art do not create but imitate. [...] sacred art vanished and left behind only the halo which surrounded its servants.' Gurdjieff defines art in relation to craft. With **knowledge** the shoemaker's craft 'may be sacred art too, but without it a priest of contemporary art is worse than a cobbler' (*Views*, 1918: 35–6; also *Views*, 1924: 182–6; see also **fall; influences**).

Webb (1980: 509–13) looks at Pythagoras as the prime source of all theories of 'Objective art' based on mathematical canons of proportion. Gurdjieff's pupils accept *Tales* as an objective work of art (see Orage in *Teachings*: 126).

At the turn of the nineteenth century, artists had become mystics and striven for the **Absolute**, and in the 1920s art was still seen to some extent as an alternative to religion. However, experiences of World War I had created a demand for alternative values (Webb 1980: 174). Art had a high profile in Paris, where there was a rich cultural mix of Dadaists and Surrealists, Russian music and dance, English-language writers, and visual artists. Gurdjieff offered his pupils an alternative to art practice by pointing out their inability 'to do' anything and by directing them towards 'Objective art' (see 'Art', Chapter 30 of *Tales*).

Further reading

It is worth comparing Gurdjieff's ideas concerning the value of the subconscious with early Surrealist practices that aimed to bring the Surrealists into contact with their unconscious functioning; on this subject, see Williams 1987. For an analysis of the Harlem Group's 'Objective art' writings, see Woodson 1999.

ASCENDING OCTAVE *see* **Law of Octaves**

ASHOK

An Ashok or Ashik, from the Turkish *asiq*, is a minstrel singer, literally a 'lover' (Reickl 1992: 385). Gurdjieff writes in *Meetings* that his father was an Ashok or bardic singer and that he accompanied his father to three song contests. Gurdjieff's teachings were influenced by this tradition (see **oral tradition, turkic**).

ASSOCIATIONS

Associations can be harmful or helpful. Gurdjieff gives the example of different associations with the word 'world' (see **world/s, all worlds**) and shows how these make it difficult for people to understand one another (*Search*: 74–5). People who are not 'individuals' seem to be; this is because they have differing sets of associations (*Search*: 388). We think and feel by chance associations called up by memories or things within our field of consciousness. The constant flow of associations captivates and binds us, preventing our objectivity and freedom; as long as we are alive associations never stop: they continue, even in deep sleep (*Views*, 1918: 45; 1923: 117).

Associations are made mechanically between an inner state, e.g. happiness, and some accidental occurrence, e.g. a sound. Thereafter the sound will trigger happiness. Man's world-concept is entirely defined by the character and quantity of those associations (*Views*, 1924: 74). Gurdjieff suggests that pupils sit alone for an hour, with relaxed muscles, allow associations to flow without identifying with them, tell them that if they allow you to do as you want now, then later you will grant their wishes (*Views*, 1930: 92).

Gurdjieff gives examples of how useful associations were formed in people through ritual. On feast days in Persia and Armenia in former times, associations were used to reinforce states, e.g. people would receive a 'special drink' or 'smoke', and then under this influence handle animals they would normally be fearful of. The associations induced would free people from fears (*Views*, 1924: 180–1; see also **narcotics**).

'Only associations of a certain strength in one centre evoke corresponding associations in another', but all associations *do* reach the **formatory apparatus** (*Views*, 1923: 128). This is contradicted by Gurdjieff's later statement that there are associations in all centres but that 'they *do not* reach the formatory apparatus, and so are not manifested' (*Views*, 1923: 132, my emphasis).

The number of associations a person has affects their perception of time (*Views*, 1924: 123; see also **time/the eternal**).

Through struggle, factors can be crystallised for conscious associations (*Voices*: 274).

Further reading

For Orage's interest in John Watson's Behaviorism, see Taylor 2001: 219, Watson 1914; see also King 1996 [1927].

ASTRAL BODY *see* bodies

ASTROLOGY

Sumerian astronomy/astrology (*c.*3000–1500 BC) established a form of the **zodiac** and a method of interpreting and interrelating the celestial and mundane worlds (see Van der Waerden 1949: 6–26, in Campion 1994: 88). The mythology and number symbolism derived from these observations entered European culture via Hebrew and Christian texts, and also through Greek philosophy and science. Some of these ideas were incorporated into the Christian tradition, others were rejected by Christianity and became part of the Occult tradition. In this way astrological symbolism permeated European culture (see Hopper 1938; Webb 1976).

In *Tales* Beelzebub asserts the superiority of Sumerian civilisation above all others; the influence of astrology can be found directly in Gurdjieff's cosmological teaching, his Laws of Three and Seven, and indirectly in the structuring of his texts and his use of the astrological system of correspondences within their narrative framework. His **Laws of Duality**, **Three** and **Seven**, and the four **bodies** of man, are largely derived from Western European occult sources, he drew specifically from **Theosophy** (see Wellbeloved 2001a: 35–63; see also **number/numerology**).

Type can be equated with astrological sign. Gurdjieff refers to the legend that the twelve apostles each represent a type, but says that some maintain there are more than twelve types (*Search*: 246). Signs are usually thought of as the twelve solar signs; however, there are also lunar signs corresponding to the twenty-eight 'lunar mansions': these consist of a division of the ecliptic into twenty-eight arcs, each of 'which correspond[s] approximately with the daily mean motion of the Moon through the ecliptic' (Gettings 1987: 292). Gurdjieff recounts his search for the twenty-eight types of person necessary for his observation and experiments (*Herald*: 23; see also **enneagram**; **planetary influence**).

Gurdjieff's cosmology stresses the correspondence of macrocosm with microcosm: the law 'as above so below' is expressed everywhere, 'we have within us the sun, the moon and the planets, only on a very small scale' (*Views*, 1924: 188). Thus a study of the macrocosm will illuminate the microcosm and vice versa.

> Astrological signs were originally 'invented' to synthesize the particular characteristics against which a given individual would have to fight [...] in the course of his life on earth

Gurdjieff indicated ways in which a person may benefit from interpreting the characteristics of his own sign (Peters 1976 [1964, 1965]: 321–5).

Gurdjieff's definition of substances as 'carbon', 'oxygen', 'nitrogen' and 'hydrogen' corresponds to the astrological **elements** fire, earth, air and water. Each of these substances may be the conductor of one of the three forces in his Law of Three (*Search*: 89–90). In astrological terms, Gurdjieff's active force represents the cardinal mode, the passive force the fixed mode and the reconciling force the mutable mode. This description of the four elements being acted on by three forces also stands as a definition of the zodiac, whose twelve houses are made up of three sets of four elements, each set being activated by the three astrological forces (see Figure 1).

Four Elements

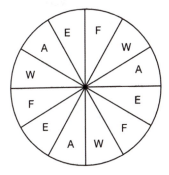

1. Carbon – Fire
2. Oxygen – Earth
3. Nitrogen – Air
4. Hydrogen – Water

Three Modes

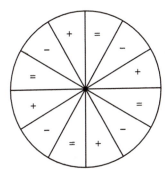

1. + Cardinal – Gurdjieff's First Active Force
2. – Fixed – Gurdjieff's Second Passive Force
3. = Mutable – Gurdjieff's Third Reconciling Force

Four Elements as Conductors of Three Forces

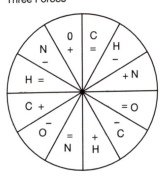

The Zodiac as Twelve Signs

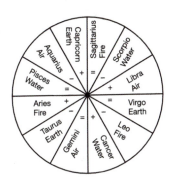

Figure 1 Astrology: Four elements and three forces

15

Figure 2   Astrology: Elements, signs, centres, Gospel writers

Element	Part of man acted upon	Zodiacal sign	Zodiacal activity	Gurdjieff's centre	Gospel writer and his symbol
Fire	Spiritual	Aries Leo Sagittarius	Creating	Sex	Mark: Winged lion
Earth	Physical	Taurus Virgo Capricorn	Building	Instinctive	Luke: Winged bull
Air	Intellectual	Gemini Libra Aquarius	Communi- cating	Intellectual	Matthew: Winged man
Water	Emotional	Cancer Scorpio Pisces	Feeling	Emotional	John: Eagle

Note: This table shows the elements and the activities ascribed to them in relation to the signs of the zodiac, to Gurdjieff's centres and to the Gospel writers.

For the relationship of astrological elements and signs to Gurdjieff's centres and the symbols of the gospel writers, see the table in Figure 2.

The tradition of numerologically and astrologically structured texts was a literary modernist interest in the 1920s. Largely due to Frazer's *The Golden Bough* (1994 [1890–1915]), there was interest in the idea that archaic epics were zodiacally structured. Blavatsky had suggested that the twelve cantos of Nimrod represent the zodiac (1988 [1888]: vol.2, p.353; Blavatsky cites Smith 1882: 236, however, I have not found this text); the twelve tablets of the epic of Gilgamesh also suggested a zodiacal structure (Campion 1994: 100). These interests flourished at the time Gurdjieff began writing *Tales*, his own epic. Indeed he used the zodiac in the structure of *Tales*, as well as in *Meetings*, *Life* and *Herald*.

Each of Gurdjieff's four texts can be seen as representing one of the three forces in his Law of Three: the positive, the negative, the evolutionary third force and the involutionary third force. In astrological terms:

- *Tales* is lunar, passive/destructive and female; it represents the fixed mode, in terms of Gurdjieff's Law of Three, and it expresses the second, passive or negative force. Its purpose is to destroy the reader's 'world-view'.

- *Meetings* is solar, creative/active and male; it represents the cardinal mode; in terms of Gurdjieff's Law of Three, it is the first active or positive force. Its purpose is to create a new world.
- *Life* is mercurial, reconciling and androgynous; it represents a positive mutable mode; in terms of Gurdjieff's Law of Three, it represents the third, reconciling force. Its purpose is to help the reader to awaken in the new world, in the present, and as such represents the eternal and a positive evolutionary third force.
- *Herald* is also mercurial, reconciling and androgynous, but represents a negative mutable mode; in terms of Gurdjieff's Law of Three it represents a negative third, reconciling force; its purpose is to announce the future benefit of his writings, as such it is temporal and involutionary.

Many of Gurdjieff's pupils would have been familiar with Theosophical cosmology and astrology, and in this way prepared for his teaching. In Leo (1989 [1913]: 74), for example, can be found four interpenetrating bodies similar to Gurdjieff's but expressed as triads of elements (see Figure 3; Blavatsky 1988 [1888]; Webb 1980).

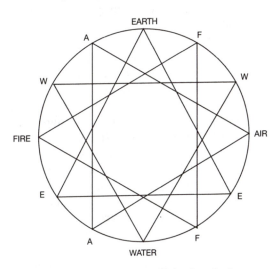

Figure 3 Astrology: Theosophical/Gurdjieff's bodies: the interpenetrating fire, earth, air and water bodies of Theosophical astrology can be related to Gurdjieff's four interpenetrating bodies, see **bodies**.

There was a growing focus on astrology as a tool for psychological learning (Rudhyar 1963 [1936]). The diagram of the zodiac relates to time, a major theme in Gurdjieff's writings (see **time/the eternal**).

Further reading

For late nineteenth-century astrology, see Massey 1883 and Sepharial 1898; for Theosophical astrology and astrology-related ideas, see Blavatsky 1988 [1888]; Kingsford's preface to the 1886 reprint of Weigel 1886 [1694]; Leo 1989 [1913]; Bailey 1982 [1951]. For psychological/Jungian astrology, see Rudhyar 1963 [1936]; for academic works relating to astrology, see Campbell 1980 and Curry 1992; for a contemporary Jungian psychological interpretation of astrology related to Ficino, see Moore 1990. For astrology and literature, see Eade 1984; Fowler 1964; North 1988. See also Wellbeloved 2001a: 35–63 and Campion 1994.

ATMOSPHERE

Everything living is surrounded by an atmosphere. Each atmosphere has a certain size. Factories and humans each have atmosphere composed of different elements, and each has its specific 'smell'. Some of the substances produced in a man's organism are used for the transformation of other matters, but others go into his atmosphere and are lost. Particles within the space of the atmosphere are attracted by the organism. However, beyond certain limits particles become torn off from the atmosphere. This happens when the shape of the atmosphere is stretched out of its spherical shape due to strain or danger. Particles of a man's atmosphere may dissolve or may remain attached to his clothing or belongings, in which case they can be acted on by magnetism, hypnotism and telepathy (see **hypnosis/hypnotism**; **magnetism/animal magnetism**; **telepathy**). Magnetism acts directly, hypnotism at a distance and telepathy at a greater distance from the atmosphere. A telepathic person can follow the 'trail' of particles and form a connection with his own matter, so that he can act on a man's mind; if he has an object belonging to a man, he can make a clay or wax image around it, and as he acts upon it he will act upon the man (*Views*, 1918: 211–12; see also **magic/magician**; **occult/occult revival**).

Physical and astral elements mix together to make a third substance, which forms an atmosphere around a man. Just as one planet loses or gains atmosphere due to other planets, so a man is surrounded and affected by the atmospheres of other men. When atmospheres are sympathetic to each other, a connection can be made and 'lawful results occur'; the quantity of the atmosphere stays the same, but the quality changes.

> Man can control his atmosphere, it is like electricity, having positive and negative parts; one part can be increased and made to flow like a current.

> (*Views*, 1930: 93)

Both the Earth and men have radiations that form their atmospheres. These radiations reach definite limits. In men the vibrations given off by the processes of active reasoning can expand for hundreds or thousands of kilometres, while the vibrations resulting from sensation cannot expand beyond two hundred metres. Vibrations, from active and passive thinking, feeling, and instinctive functioning, form an atmosphere around a man, 'analogous to the spectrum of colours'. The closer people are to each other, the more intimate is the mixing of their atmospheres, and the better the contact between their specific vibrations (*Life*: 175–7; see also **emanations**).

ATOM

Atoms of matter are small particles of matter that are indivisible in their given world; the atoms of the **Absolute** alone are indivisible. In each of the descending worlds of the Ray of Creation (see **ray of creation; world/s, all worlds**), the number of primordial particles corresponds to the number of laws in that world, and becomes correspondingly denser and slower in each succeeding world. Each atom is the smallest quantity of a substance that possesses all its chemical, cosmic and physical or psychic properties, and its degree of intelligence (*Search*: 87–9, 206). The term 'atom' can refer to elements (see **hydrogens, table of**), but may also be used of 'compound matters which possess a function in the life of man or the universe', i.e. an atom of bread or of water (*Search*: 175–6).

Gurdjieff referred to the nine numbers involved in the octave, seven notes plus two intervals, 'as though around every point, nine more subordinate points were grouped; and so on to the atoms of the atom' (*Views*, 1914: 34–5).

Further reading

The chief Greek atomic theorists were Leucippus, Democritus and Epicurus. The Greek *atomoi* (literally 'uncuttables') was translated into Latin by Lucretius as *primordia* ('first beginnings'), see Gaskin 1995; Russell 1996.

ATTACHMENT

Man is attached to all aspects of himself including his own stupidity and even suffering. Attachment to things keeps a thousand petty 'I's alive in him (*Search*: 218).

See also: **identification**

Further reading

For Buddhist teaching on attachment, see Walpola 1967.

ATTENTION

Attention can be the directing of the thinking centre's activity (*Search*: 110). Attention may be taken from us mechanically or it may be actively directed towards some inner or outer activity. In **self-remembering** the attention is divided: part flows to observe the self and part to an outward or inward event or phenomenon (*Search*: 118–19, 179). Attention can be directed to sensing parts of the body (see **sensation/sensing**; see also **energy**; **exercise**; **stop exercise**).

Observation of attention allows a man to distinguish between the work of different parts of **centres** (*Search*: 56). Each of a man's centres has attention in proportion to the energy and elements it receives. Usually the mind receives less than the body and feelings, and so it usually has less attention. Here Gurdjieff equates attention with memory. He says that the memory of the mind is short and ends when the material received has been used up (*Views*, 1923: 224–5). Gurdjieff suggests to a questioner that a way to begin to acquire attention is to stop restless movements, which betray a lack of authority. Without attention, **self-observation** is impossible (*Views*, 1930: 90).

Attention may be automatic or mechanical; the pupil must distinguish between these. **Music** can be used to divert some of our mechanical functioning. When carrying out tasks to music, the pupil should listen automatically; initially the attention will stray to the music, later it will be possible to listen to the music and to other things automatically. Through 'full, deep, highly concentrated attention' the pupil can 'taste' the difference between these two kinds of attention and so 'be able to discriminate between our incoming thoughts, information on one side and differentiation on the other' (*Views*, 1923: 220). In *Life* (p.140), Gurdjieff seems to express this differentiation by writing that he was looking at someone automatically, because the whole of his attention was in another place.

Attention in its passive state is the result of actions in all three centres, but the whole attention can be directed at something either within or outside a man, with the result that all the automatic associations continually flowing in him will cease to hinder him. Attention can also be divided into two or three parts; Gurdjieff gives an exercise for the attention (*Life*: 112–13, 138–42; see also **dreams**). Attention only in the mental centre is psychopathic attention; attention is made when associations of thought and feeling work together with memory (Patterson 1999: 90).

AUTOBIOGRAPHICAL WRITINGS

Gurdjieff mythologised his life and so it is not possible to accept these events and dates as accurate. Each of his texts contains autobiographical material, but this is shaped according to the function of the specific text. Thus the roles that Gurdjieff presents himself playing vary in all four texts. Gurdjieff gives his reader clues to this unreliability, through anomalies and contradictions in his texts. In *Meetings*, for example, he refers to the regular life led by his father, who always went to bed early and made no exceptions to this rule. However, Gurdjieff contradicts this by recounting a specific event when his father stayed up all night, and also states that his father would sometimes 'sit all night pondering the meaning of the ancient legends and sayings' (*Meetings*: 34, 45). While some of the events narrated in *Life* did take place, others did not, or took place differently, or on dates other than those Gurdjieff gives (see Taylor 2001: 168–72, and more fully 1998: 179–205; see also **writings**; **zodiac**).

The period of Gurdjieff's wanderings (*c.*1885–1910) and the years following (up to 1924) correspond to a time of archeological and anthropological exploration. The discovery of ancient places, artefacts and literature led to an interest in and re-evaluation of ancient cultures. Gurdjieff's 'myth' reflects these interests.

Further reading

For an account of archeological activities from 1860 to 1970, see Glyn 1981: 98–157; for the 'myth' of Gurdjieff – an account of his life based on autobiographical writings and the writings of others – see Moore 1991.

'B' INFLUENCES see influences

BARRIERS

Barriers are more difficult than the initial tasks a teacher sets a pupil. Once a barrier has been passed, the pupil can not return to how he was; if he is then unable to surmount the next barrier, he will remain stuck between them. Sometimes barriers are tests in which the pupil may be treated unfairly to see how he reacts, this will reveal his true nature. One of the principal barriers to overcome is constant lying, which usually goes unnoticed (see **lies/lying**); another is the conquest of unreal fears (*Search*: 228–31).

See also: **corns**

BEELZEBUB'S TALES TO HIS GRANDSON

Gurdjieff's text has the double title *An Objectively Impartial Criticism of the Life of Man or Beelzebub's Tales to His Grandson*, but is usually referred to by the second part of the title only.

In this, the First Series of his complete text *All and Everything*, Gurdjieff warns his reader that his aim is to destroy the reader's 'mentation and feelings' about 'everything existing in the world'.

The name of Gurdjieff's hero, Beelzebub ('Lord of the Flies'), is a derogatory Hebrew renaming of the pre-Judaic Caananite god Baal, while Hassein (Beelzebub's grandson, whose name has the same Arabic root as Hussein, the name of Muhammad's son) suggests the post-Christian religion of Islam. Freud (1990 [1939]: 381–6) recognised Judaism and Christianity as expressing a relationship between father (Judaism) and son (Christianity). In this light, Gurdjieff's choice of grandfather and grandson suggests a pre-Judaic and post-Christian relationship.

Tales follows the form and function of classical epic in which a prince or important youth is given all the contemporary knowledge available by his vizier or other wise person. The word 'tales' suggests both the telling of stories, as in *The Thousand and One Nights*, and also the telling of fictions or lies (see **lies/lying**).

This text used to be referred to by **Work** pupils as *Beelzebub,* but because of fears that this might be interpreted as in some way Satanic, some Work groups now refer to it as *Tales.* Justification for this can be seen in the refusal of a commercial company in the UK in 1996 to carry out work for a conference on *Beelzebub's Tales to His Grandson.* The title of the conference was changed to obviate further difficulties.

Although Beelzebub, as a character in *Tales*, does indeed tell lies, he can be more usefully regarded as a Romantic anti-hero, a personification of the Fall, who is pardoned and redeemed (see also **theosophy**).

Tales: An outline

Tales is a Fall myth which contains many layers of Fall narrative and symbolism. Gurdjieff writes in general about the fallen nature of man, and in particular about Beelzebub's Fall and Redemption. Beelzebub rebels against His Endlessness (God) and is banished to a distant Solar system (ours). He spends his exile in observation of the solar system, and of Earth and men in particular. He visits Earth six times and witnesses its life-span from just after its creation until 1922. Because of the help he gives to mankind, Beelzebub is pardoned and returns to his home-planet Karatas.

The tales are told to his thirteen-year-old grandson Hassein on board a spaceship travelling to and from a conference on another planet, shortly after Beelzebub's return from exile. He has taken Hassein with him so that the time of the journey might be spent in teaching him. Hassein learns about the creation of Earth and of men, and of subsequent disasters and Falls. These give Hassein an intellectual grounding in the theoretical structure of the universe and also develop in him an emotional relationship to, and a compassion for, the fate of men.

During the return journey with Hassein, Beelzebub is revealed as having reached a state of perfection second only to the highest in the universe. His final message for humanity is that only through a constant memory of death, that we will die, that everyone we see or think about will also die, will we be able to find compassion and love for one another. Beelzebub suggests that consciousness of death can destroy the ego. This is necessary because the ego's tendency to hate is the cause of all men's abnormalities.

Within this narrative framework Gurdjieff gives his teaching about the degenerate state of humanity, about the cosmological **Laws of**

Three and **Seven**, and about the possible 'way' to liberation. (For the influence of the occult on Gurdjieff see the introduction to this book and entries on **occult** and **music**.) The influences of the oral tradition (see **oral tradition/oral transmission**) and literary modernism both serve to encourage the use of literary strategies that result in multivalence. Gurdjieff uses humour, paradox and inconsistencies within his narrative to subvert the reader's attempts to arrive at a certain knowledge or final understanding of what he has read, thus inducing a continuing and changing experience of the text, and a continuing and changing experience of the reader himself. Just as the content of Gurdjieff's text remains open to differing interpretations, so the overall numerological structure of the text into books and chapters serves the same purpose in offering the reader a multiplicity of possible numerological interpretations (see also **number/numerology**; **writing**; **zodiac**).

The Biblical themes of Fall, Creation and Redemption expressed in the overall structure of the texts of *All and Everything* are also expressed by the division of *Tales* itself into three books. (An earlier plan for the contents of the three books is given in *Herald*: 50–5.) Gurdjieff shows a table of contents for the three books in which Book 1 has thirty chapters, Book 2 has eleven chapters and Book 3 has seven chapters. The forty-eight chapters of *Tales* has a numerological significance because, according to Gurdjieff's **Ray of Creation**, forty-eight is the number of laws man is subject to on Earth.

Gurdjieff's Laws of Three and Seven are largely derived from astrological cosmology (see **astrology**). The forty-eight chapters of *Tales* may be understood as twelve sets of four chapters ($4 \times 12 = 48$), each set of chapters occupying a sign of the zodiac (see Figure 35 in **zodiac**; see also Wellbeloved 2001a: 73–5; **number/numerology**; **writing**).

The **Foundations** favour listening to Gurdjieff's texts without analysis, in order for them to reach the subconscious. However, Gurdjieff's instructions were that his texts required three readings, each of which was equivalent to one of the three forces in his Law of Three. We should read first as we have become mechanised to read (i.e. passively), second 'as if' we were reading aloud to another (i.e. actively) and third we are to try to fathom the gist of his writings (i.e. a reconciling mode). (See Wellbeloved in Scullion 2001: 45–64; see also **oral tradition/oral transmission**; **oral tradition, turkic**; **myth**; **writings**.)

A slightly shortened edition of *Tales*, with some alterations, was published at Jeanne de Salzmann's behest in 1992. However, this has not replaced the first edition, which remains in print and is the edition favoured by most Work students.

Further reading

For Work pupils' commentary on *Tales*, see Orage in *Teachings*: 125–215 and Blake 1977; for relevant forms of story-telling, compare West 1988 on Hesiod's *Theogony* and *Works and Days*, and Caracciolo 1988 on *The Arabian Nights*.

BEING

In order to evolve, a man needs to develop both **knowledge** and being. Just as there are different levels of knowledge, so there are different levels of being (e.g. the being of a mineral is not the same as the being of a plant or the being of an animal). The beings of two men may vary more than the being of a mineral and an animal. People of Western culture value knowledge without realising that a man's knowledge is dependent on his level of being.

If knowledge develops more than being, the man knows but is powerless to do (a weak yogi); if being outweighs knowledge, a man can do but does not know what to do (a stupid saint). There are 'entire civilisations [that] have perished because knowledge outweighed being or being outweighed knowledge.' Modern man's being lacks unity, 'lucid consciousness', 'free will', a 'permanent ego or I' and the 'ability to do'. If a man wants knowledge then he must change his being, to do that he must wake up from **sleep**. The relationship of knowledge to being determines **understanding**. Mechanicality can only be understood when it is felt with the whole mass, the whole being (*Search*: 64–8; see also **law of reciprocal maintenance/reciprocal feeding** for how all creatures of every degree of being are defined).

'With a development of being we can find a higher state of **consciousness**' (*Views*, 1922: 79). Gurdjieff writes that as a result of his teaching and with the help of his writings his past pupils have the necessary data to enter the path to real being (*Herald*: 83).

See also: **levels of being; man; presence**

Further reading

Taylor (2001: 222–3) draws attention to a relationship between Edmund Husserl's (1859–1938; see Husserl, *The Idea of Phenomenology*, 1999) [1910], Martin Heidegger's (1889–1976; see Heidegger, *Being and Time*, 1996 [1927]) and Gurdjieff's notions of being (see also Krell 1997: 13).

BEINGS

One-, two- and three-brained beings are terms used in *Tales*, see
brains, centres.

BELIEF

A pupil should only believe something if his work produces the same
result time after time (*Views*, 1924: 201; see **faith**). Belief is a weakness
that must be destroyed. A person who believes, identifies with his
belief; when he wishes to pass on his beliefs with his **emanations** he
loses his energy. But if he does not believe, he can transmit something
to another in an impartial way (*Voices*: 70).

BLOOD/BLOOD RELATIONS

There are customs of blood brotherhood in which men mix their
blood together in a cup and drink it. The rite that took place at the
Last Supper of Christ with his disciples was a magical ceremony similar
to blood-brotherhood rituals. Christ used his blood and flesh, not
bread and wine, to form a link between his astral body and his disciples
(*Search*: 96–7; *Views*, 1918: 211; see also **enneagram**). For
transformation of blood by animal magnetism, see hypnotism and
magic (see **hypnosis/hypnotism**; **magic/magician**). For the
'blood' of the astral body, referred to in *Tales* as 'hanbledzoin', see
magnetism/animal magnetism.

In the **group meetings during World War II (1940–4)**,
Gurdjieff emphasised the importance of blood relations above all
others. We are links in the chain of our blood, and it is an honour to
be so; we have responsibilities to repair the past for the good of the
future. Husband and wife are defined as being of one blood only if
they have children. Through an exercise that Gurdjieff gives, and
through sending **emanations**, a pupil can help his brother who can
receive a contact through his blood (*Voices*: 175, 155, 73; see also
justice; **remorse**). However, Gurdjieff also said not to trust anyone,
neither brother nor sister (see **sincerity**).

BODIES

As well as the physical body, man may develop three other bodies: the astral body, the mental body and a fourth or causal body. The astral body is not present in everyone. It has to be formed by a crystallisation, which is the result of an inner struggle between 'yes' and 'no' that can form a unity in man. Such a body can survive death and may also be reborn in another physical body; if not, it will eventually die, as it is not fully immortal. However, the inner struggle engaged in is not always successful. For example, a monk who is afraid of sin: although the struggle may form something in him, it is formed on the wrong foundation and so he cannot develop further.

A fully developed man has four bodies. These are

> composed of substances which become finer and finer, mutually interpenetrate one another and form four independent organisms, standing in definite relationship to one another but capable of independent action.

> *(Search: 40)*

In terms of the **Ray of Creation**, the materiality of the four bodies relates to the materiality of the worlds (see Figure 4).

The physical body is composed of earthly material and after death returns to earth; the astral body, composed of planetary material, may

Figure 4 Bodies: Ray of Creation and number of laws

Ray of Creation	Bodies	Number of laws
The Absolute		
All Worlds		
All Suns	Causal body	Under 6 laws
Our Sun	Mental body	Under 12 laws
The Planets	Astral body	Under 24 laws
The Earth	Physical body	Under 48 laws
The Moon		

Note: This table shows the materiality of the four bodies in relation to their place in the Ray of Creation.

27

survive death for a while; the mental body, composed of solar energy, can survive the astral body; the causal body is composed of material from the starry world beyond the solar system and is immortal within the solar system. Only the fourth body completes the development possible for man, to it belong real will, real 'I', the soul, the master (see **master; soul; will/free will**). However, **mortality** is universal, with the exception of the **Absolute** (*Search*: 93–4, 91).

Gurdjieff gives definitions of these bodies according to Christian, Theosophical and certain among what he calls 'Eastern teachings'. The Christian definition gives the Carnal, the Natural, the Spiritual and, according to esoteric Christianity, the Divine Body. In Theosophy these are termed the Physical, the Astral, the Mental and the Causal Body (i.e. a body that causes its own actions independently of external causes). In 'Eastern teachings', the bodies are represented by the **carriage, horse, driver and master**. Sometimes these bodies are in good order, but their connections are not working.

These bodies are not possessed by ordinary man, who has one body, governed by outside influences that produce desires, thoughts coming from the desires, and multiple contradictory wills created by the desires. In a man with four bodies, the first body obeys the desires of the second body, subject to the thinking consciousness of the third body, which itself obeys the one individual permanent 'I', will and consciousness of the fourth body. Gurdjieff gives an 'Eastern' analogy for the functions and growth of the four bodies (see **alchemy**; *Search*: 40–3, 92–3; *Views*, 1924: 217). All religions and ancient teachings contain indications of how to acquire a fourth body and immortality (see **soul; ways/fourth way**).

Under certain conditions, the astral body can be seen, separated from the physical body and photographed. The astral body can also be detected because it has functions that the physical body cannot have. As a result of specific exercises, man can develop a ring of small bones around the neck, known as Buddha's necklace, which connect the physical body to the astral body. If the astral body lives on after death, it can be contacted by anyone who possesses one of the bones (*Search*: 62–3). The astral body is made of the same matter as the physical body, but each cell is permeated by emanations of Si 12 (see Figure 19 in **hydrogens, table of**); when these emanations crystallise the astral body is formed (*Search*: 254–9).

The astral body and the mental body are necessary for the higher centres to function fully in relation to the lower centres. The higher emotional centre requires the astral body and the higher intellectual centre requires the mental body. The fourth body is required for a full functioning of all centres over which there is full control (*Search*: 197; see also *Views*, 1924: 214–18).

In the 1940s Gurdjieff taught that there are two bodies, the organic and the psychic, and focused on the need to control the organic body, which is an animal that desires food and sleep: one must feel it as a stranger, subdue it, train it and make it obey. The psychic body has other needs, aspirations and desires; it belongs to another world. There is conflict between these bodies that the pupil must reinforce with will. He can use this struggle to create a third state, different from the other two, which is the master and united to something else (*Voices*: 164). The body must be educated consciously with the head, never allowed to do what it wants, be made to do everything that it does not love, inured to struggle, made submissive. An intelligent person has his body enslaved; if the body directs, the person is a nullity, a peasant. The more desire there is to direct the body, the more it will oppose this, and in resisting the pupil will gain strength. A pupil, in whom two parts (intellect and emotions) do function, is advised to starve himself, to govern his body mercilessly, to make it suffer (*Voices*: 66, 198).

Tracol (1994: 97) writes that Gurdjieff evoked respect for the body, that there are misunderstandings about what Gurdjieff said 'or wrote about the necessity to compel the body to obey higher imperatives' (from an interview in *Parabola* IX (4), 1984).

Further reading

For Egyptian multiple bodies, see Wallace Budge 1973 [1911]; for Theosophical multiple bodies, see Leo 1989 [1913].

BRAINS

Gurdjieff distinguished between one-, two- and three-brained beings. Worms are one-brained, sheep are two-brained and men are three-brained. Brains correspond to **centres**: the first brain corresponds to the moving centre, the second to the emotional centre and the third to the intellectual centre. Each brain has its own life-span, so one brain may die before another. Each brain, according to its quality of matter, can be called an individual entity, a **soul** (*Views*, 1924: 122–3; 1923: 134; see also **beings**).

Men have corrupted dogs and horses by trying to make them almost human; even though they are two-brained animals and cannot acquire the third brain necessary to become human, still they wish for the impossible. For this reason, we must take care of them and be kind (Peters 1976 [1964, 1965]: 76).

Further reading

For an account of how the structure of the human brain mirrors its evolution, see MacLean 1990; for an incorporation of this into Work terms, see Buzzell 1996.

BREATH/BREATHING

In 1924 Gurdjieff remarked that 'all Europe has gone mad about breathing exercises' and that he had healed people who ruined their breathing through them. There are three kinds of breathing: first, normal breathing; second, inflated or artificial breathing; third, breathing that is modified by movements. Normal breathing goes on unconsciously and is controlled by the moving centre. Inflated breathing is artificial and occurs when a person changes their breathing according to patterns of counting inhalations and exhalations. This is not done through the moving centre but through the **formatory apparatus**, which has access to a different set of muscles. Breathing can only be carried out by the formatory apparatus for a short time, as its work is 'worse' than that of the moving centre. The aim of this method of breathing is to get the moving centre to imitate the breathing of the formatory apparatus, but many other conditions are needed to achieve this. Gurdjieff connects this type of breathing with yogi breathing and with special breathing used in mental prayer in Orthodox monasteries. However, there is a risk that the moving centre will not restart breathing, in which case the person would die. This is not something to attempt from books. The third kind of breathing is where breathing is induced and modified by movement and postures, the specific movement depending on the person's **type**. If a person knows how to control his breathing he can control his organism (*Search*: 387–8; see also **time/the eternal**).

The rhythms of organs in the body are interconnected. Artificially controlled breathing can disturb the rhythm of the lungs and also, if continued, of the stomach and all other organs. It is better not to experiment with breathing unless the machine is understood in all its parts, otherwise illnesses may be caused (*Views*, 1924: 164–6; see also *Meetings*: 188–90). Bennett (1976 [1973]: 220) writes that, although Gurdjieff warned against breathing exercises, he did teach many to him and to other pupils throughout his teaching period. Bennett further notes that Gurdjieff explained the principles of right breathing in a series of lectures at the Institute in 1923. Ouspensky also records experiences of changed states of consciousness that arose due to breathing exercises (*Search*: 260–6).

Further reading

See Kornblatt's chapter 'Russian Religious Thought and the Jewish Kabbala' (Rosenthal 1997: 78), which refers to techniques of practical Kabbala that, in common with other occult practices, use breathing, counting and repetitive prayer.

BUFFERS

Buffers are gradually created within a person through education and imitation of other people. They function to prevent a man from recognising the many forms of contradictions within him (i.e. of feelings and opinions). Without buffers a person would experience constant **friction**, he would feel the reality of his multiple 'I's, he would feel mad. Buffers allow a person to always be in the right, not to feel his conscience and to lie incessantly to himself and to others (see **conscience**; **lies/lying**). A person needs some control, even if it is artificial. Only a person with conscious control (i.e. will) can live without buffers. Therefore, in order to destroy buffers, a person must develop will (see **will/free will**). During the process of destruction he must depend on another who has already developed his own will (*Search*: 154–64; see also **schools**).

Gurdjieff taught, perhaps in an echo of Christ's teaching (Luke 18: 16–17 [King James Version]), 'we must destroy our buffers. Children have none, therefore we must become as little children' (*Views*, 1922: 40; see also **essence**).

Further reading

See also Meyer 1992: Saying Four: 'The person old in days will not hesitate to ask a little child, seven days old, about the place of life, and that person will live.'

'C' INFLUENCES *see* influences

'CARBON'

One of the four states of **matter**.

See also: **elements; hydrogens, table of**

CARRIAGE, HORSE, DRIVER AND MASTER

Gurdjieff relates the four **bodies**, parts or functions of man to a carriage, horse, driver and master. The carriage represents the physical body/instincts, the horse the astral body/emotions, the driver the mental body/mind and the master the causal body/I, consciousness and will (see **'I'/identity**; **consciousness**; **will/free will**). In order for the team above to function usefully, each part/body must be formed and in good working order, and there must be some means of connection between the bodies/parts. Work on the self is work on both the 'bodies' and the 'connections'.

Work begins with the driver, who must wake up so he can hear the master's voice. He must learn the master's language, so as to understand him; he must also learn to care for the horse and harness it correctly to the carriage, otherwise even if he understands the master he cannot carry out the master's wishes. If the mind controls the emotions, they will pull the carriage (the body) after them. The connections needed are the understanding between driver and master, the reins between the driver and horse, and the shafts and harness between horse and carriage.

When the four bodies are formed and connected, all are controlled by the master/I, consciousness and will. If there are three bodies, control comes from the driver/mind; if there are two bodies, control comes from the horse/emotions; and if one body is formed, then control comes from the carriage/physical body. Because the natural common language between mind, feelings and body has been lost, we must establish an artificial or 'fraudulent' means of communication. We can do this by applying general exercises that are possible for everyone and specific methods applied subjectively for individuals. The feelings and body have degenerated and formed a 'crust of vices', and so, in order to establish communication between them, it is first necessary to 'correct old sins'. At present, there are only a series of passengers, no permanent master in the carriage (*Views*, 1923: 221–6). After a certain stage in the Work, which Gurdjieff referred to as 'Philadelphia', there is a master who arranges everything (*Views*, 1924: 191–2; see also **love**; **soul**). Sometimes, accidentally, there may be a substance that allows the driver to hear. One such substance is formed when we suffer (*Views*, 1924: 100; see **suffering/pleasure**).

Gurdjieff also equates the carriage, horse and driver with the **body**, **essence** and **personality**. Essence is the horse, and the essence likes or dislikes according to **type**. However, we consider mechanically in essence and so we like or dislike one another mechanically (*Views*, 1924: 144; see also **considering**).

In this comparison of bodies to carriage, horse and driver, 'Gurdjieff followed the *Upanishads* and Plato' (Webb 1980: 144).

CENTRES

The activity of the physical body is regulated by several different 'minds', which are termed 'centres'. Gurdjieff referred to different numbers of centres, from three up to seven. The seven centres, defined in terms of three storeys, are the moving, instinctive and sex centres that form the lower storey; the intellectual and the emotional centres that form the middle storey; and two higher centres, the higher emotional and the higher intellectual centres, that form the upper story. If one centre develops at the expense of the others, this makes for a lopsided person, incapable of further development (*Search*: 55, 282).

The functions of the centres can be recognised. The intellectual centre comes to conclusions by making comparisons; the emotional centre always responds to experiences as pleasant or unpleasant, it is never neutral; the sensations of the instinctive centre, from the five senses and the inner functions of the organism (e.g. heartbeat, digestion), are neutral in-born reflexes. The moving functions are not reflexes and must be learned through imitation. Individuals do not only perceive the world through one or another of the centres predominating, they may also experience it through a combination of centres, such as thoughts and sensations or thoughts and emotions. All these functions are interconnected. Each centre has a thinking, an emotional and a moving part, as well as its own associations, memory, imagination and the ability to **daydream**. Centres do not always function in an appropriate way. One centre may attempt to do the work of another for which it is not suited: e.g. thought may interfere with emotions, movements or sensations, which accounts for people being unbalanced or neurotic (*Search*: 109; see also **formatory apparatus**)

Each centre works with a specific **'hydrogen'**. The centres are like machines working on fuels of different qualities. Gurdjieff said that the intellectual centre works with hydrogen 48, the moving centre with hydrogen 24, the emotional centre can work with hydrogen 12, but mostly works with hydrogens 48 and 24. These lower centres are undeveloped in man. The higher emotional centre works with hydrogen 12 and the higher intellectual centre with hydrogen 6 (*Search*: 194–7, 279).

However, the higher centres cannot be accessed unless the lower centres function with their correct level of energy. This establishes a connection between lower and higher centres. The speed of our usual emotions is so much slower than that of the higher emotional centre that we are unable to hear the voices that speak and call to us from the higher emotional centre. As he is, a man may receive 'mystical' or 'ecstatic' experiences belonging to higher centres, but will be unable to retain an accurate memory of them. **Symbols** are used to help to make contact with the higher intellectual centre; **myths** are used to help to make contact with the higher emotional centre (*Search*: 194–7, 279; see also **three-storey factory/digestion of three foods**).

Each centre is a motivating force and also a receiving apparatus for **influences** that dictates how a man functions. The lower centres (sex, instinctive and moving) are divided into positive and negative. An impression may fall into both parts of the centre, the 'yes' and the 'no'. This results in laughter, which pumps out excess energy that might otherwise become negative and poisonous. Higher emotional and higher intellectual centres are not divided into two, and hence there is no laughter in those centres. Gurdjieff suggests that this has a bearing on why there is no mention of Christ laughing in the Gospels. As well as being divided into positive and negative parts, the centres are also divided into a thinking, feeling and moving part, and each of these three parts is divided again into three. In each of these parts there are rolls connected in various directions. What is called 'individuality' in people is a difference of 'rolls' and 'associations' (*Search:* 115, 236–7; see **associations**; **rolls**).

Independent work, including **super-efforts**, is impossible for man due to the fact that his centres are always connected, so that even if he wishes to change, for example, his thinking, any habitual posture or emotion will trigger habitual thoughts. Thus a pupil needs a **teacher** (*Search*: 347).

Ouspensky connected his understanding of time in different cosmoses with the speed of centres. Gurdjieff spoke about the enormous difference in the speed with which different centres functioned (*Search*: 339; see **moving/instinctive centre**; **time/the eternal**).

Centres never sleep, they continue to associate; what we call memory, attention or observation is the observation of one centre by another. There are five links between the seven centres; depth of sleep is characterised by the number of links that are broken. There is a subjective state in which a man may be active. However, the objective state of activity is one in which all centres are connected (*Views*, 1923: 117–18; see also **dreams; sleep**).

Each centre has the capacity to feel joy, sorrow, cold, heat, hunger and tiredness. A distinction must be made between the manifestation of a centre and the manifestation of a man: the latter is the result of a definite proportion of postures in each centre functioning in relation to each other (*Views*, 1922: 136–7; see also **machine/mechanicality**). Each centre or brain has a mainspring that unwinds during the course of life: 'thinking resembles the unwinding of a reel of thread', and when all the thread is unwound life ends. It is also possible for some centres to die while a man lives on in only one or two (*Views*, 1924: 121–3).

Centres are without critical faculty; they record everything they hear and have an indiscriminate belief in whatever they record. It is necessary to bring centres together. When a person looks with one centre only, he is under hallucination; with two centres together he is half-free, and with three centres together he cannot be under hallucination (*Views*, 1924: 263, 192; see also **self-observation; self-remembering**).

Information given about memory in centres is contradictory. Gurdjieff says 'that each centre *has its own memory* and associations. That each centre consists of three parts: the thinking, the emotional and the moving' (*Search*: 109, my emphasis). This is supported in *Views* by his statements that the centres/brains are animate and, taken singly, are individual animals in themselves that can and do live independently: 'Each brain has a definite, independent, specific existence. In short, according to the quality of its matter, each can be called an individual entity, a **soul**. In the centres life, associations, influence and existence are psychical (*Views*, 1923: 134). However, he also says that 'by itself a center has no consciousness, *no memory*', that it is a 'chunk of a particular kind of meat' that merely possesses the capacity to record, that consciousness and memory occur only when one centre watches another, that our mind and the other centres have no critical faculty, no consciousness, *that memory only exists when one centre watches another and records* (*Views*, 1923: 262–3, emphasis added).

Gurdjieff's seven centres relate to the seven Hindu *chakras* or energy centres, which were introduced into popular occultism via the Theosophists. However, seven centres also appear in the works of Renaissance mystics (Webb 1980: 533; see also **astrology**).

See also: **emotional centre/emotions, feelings; intellectual/thinking centre, intelligence; moving/instinctive centre; sex centre**

CENTRE OF GRAVITY

Each of man's three **machines** has a centre of gravity, also referred to as a **soul**. For the body the centre of gravity is the moving centre, for the personality it is the intellectual centre and for the essence the emotional centre (*Views*, 1922: 137).

In a group meeting, a pupil says that through work she finds a centre of gravity in the head, which allows her to de-identify. Because she has found this, Gurdjieff is content with all his being. However, the centre of gravity for the presence is defined as the solar plexus, which is the centre for feeling. Gurdjieff also suggests that creating an **ideal** will save a pupil from automatic attachments. If the pupil thinks about this consciously and automatically, this will grow and form a centre of gravity (*Voices*: 86, 93, 69).

CHIEF FEATURE

Each person has a chief feature or chief fault around which his 'false personality' is built. The teacher of a group must help members individually to see this chief fault, the struggle against which will form the individual's own path. Sometimes the person forms around his chief feature. Gurdjieff was ingenious in his definitions and said that, if people disagreed about their chief feature, this showed that he was right. People should struggle with the involuntary manifestations of their chief feature, which is usually discerned by those around them. Nicknames sometimes define chief feature well (*Search*: 226–7). Chief feature 'arises from one or more of the seven deadly sins, but chiefly from self-love and vanity' (*Journey*: 87).

CIRCLES OF HUMANITY

There are different circles of humanity: esoteric, exoteric and outer (see **conscious circle**).

CIVILISATION

Contemporary civilisation is Fallen and compared unfavourably with ancient civilisations in all of Gurdjieff's writings. Civilised people have exactly the same interests as 'ignorant savages'. Modern civilisation is based on violence and slavery; fine words about progress are merely words (*Search*: 51). Modern civilisation, while it has an unlimited scope for influence and opened man to new horizons in science and technology, nevertheless failed to educate people harmoniously (see **harmony/harmonious/harmonic**). As a result people are deprived of the faculties proper to their **type** and no longer function as an indivisible whole as they did in the Babylonian civilisation (*Herald*: 27–8).

CONSCIENCE

'Conscience in the sphere of emotions is what consciousness is in the sphere of the intellect.' Conscience is a state in which a man feels within him everything that he feels, without **buffers**. But a man whose thousands of inner feelings are contradictory cannot bear the shame and horror of such an experience, and so he must either destroy his contradictions or his conscience. Gurdjieff taught people to find conscience, and this is not the same as morality. While behaviour according to conscience is universal and cannot be contradicted, behaviour according to morality, which consists of buffers, is not universal: two men who are moral may have quite contradictory morals. The work of awakening conscience involves much **suffering**, but if a man persists he will experience moments that are a foretaste of the joy of a clear conscience (*Search*: 155–7; see also **alchemy**).

Everyone has a conscience. It was formed in us through the ages, but it has become 'crusted over' and does not function. When behaviour is guided by conscience it is in accordance with the commandments, but a conscienceless person cannot be moral. The ordinary circumstances of life, shock, bereavement, great sorrow or insult can temporarily awaken conscience, and conscience then unites the usually separate personality and essence. When a man begins to work, conscience can help him to be calm and thus have time for work. Later, conscience serves another purpose (*Views*, 1924: 239, 247–8; 1914: 251).

Gurdjieff quotes his father's saying 'Truth is that from which conscience can be at peace' (*Meetings*: 46).

The difficult conditions in Gurdjieff's Institute created frictions between a man's conscience and his automatic functioning. This enabled pupils to see their own inner emotional contradictions and to remember their aim (*Meetings*: 270; see also **good and evil**).

In *Tales* the Very Saintly Ashiata Shiemash teaches men that the way to access the conscience, buried in their subconsciousness, is through **conscious labour and intentional suffering**, also referred to as 'being-Partkldog-duty' (see **duty/striving; remorse**).

Contemporary people lack the 'scruple-of-conscience' that would compel them to act frankly, even if this was against the wishes of their waking consciousness (*Herald*: 74).

In the **group meetings during World War II (1940–4)** Gurdjieff called upon pupils to suffer remorse of conscience especially focused on the relations of children and parents. However, his suggestions run contrary to a conventional Christian understanding of familial duty.

CONSCIOUS CIRCLE OF HUMANITY

Any evolution of humanity can take place only through the evolution of a group of conscious people. If there were 200 conscious people, they could change life on earth. There may not be enough people in the group, or they may not wish to effect change, or it may not be the right time to effect change for humanity. We on the outer circle of humanity cannot know about these people until we become like them. They have:

> attained the highest development possible for man, each one of whom possesses individuality in the fullest degree, that is to say, an indivisible 'I', all forms of consciousness possible for man, full control over these states of consciousness, the whole of knowledge possible for man, and a free and independent will.

They are in agreement with one another and their actions lead to a common aim and are based on common understanding (*Search*: 309–11; see also **esoteric; evolution**; for the origins of the notion of the conscious circle of humanity, see **masters** and **Theosophy**).

Ideas of specially evolved members of a conscious circle of humanity were in accord with contemporary notions that extended Darwinian evolution to describe a Nietzschean evolution of man into a super-race.

CONSCIOUS LABOUR AND INTENTIONAL/ VOLUNTARY SUFFERING

The consequences, for humanity, of the Biblical Fall are toil and suffering. Toil to grow food and suffering to give birth to children. The practice of conscious labour and voluntary suffering is active rather than passive, an evolutionary rather than involutionary response to the Fall (see Genesis 3 [King James Version]; see also **duty/ striving**; **suffering/pleasure**). Bennett (1976: 221) connects the Sufi *riyazat* and *inkisar*, *'discipline, austerity and voluntary suffering'*, with *Gurdjieff's conscious labour and intentional suffering.*

CONSCIOUS SHOCK

Shocks are needed for vibrations to flow on, in either an involutionary or evolutionary direction (see **law of seven**). The shocks required for involution are mechanical, the shocks required for the continuation of vibrations in an evolutionary octave must be conscious. A pupil can give himself two conscious shocks, in order that the food he takes in can be transformed to its highest level; these shocks are connected with air and impressions (see **three-storey factory/digestion of three foods**).

CONSCIOUSNESS

Organs and parts of the body each have their own consciousness (*Search*: 53).

Men believe that they are conscious, but experience of **self-remembering** will show them that this is an illusion. Consciousness can only be known within, in the moment when it appears. These moments are very short and separated by long periods of functioning in unconscious mechanicality (see **machine/mechanicality**). Consciousness has a recognisable 'taste'. It exists in different levels and fluctuates, now present, more often absent (see **levels of being**). Just as conscience is the state when a person feels all that they feel, so consciousness is a state when a person 'knows all at once' everything that he knows, and realises how little and how contradictory this knowledge is (*Search*: 116–17, 155; see **art**; **fear**).

The psychical and physical functions of man work with four different states of consciousness. The first is ordinary sleep, in which any **impressions** that reach him arouse fantastic **dreams**. The second state is waking sleep, wrongly called 'clear consciousness'. This seems to be a better state than sleep. However, a man does not self-remember, and so he cannot control his thoughts, his emotions or his **attention**, and unlike in passive sleep he is more dangerous because he can act (e.g. he can wage **war**). The third state is self-remembering, a state that cannot be created by wish or decision alone, in which man can see that usually he sleeps and feel the need to awake. The principal obstacle to acquiring this state is that people imagine that they already possess it. The fourth state is objective consciousness, in which man can see the real world. This state, referred to in many religions as 'enlightenment', may sometimes occur, but the only right way to this state is through self-remembering, through work on oneself that results in inner growth (see **work, to**). The two higher states of consciousness are connected with the higher **centres**: the higher emotional and higher intellectual centres. These are fully developed and functioning, but because of our waking sleep their work fails to reach us (*Search*: 141–5; see also **being**; **subconscious**; **unconscious/unconsciousness**).

Further reading

For cosmic consciousness and evolution, see Bucke 1969 [1901] and May 1993; for conscious evolution in Work terms, see King 1996 [1927]; for the evolution of consciousness and the 'Aquarian frontier', see Rozak 1975.

CONSIDERING

Internal considering is a kind of **identification** and prevents **self-remembering**. It takes several forms. A man takes personally what others think of him and wastes energy in thinking about it. He is capable of taking society as a whole, or even the weather, as personally unjust to him in not fulfilling his own requirements. Other forms of considering are the fear that he is not considering another person enough and the belief that he 'ought' to do this or that. These 'oughts' spring from fear of the other: 'ought' should rightly be connected with **aim**.

  The study of considering must form part of **self-observation** and observation of others. Right external considering occurs when a man remembers that men are **machines** and cannot help the way they function. This is especially important in relation to other people in the **Work**. It is necessary to stop internal considering in order to produce the second conscious shock (see **three-storey factory/digestion of**

three foods). External considering is impossible for someone who is 'seated in his **chief feature**' (*Search*: 151–4, 191, 267). We always consider in essence mechanically. Every influence evokes a corresponding considering. When you are free internally of other people's opinions, you will be free of the people around you and know whether to 'offer the other cheek' or not (*Views*, 1924: 144, 249–50).

CORNS

Gurdjieff used a process of finding a person's most sensitive 'corn' and then 'pressing' it hard. This process removed the 'masks' that people habitually wear and so helped Gurdjieff to see into their inner worlds; this provided him with 'inner riches' (*Life*: 44, 51–3). For example, Gurdjieff ridiculed his pupil Jean Toomer in public, calling him a 'picaninny' (Taylor 1998: 89).

COSMOLOGY

Gurdjieff's teaching on the cosmoses, as recorded in *Search* by Ouspensky, was given between 1915 and 1918.

See also: **evolution/involution; Law of Octaves; Law of Seven; Law of Three**

Further reading

For contemporary influences, see Fedorov 1990 and Blavatsky 1988 [1888]; for the importance of cosmic thinking in Russia, see Burke in Rosenthal 1997.

COSMOSES

There are seven cosmoses, which exist one within the other. These are:

1 Protocosmos
2 Ayocosmos/Megalocosmos
3 Macrocosmos
4 Deuterocosmos
5 Mesocosmos
6 Tritocosmos
7 Microcosmos

They can be related to the **Ray of Creation** (see Figure 5). The last three 'notes' in Figure 6 are defined differently from those in the Ray of Creation (*Search*: 137).

'Each cosmos is a living being which lives, breathes, thinks, feels, is born and dies' (*Search*: 206).

The quantitative interrelation between the worlds in the Ray of Creation is not the same between all worlds; for example, it is much greater between All Suns and Our Sun than it is between the Earth and the Moon. However, the interrelation between cosmoses is constant and is always that of zero to infinity. This relationship can be expressed in terms of **dimensions** (see also **relativity**; **time/the eternal**).

Each cosmos can be studied in relation to itself, and defined in relation to the larger cosmos above it and to the smaller cosmos below it. In order to define himself, man as Tritocosmos needs to do so in relationship to the Mesocosmos (the planets of our solar system) and

Figure 5 Cosmoses: Cosmoses in relation to the Ray of Creation

	Ray of Creation	Cosmoses	
Do	The Absolute	Protocosmos	The first cosmos
Si	All Worlds	Ayocosmos	The holy or 'great' cosmos
La	The Milky Way	Macrocosmos	The large cosmos
Sol	Our Sun	Deuterocosmos	The second cosmos
Fa	All Planets (the Earth)	Mesocosmos	The middle cosmos
Mi	Man	Tritocosmos	The third cosmos
Re	Atom	Microcosmos	The small cosmos

Source: From information in **Search**: 205.

Figure 6 Cosmoses: Last three notes of the Ray of Creation

	Ray of Creation from Search: 205	Ray of Creation from Search: 137
Fa	All Planets	The Planets
Mi	Man	The Earth
Re	Atom	The Moon

the Microcosmos (the atom). As he becomes conscious of the life of the planets, he will also become conscious of the life of atoms.

However, the Tritocosmos can also be taken as all living beings (i.e. organic life on earth), while the Microcosmos ('the small cosmos') can be taken as any individual living being (i.e. man, animal or plant). Gurdjieff refers to the cosmoses using both definitions. Ouspensky understands the second version as more useful and points out that Gurdjieff uses this definition (the Microcosmos as man) in 'Glimpses of Truth' (*Views*, 1914: 22; also referred to in *Search*: 214). Ouspensky goes on to define other Microcosmoses: if the Microcosmos is man, then the Microcosmos below him will be the cells in his body; one cell, composed of milliards of molecules, comprises the third Microcosmos; and the fourth Microcosmos will be that of the electron (*Search*: 205–8).

The correspondence of macrocosm and microcosm is expressed by Gurdjieff:

> it is possible to study the sun, the moon. But man has everything within him, I have inside me the sun, the moon, God. I am – all life in its totality.

(*Views*, 1924: 102)

See also: **allegory/analogy; astrology; dimensions**

Further reading

Rosenthal 1997.

CRYSTALLISATION

When, through inner work, a man has accumulated enough fine matter in himself, new bodies (the astral, mental and fourth bodies) can form and crystallise within him. Salt added to water will dissolve, but when the solution is saturated with salt the crystals no longer dissolve. In the same way, the material required for the formation of a soul is usually dispersed, but when there is a surfeit the crystallised material takes the form of the physical body and is a copy of it (*Views*, 1924: 202, 215; *Search*: 180, also 255–6).

See also: **bodies; friction**

Further reading

For Valentin Tomberg's Christian Hermetic repudiation of Gurdjieff's view on crystallisation, see Anonymous (1991: 341–72). Tomberg, who came from St Petersburg and was a pupil of Rudolph Steiner, had a common interest with Ouspensky in Tarot.

DANCES/DANCING

Moore (1991: 351) defines seven categories of dance created by Gurdjieff with the aims of transmitting esoteric knowledge and of providing a means of harmonious evolution for the dancers. These are:

1   rhythms (harmonic, plastic and occupational)
2   the six preliminary exercises or 'Obligatories'
3   ritual exercises and medical gymnastics
4   women's dances
5   men's ethnic dances ('Dervish' and Tibetan)
6   sacred temple dances and tableaux
7   the thirty-nine Movements of Gurdjieff's last, partly enneagrammatic, series

The dancers obey the strictly defined movements of:

> arms, legs, and head [and] must often conform to independent contrapuntal rhythms; interior exercises in sensation and counting in canon may be added, and silent or spoken prayer.

This is made possible only 'by the dancer's mobilised **attention** equipoised among intellect, feeling and body' (see **bodies**). The transmission of dances is direct from teacher to dancer. Diaghilev attended performances of Sacred Dances at the Institute and wished to present them in one of his Ballets Russes seasons. Some movements are shown in the 1979 film of *Meetings with Remarkable Men*. 'Nearly ten archival films' have been made, directed by Jeanne de Salzmann, which can be seen only by invitation (Moore 1991: 352–3).

In Essentuki in 1918 Gurdjieff began teaching rhythmic exercises to music and also Dervish dances; the first public performance was in Tiflis in 1919. In 1920 in Constantinople he continued to prepare people to take part in a ballet or revue, which included Dervish and Eastern dances. Pupils had to acquire control over themselves and in this way approached 'the disclosure of higher states of consciousness'. According to Gurdjieff, the ballet should become a **school** (*Search*: 372, 382; see also **music; struggle of the magicians**).

The practice of movements can be useful for everyday life only if they take into account a man's constitution, and if breathing, thought and a man's old characteristic movement also takes part. They are useful for self-perfection if we add to the above normal feelings and sensations, and also special feelings and sensations that we aim to acquire (*Views*, 1923: 174–5).

> Dances are for the mind. They give nothing to the **soul** – the soul does not need anything. A dance has a certain meaning; every movement has a certain content.
>
> (*Views*, 1924: 181)

Gurdjieff describes the use of dance to represent the laws that govern the movement of planets (*Views*, 1914, 'Glimpses of Truth': 31).

Gurdjieff defined himself, among other definitions, as a teacher of dancing. He may have been influenced in making this role central to his teaching at the **Institute** in France by his experience of 'Rhythmische Gymnnastik', a system of rhythmic gymnastics (anglicised as 'Eurythmics'), that was taught by Emile Jaques-Dalcroze (1865–1950), first in Russia and later at the Dalcroze Institute in Hellerau, Germany. Gurdjieff adapted aspects of Eurythmics, just as earlier he had adapted Eastern dance forms, to his own ends (Webb 1980: 187–91). In 1923 Gurdjieff's pupils gave a performance in Paris; he also chose to introduce himself in America via performances in New York, Boston and Chicago in 1924. (See Bennett 1976: 226–7 for an extract from the programme notes for these performances.) Gurdjieff stopped teaching movements when he began to write around 1924, but resumed in Paris during World War II and continued until a few weeks before his death in 1949 (Bennett 1976: 222).

DAYDREAMING

Daydreaming is without **aim** and achieves nothing. The motive for it lies in the **emotional** or **moving centres** that recreate past experiences, whether pleasant or unpleasant. It is mostly carried out by the **intellectual centre**, which is lazy and avoids effort, although other centres also have their own forms of daydreaming. Many people spend much of their lives in unpleasant daydreams; these imaginings and daydreams are the wrong work of the intellectual centre and form an important subject for **self-observation** (*Search*: 111).

See also: **dreams**

DEATH/REBIRTH

A man's ability to resist external influences is the very thing that enables him to resist the death of the physical body (*Search*: 31). Nothing is immortal, 'even God is mortal', though there is a great difference between these mortalities (*Search*: 91).

With reference to a question asked about the wave of emotion that appeared to have made a change in the robber on the cross next to Christ, Gurdjieff said that this took place during terrible suffering and 'refers to the idea of man's last thoughts and feelings at the moment of death'. In ordinary life these thoughts are replaced and so there is no prolonged wave of emotion, which could lead to change (*Search*: 349).

A man must die to his small 'I's, not gradually as in the process of waking up, but '*all at once and forever*' (*Search*: 218–19, emphasis as the original). This seems contradicted by the reply Gurdjieff gave when his 1916 group told him that their friends now found them colourless. Gurdjieff explained that this was because they had begun to die, although it was 'a long way to complete death but still a certain amount of silliness is going out of you' (*Search*: 245). In 1924 Gurdjieff said that the death of false confidence, of personality, must occur before rebirth is possible, but as our machines are complicated, this breaking down process is long and difficult. Christ and other teachers spoke of the death of our inner tyrant, which may take place during our lifetime (*Views*, 1924: 86, 238).

Gurdjieff's hero in *Tales*, Beelzebub, says that the 'sole means' for saving men is for an organ to be implanted in them, like **kundabuffer**, but one that makes them remember the inevitability of their own and other people's deaths. Only this can destroy the egoism which causes them to hate each other (*Tales*: 1183; see **egoism/egoist**). Beelzebub explains that death provides a release of energy that goes to sustain the **Moon**. If this quality of energy is too low, nature has to make up for quality by a higher number of deaths, thus **wars** are necessary (*Tales*: 1098–9).

At death the physical body disintegrates: the parts from the Earth return to earth, 'parts which came with planetary **emanations** return to the planetary world; parts from the earth's atmosphere return there' (*Views*, 1924: 216; see also astral and higher-being bodies in **bodies**). There is no need for resurrection of the physical body, because if there is a soul it can get along without it. If a man were deprived of his illusions, interests, cares, expectations and hopes, he would become empty, only psychologically alive; this would be the death of 'I', of everything false (*Views*, 1924: 238–9).

> Only the complete realization by man of the inevitability of his own death can destroy those factors, implanted thanks to our abnormal life, of the expression of different aspects of our egoism, this cause of all evil in our common life.
>
> Only such a realization can bring to birth again in man those formerly present divine proofs of genuine impulses – faith, love and hope.
>
> (*Life*: 159–60)

In 1936 Gurdjieff referred to his own death and rebirth after his car accident, saying that he was born in 1924 and is not yet of responsible age (Patterson 1999: 105).

Gurdjieff's insistence on the necessity for remembrance of death echoes *memento mori*, the Christian injunction to remember death.

See also: **good and evil; recurrence/reincarnation**

Further reading

Tracol 1994: 13–21 [1985].

DENYING FORCE *see* **forces; Law of Three**

DEPUTY STEWARD *see* **'I'/identity; steward/deputy steward**

DESTRUCTION

Gurdjieff viewed destruction as a necessary part of his teaching. *Tales* aims to destroy its readers' world-view, just as Gurdjieff's teaching methods and theory aimed to destabilise, discourage and shock his pupils in order to help them to destroy their vanity, egoism and habitual view of themselves.

See also: **aim; corns**

DERVISHES   *see* **dance; music; Sufi/Sufism**

DESCENDING OCTAVE   *see* **Law of Octaves**

DIAGRAM OF EVERYTHING LIVING   *see* **Law of Reciprocal Maintenance/Reciprocal Feeding**

DIFFICULTIES

Although this is not a specific term that Gurdjieff used, his teachings (as recorded by Ouspensky) outline an almost insurmountable set of difficulties and dangers for prospective pupils. Overall, these difficulties correspond to a Gnostic view of life on earth.

Some of these difficulties are because we live in a dark part of the universe, remote from the centre and under the limitations of many laws. There are planetary forces against evolution in general and against individual **evolution**, which is not necessary and is very difficult, against nature and against God (*Search*: 81, 46–9; see also **gnosticism**).

The pupil's evolution is only of interest to himself, and no one is under the obligation to help him; the forces opposing his evolution must be outwitted (*Search*: 58). The pupil may not be able to discriminate between esoteric and exoteric **influences**, and therefore he may not develop a **magnetic centre** or he may form a wrong magnetic centre. A man's **machine** may be too damaged to repair. His **personality** may not be sufficiently developed, and so his **essence** may be deformed or dead. This system is for those who have already sought and burned themselves (*Search*: 202–3, 229, 164, 244).

The pupil cannot recognise a possible guide. If the pupil does attract a **teacher**, the teacher may not be from an esoteric centre. The teacher may be genuinely deceived, he may trust another who is deceived or he may intentionally deceive the pupil and lead him far from the true way. Pupils cannot recognise the wrong way (*Search*: 202–3). However, pupils must recognise that they do not exist and become conscious of their own nothingness (*Search*: 160).

The pupil must accept, obey and totally trust his teacher; he must never tell lies or suppress the truth: the most insignificant lie will bring his work with the teacher to an end (*Search*: 270, 229). A true teacher may treat a pupil badly or unfairly as a test (*Search*: 228–9).

Once the pupil enters onto the 'stairway' leading to the 'way', the pupil is dependent on others on the 'stairway'. If they fall, he will fall; if he fails to put anyone on the step beneath him, he will fail (*Search*: 201–2).

When he begins work, a pupil's machine is malfunctioning: he wastes energy, he has no will, individuality or ability to 'be' or to 'do' anything (see **being**; **doing**; **energy**; **will/free will**). His **centres** function with the wrong energy, he cannot remember himself however hard he tries, he is unable to be responsible, he lives in **dream** and illusion, his relations with others are mechanical (see **machine/mechanicality**), he cannot **love**. Because he is ruled by internal **influences**, external influences cannot reach him, and mistakes can never be redeemed.

The death of 'I', which is necessary, is possible in principle, but is more difficult than becoming a multi-millionaire through honest work (*Views*, 1924: 239).

Ouspensky, reflecting on the difficulties of the Fourth Way, wrote that as pupils realised how complex and diverse the methods of work were they saw more clearly the difficulties of the way, understanding that they needed great knowledge, 'immense efforts' and help that they did not have the right to count on. They realised that even to start on the work seriously required exceptional phenomena 'needing thousands of favourable inner and outward conditions'. In the face of such difficulties many of them lost the desire to make any kind of effort. But they learned that this was a stage that pupils pass through. A pupil must relinquish large, distant achievements, and be able to value what he gets today without thinking of tomorrow and what he may get then (*Search*: 360).

If men could invent difficulties and sacrifices for themselves they could go far; however, this is not possible and so they need direction from a teacher. Starting and continuing to work is difficult because life runs too smoothly (*Search*: 240).

The accumulation of difficulties seems to lead a pupil to acknowledge complete helplessness and to willingly subjugate himself to his teacher; in fact, this is one of Gurdjieff's demands (see **slavery/slaves**). Yet Gurdjieff, while teaching that the pupil's *mind has no critical faculty of itself* unless one centre watches another, also demanded a critical and questioning mind. 'If you have not *by nature* a critical mind your staying here [the **Institute**] is useless' (*Views*, 1924: 263, aphorism 27, 275, emphasis added).

It is paradoxical that while Gurdjieff seemed on the one hand a prophet of doom, disaster and hopelessness, he still generated a feeling of 'great hope and encouragement'. Peters remarks that this paradox, although a potentially dangerous thing, was itself useful in that it could stimulate people to work against seemingly impossible odds (Peters 1976 [1964, 1965]: 234).

Gurdjieff introduced a different set of difficulties for pupils in his **group meetings during World War II (1940–4)**.

From the above we might conclude that the constant demands on the pupil to make efforts, in the face of an intensifying acknowledgement of his own inherent inability to 'do' anything, constitutes the major paradox of the teaching. This paradox does not exist in the receptive form of Work introduced by de Salzmann (see **new work**; **presence**).

DIMENSIONS

The interrelationships of cosmoses are examined in terms of dimensions, which are expressed in terms of space as a point, a line, a plane, and then three-, four-, five- and six-dimensional bodies. The fourth dimension is time, which contains a finite number of possibilities; the fifth is eternity, 'the infinite existence of every moment of time', ' the eternal existence or repetition of the actualised possibilities'; and the sixth dimension is beyond time and contains the actualisation of all possibilities. These dimensions are in the relationship of zero to infinity, and this is the relationship between cosmoses. Thus for each cosmos the one below it will be perceived as three-dimensional, while the one above it will be five-dimensional: e.g. for man, organic life on Earth is three-dimensional, and his own life is experienced in four dimensions (*Search*: 208–13).

See also: **time/the eternal**

Further reading

See Ouspensky 1984 [1931]: 67–112.

DISAPPOINTMENT

For a person to be willing to enter the **Work** he must be disappointed in himself and in his life in whatever area his interests lie. He must be convinced that there is something to learn, but that he will not be able to learn it by himself. The Work is for 'those who have already sought and burned themselves'. A man who has neither sought nor been burned will not be interested in the Work (*Search*: 244). Most of the pupils at the Institute were 'misfits', people who were dissatisfied with life. Gurdjieff himself explained that this dissatisfaction was 'practically essential' (Peters 1976 [1964, 1965]: 309).

See also: **Gnosticism**

DOG

For 'bury the dog', see **writings**; for 'die like a dog', see **toast of/to the idiots, the Science of Idiotism**.

Gurdjieff referred to weaknesses, things crystallised in a person by education and life, as 'dogs' that must be 'killed'. It is impossible to kill them outright because once something is crystallised it is there permanently. However, the 'dogs' must be overcome, they must not control you. They must be turned into functions, and as functions they may be an asset. The 'dogs' gather around 'villages' (i.e. the **centres**). Gurdjieff advises pupils to get rid first of the dogs around the sex centre (*Voices*: 236).

See also: **Nature/Great Nature/the Common Mother**

Further reading

On Sufism and dogs, where 'nafs' (inner dogs) represent selfish, ego desires, see Nurbakhsh 1989.

DOING

Man is a **machine** and as such cannot 'do' anything. This must be understood not just intellectually but felt with the 'whole mass' and never forgotten. In order to do, it is necessary to be (see **being**). Progress and civilisation cannot come about as a result of mechanical 'happening'. Each small 'I' does what it wishes; there is no permanent 'I'. 'Doing presupposes an **aim**.' However, mechanical man is unable to fulfil an aim (e.g. to follow Christian precepts) because all his actions are controlled by external circumstances. Real doing is a form of **magic**; there is also imitation doing, brought about through deception on the part of a black magician (*Search*: 21–2, 99, 52, 54, 59, 102, 113, 226, 316–17). 'To do means to act consciously and according to one's will' (*Views*, 1924: 69).

In contrast with this, Gurdjieff also exhorted pupils,

> you must find a teacher. You alone can decide what it is that
> you wish to do. Search into your heart for what you most
> desire and if you are capable of doing it, you will know what
> to do.

> (*Views*, 1922: 81)

The ability to do can not be acquired by the mind. Even though only the mind cares about the future, the possibilities for change regarding 'doing' lie in the **body** and the feelings, although these two care only about the present moment (*Views*, 1923: 221–3).

Gurdjieff's teaching on the inability to do was affirmed for his pupils by their witnessing the war in Russia. In November 1916 the war was ending, irrespective of any ideas about continuing or stopping it, nor could anyone 'do' anything to avert the coming crash (*Search*: 316). The inability to do is expressed in the psychology of Behaviorism, which had its origins in Russia. King (1996 [1927]), in the earliest publication of Gurdjieff's ideas, entitled his book *Beyond Behaviorism*.

Further reading

For Behaviorism, see Watson 1914; for post-World War I willingness to give up responsibility for doing, see Williams 1987.

DREAMS

A person who dreams at night is using up energy that he did not use during the day. Dreamless sleep, when all the connections between **centres** are broken, is the most productive for man. Dreams are caused by one centre observing another; dream and half-dream states slow down the body's manufacture of the energy it needs (*Views*, 1923: 119).

In sleep a man's **attention** 'is stored up' for subsequent manifestations, but due to disharmony in the daily expenditure of energy the attention may make dreams from the associations flowing in him (*Life*: 138–9).

Gurdjieff's teaching on dreams represents a notable diversion from the value usually given to dreams and their interpretation in the prophetic and occult traditions, as well as in the psychologies of Freud and Jung. This is surprising because of the value Gurdjieff gives to the interpretation of symbol and myth. Maurice Nicoll, a Jung-trained psychiatrist who spent a year at Gurdjieff's **Institute** and later became a **Work** teacher in the United Kingdom, writes that the Work discourages the study of dreams because once attention is paid to them they are altered. However, he also refers to a conversation in which Gurdjieff told him that though most dreams were chaotic and valueless because they came from the moving/instinctive centre, dreams could come from other centres, including the higher centres. Nicoll (1992 [1952–6]: vol. 1, pp.352–7, 369–71) suggests that higher centres are constantly sending influences to help us, which we do not hear; sometimes these come in the form of dreams.

Gurdjieff told his group that he spent fifteen years learning not to dream (*Voices*: 159).

Tracol (1994: 54, undated) says he would be tempted to forget dreams, if he didn't feel how many secret links united his daydreams with his nocturnal dreams: although his day is bathed in dreams he does not know 'what couplings' take place between these two sets of dreams. De Salzmann does not decry dreams, she comments briefly on a dream told her by Ravindra (1999: 81).

Further reading

Nicoll 1920; see Kelsey 1991 [1973] on dreams in the Bible.

DRUGS *see* narcotics

DUTY/STRIVING

In *Tales* Gurdjieff expresses, via his character Ashiata Shiemash, five duties or strivings carried out by people who were working consciously on themselves:

1   To have in their ordinary being existence everything satisfying and really necessary for their planetary body.

2   To have a constant and unflagging instinctive need for self-perfection in the sense of being.

3   The conscious striving to know ever more and more concerning the laws of World-creation and World-maintenance.

4   The striving from the beginning of their existence to pay for their arising and their individuality as quickly as possible, in order afterwards to be free to lighten as much as possible the sorrow of our COMMON FATHER.

5   The striving always to assist the most rapid perfecting of other beings, both those similar to oneself and those of other forms, up to the degree of the sacred 'Martfotai' that is up to the degree of self-individuality.

(*Tales*: 385–6)

'Being-Partkdolg-duty' is a term used in *Tales*; it means 'obligation' in three languages: Armenian, Russian and English (Bennett 1976: 221). To carry out 'being-Partkdolg-duty' is **conscious labour and voluntary suffering**, and can be expressed as:

an intellectual duty to strive to understand the meaning and aim of existence, an emotional duty to feel the weight of the maintenance of everything existing, and a physical duty to make the planetary body the servant of your aim.

(Orage, in *Teachings*: 175)

Man's duty is to prepare for the future in the present moment, and also to repair the past (*Teachings*: 109). Gurdjieff gave students exercises for repairing the past of their families, for helping members of the family who were dead (see Bennett 1962: 254–5).

Throughout *Tales* Gurdjieff emphasises the necessity for man to strive against nature; to become active in relation to the forces of involution towards which he is usually mechanically passive. There are no recommendations in *Tales* that a person may be 'worked upon' or receive from above without striving (see **new work**). Some Work pupils take the five strivings as practical aims. However, there are apparent contradictions between these and Gurdjieff's other teachings: for example, Gurdjieff's injunctions to pupils to make **super-efforts**, that it is better to die making an effort than continue living in sleep (*Search*: 232), goes against the first striving; and his notion about self-perfecting, that only a conscious egoist can help people (*Search*: 103), precludes the fifth striving, at least until the person has already self-perfected.

EDUCATION

Gurdjieff expresses a low opinion of contemporary education in his writings, especially in *Tales*. Children are obliged by law to go to school, but this only educates one centre, the intellectual. Meanwhile the rest of the child, his **essence**, his ability to be moral, remains undeveloped; education is merely a mask. In order to be able to help their children, parents must first be able to help themselves. Children need sex education from about the age of four, but because they do not receive it children rarely develop normally; this education is psychologically difficult because simply explaining or forbidding something can give a child ideas. Gurdjieff recommended indirect methods for teaching, for both children and adults. This way a person learns from his own will (see **will/free will**) and can become an individual who creates rather than a machine that is created (*Views*, 1924: 124–7). Education of the emotions causes suffering and takes time; gradually the grandmothers and grandfathers became lazy and forgot (*Views*, 1924: 98–9).

See also: **corns**

Further reading

For Gurdjieff's indirect methods, see Zuber 1990 [1977]: 18.

EGOISM/EGOIST

Egoism has 'swallowed up' men's **essence**. It causes men to hate one another and is the chief cause of their abnormalities, it is unbecoming and maleficent for themselves and for 'the whole of the universe' (*Tales*: 1183; see **death**).

Gurdjieff distinguished between unconscious egoism and conscious egoism. Unconscious egoism is the striving to live solely for one's own benefit and is 'the cause of all evil in our common life' (*Life*: 159). In order to become a conscious egoist a person must die to the false confidence they have in their own self-knowledge and self-love. In that sense he must always start with himself. For example, he cannot understand others before he understands himself; if he begins to change then his children will begin to change. 'Egoism is the first station on the way to altruism, to Christianity, but it must be egoism for a good purpose' (*Views*, 1924: 125). A man can only 'be a good altruist to his nearest, when at times he can be a complete egoist' (*Life*: 54): 'it is better to be temporarily an egoist than never to be just' (*Views*: 274, aphorism 22).

Gurdjieff told a female pupil that while working she should be an egoist, forgetting God, husband, children, money; she should be a good egoist now for the sake of future altruism. However, when playing a **role** it is not possible to be an egoist with parents: **Nature** does not allow this (*Voices*: 116, 171, 105). Gurdjieff gives the example of nursing his patients for egoistic reasons. They are objects that do not interest him, he uses them to further his own understanding. He **experiments** but does no evil (*Voices*: 260). Compare the teaching on egoism with the demand for the pupil to recognise his own nothingness (see **nonentity/nothingness/nullity**).

ELEMENTS

'Carbon', 'oxygen', 'nitrogen' and 'hydrogen' are the four states of matter and equate with the occult elements fire, earth, air and water, as found in alchemy, astrology, the Kabbala and the Tarot. Gurdjieff took this terminology from *The Secret Doctrine* (Blavatsky 1988 [1888]: vol.2, p.593).

The first three elements are defined in relation to the **Law of Three**:

- 'Carbon' is a substance that conducts the first or active force and is referred to as 'C'.
- 'Oxygen' is a substance that conducts the second or passive force and is referred to as 'O'.
- 'Nitrogen' conducts the third or neutralising force and is referred to as 'N'.

The fourth substance, 'hydrogen', is regarded without relation to the force passing through it, and is referred to as 'H'. Gurdjieff's elements connect the three forces of process with the four states of matter, which correspond with the three astrological modes (cardinal, fixed and mutable) and the four astrological elements (fire, earth, air and water) (*Search*: 89–90).

In astrology the elements also express a duality of positive and negative elements. Fire and air are positive and correspond to male attributes and personifications, earth and water are negative and correspond to female attributes and personifications.

See also: **astrology; hydrogens, table of; matter**

EMANATIONS

Everything has emanations because every person and thing, the Earth, planets, our Sun, other suns and the 'source' or the **Absolute**, eats something and is eaten by something else; each of these has an atmosphere that limits its emanations. Emanations go in every direction from the Absolute. The **Ray of Creation** is one of these emanations. In space there are three mixtures of emanations: the finest, those of the Sun, reach the Earth; emanations of the planets reach the Earth but not the Sun; the Earth's emanations are shorter and do not reach beyond its atmosphere. A man is the result of the interaction of planetary emanations, the atmosphere and matters of the earth; indeed everything existing emanates matter, and has its own atmosphere. Looked at in relation to the Ray of Creation, emanations from the Absolute are the finest, those from the **Moon** the densest. Gurdjieff connects emanations to positive and negative forces, 'some things have many emanations, others less, but everything attracts or repels'. Man's **centres** also have emanations, and these combine with one another (*Views*, 1924: 188–90, 216, 204–5, 254; see also **influence**). When Solito Solano told Gurdjieff that she was most aware of emanations from her solar plexus, he said that we must know the whole body. Emanations can be stored within, and in order to accumulate them the muscles should be 'weak'. When there are enough emanations, they crystallise and there is force (Patterson 1999: 97).

In response to a pupil who taught children, Gurdjieff commented that they were more sensitive to self-remembering; it is easier for the pupil to remember himself in class because the children have not begun to emanate. What the teacher emanates is more important for the children than what he is teaching (*Voices*: 144–5; see also **exercises; role**).

Orage defines emanations as a force that does not operate through and by means of matter, and radiations as a force that does operate through and by means of matter. While radiations disperse through their own force, emanation does not diminish (*Teachings*: 201, 176).

EMOTIONAL CENTRE/EMOTIONS; FEELINGS

Emotion defines impressions according to how pleasant or unpleasant they are to the senses; it does not reason about or compare impressions and it is never indifferent to them (*Search*: 107). The disorganised feeling in our inner life causes all our misfortunes. We have neither objective, nor subjective feeling, only alien mechanical feeling (see **morality**; *Views*, 1922: 172). In order to carry out our aim we may have to manipulate or fool the horse (the emotions) because the horse only wants its food (see **carriage, horse, driver and master**). However, Gurdjieff also said that both Working and non-Working situations can be happy, but when a person begins to look for something better it means he is disillusioned. 'Blessed is he who has a soul, blessed is he who has none, but woe and grief to him who has it in embryo.' He also said that all our emotions are rudimentary organs of 'something higher': for example, 'fear may be an organ of future clairvoyance, anger of real force, etc.' (*Views*, 1924: 191, aphorism 29, 275; 1931: 194.)

The word 'feelings' is used in both *Search* and *Views*, and usually refers to emotions, but it can also refer to sensations (i.e. something felt in the body via the senses and originating in the moving centre). It is necessary to be able to distinguish between emotions and sensations because in **self-remembering** both these (and the **intellectual/thinking centre, intelligence**) need to participate. Readings and talks act as an artificial **shock** for the desires, and consequently they produce artificial results (*Views*, 1923: 229–35). In this light, we might understand the whole of Gurdjieff's cosmological and psychological teaching as an artificial shock to his pupil's desires and emotions. If this is so, and the resulting desires were also artificial, it suggests that these teachings set up a situation temporarily until the pupil can access useful emotions and desires of his own. Ouspensky writes that later he came to understand that 'work on the emotions became the basis of the subsequent development of the whole system' (*Search*: 113).

The two centres for feeling are the solar plexus and the spine brain (Patterson 1999: 97; see also **centres; self-remembering**).

Nott (*Journey*: 239) recalls Gurdjieff playing **music** on his hand organ that made Ouspensky's pupils weep, touching their higher emotional centres in a way they had not been touched in all their previous years of work. 'Gurdjieff constantly reminded his pupils: "You must feel, you must feel, your mind is a luxury. You must suffer

remorse in your feelings." ' (See also **death**; **energy**; **negative emotions**; **three-storey factory/digestion of three foods**.)

The difference between emotion and feeling is sometimes unclear in *Voices*, perhaps due to translation from French to English; sometimes emotions are connected with physical feelings (i.e. sensations). For example, Gurdjieff says 'emotion is a function of the body', that it is impossible to feel with the head: he feels pain, heat or cold with his solar plexus. These seem more like sensations, while an emotion about the sensations might be connected to pleasure or displeasure. 'Sensibility' is an English word that might usefully bridge these concepts. However, the subject-matter dealt with in **group** meetings focuses on the emotional experience of pupils rather than on the theory found in *Search*. Speaking to a female pupil, Gurdjieff refers to the psychopathy of a nonentity who imagines she wants something. 'No one can feel, it requires a special state' (*Voices*: 93, 260; on feelings of self-loathing arising from work on the self, see **remorse**).

ENERGY

All energy is material (see **matter**; **elements**). Gurdjieff uses the term **'hydrogen'** to express matter without reference to any specific force passing through it. Each of a man's functions and states requires energy of specific qualities and substances; this is also true of **Work**. Usually energy is wasted on the wrong work of **centres**; on bad moods, fantasy and **daydreaming**; on unnecessary movements and muscular tensions; on internal chatter, unpleasant negative emotions; and on a waste of the energy of **attention** (see **negative emotions**). Initially a person can save energy wasted during these processes through work on himself, via struggle against **habits**, but later on he will require even more energy and so he will need to study how his internal 'factory' produces energy. Usually the factory only produces a fraction of the energy that it is capable of producing. When this 'factory' is functioning fully, it transforms energy from the 'fuels' or **foods** that it receives (physical food, air and impressions) from dense 'hydrogens' with slowly vibrating energy to fine 'hydrogens' with quickly vibrating energy.

These different levels of energy that vibrate within matter correspond externally with different levels of the **Ray of Creation** and internally with the centres. The lower centres often work with the wrong energy; the higher centres cannot be contacted at all without the production of fine energy. This process is governed by the **Law of**

Octaves (see **three-storey factory/digestion of three foods**; *Search*: 179–80).

Through misuse of energy, a man may empty himself of energy for a long time, or even for ever (*Search*: 198).

> Energy spent on active inner work is there and then transformed into a fresh supply, but that spent on passive work is lost for ever.

> (*Views*: 275, aphorism 32)

Work requires a great deal of energy. However, the amount of energy produced in twenty-four hours remains constant, so an economical use of it will ensure that there is enough energy for work. Unnecessary tension is a major cause of wasted energy (*Views*, 1923: 115–20).

See also: **centres; sleep**

ENNEAGRAM

The enneagram is a symbol that expresses the **Law of Three**, the **Law of Seven** and their relationship to each other. It is composed of three aspects: the circle, the 3,6,9 triangle, and the six-sided figure 1,4,2,8,5,7 (see Figure 7).

The circle represents both the isolated existence of a thing as a whole, and eternally recurring process. 'The points in the division of the circumference symbolize the steps of the process.'

The 3,6,9 triangle represents the Law of Three. However, the points also represent the functioning of the octave. Point 9 of the triangle represents the first and last Do of the octave, points 3 and 6 the 'shocks' needed for the octave to flow on. These points represent places where the octave can be penetrated to make connection with what exists outside.

In the figure 1,4,2,8,5,7, the inequality of the parts into which the octave is divided is ignored. The order in which the points are joined is governed by the digits that result from the division of 1 by 7: $1/7 = 0.142857\ldots$. Whereas the circle symbolises the unity of the all, the 1,4,2,8,5,7 figure symbolises the diversity within unity (see Figure 8 showing the points of the enneagram related to the notes of the octave).

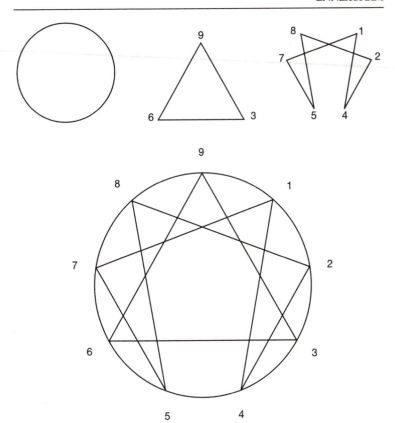

Figure 7 Enneagram: Circle, triangle and six-sided figure

In the enneagram the 'shock' at point 6 occurs in a different place than is shown in the **Ray of Creation**. In the enneagram it occurs between notes Sol and Si, whereas its 'correct place' is between Si and Do. This placement can be understood if the enneagram is read as representing the Ray of Creation in terms of its three octaves. These octaves have correspondence with the three octaves of human digestion (of food, air and impressions).

Figure 9 shows how these three octaves of digestion are represented on the enneagram. While point 9 represents the Do that starts and completes the food octave, point 3 is the Do that starts the air octave, and point 6 is the Do that starts the impressions octave; it also represents the first interval in the air octave (see also **three-storey factory/digestion of three foods**).

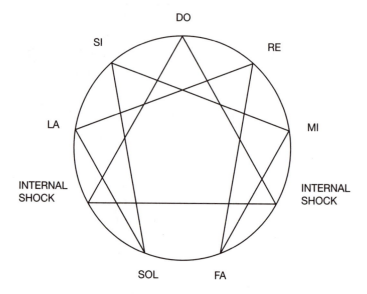

Figure 8 Enneagram related to the notes of the octave

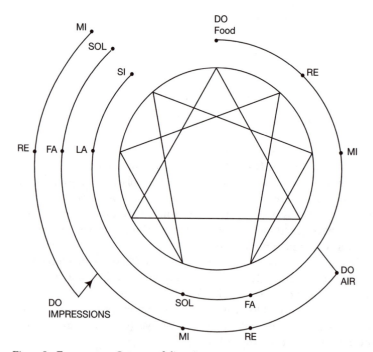

Figure 9 Enneagram: Octaves of digestion

In conformity with the Law of Three, the three 'shock' points can be taken together to represent the passive, active and reconciling nature of each 'shock'. Thus while the shock at point 3 is mechanical, the shock at point 6 requires action (see Figure 10; the triangle is as shown in *Search*: 293).

As shown in Figure 9, the enneagram can express the microcosm (the human digestive system). Ouspensky went on to use the symbol to explore the microcosm's other physical 'systems', such as the bloodstream, and also the macrocosm in terms of the planets (see *Search*: 378; Figure 11). This correspondence between macro- and microcosmoses is central to the interpretative processes of **astrology**.

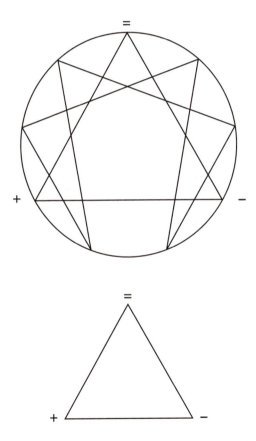

Figure 10 Enneagram: Triangle showing shocks/forces

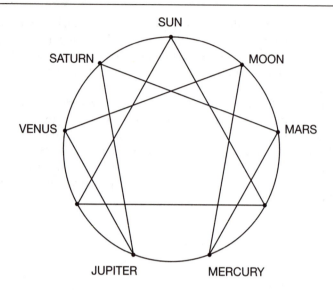

Figure 11 Enneagram: Macrocosm

Ouspensky reports an enneagram inside which were shown 'the bull, the lion, the man, and the eagle'. He connects these symbols with the four beasts of the Apocalypse and with **centres**. However, they also represent the four fixed signs of the zodiac, one in each of the elements: Taurus, Leo, Aquarius and Scorpio (see Figure 12; see also the dates in *Life*). If the enneagram is read as a symbol of the zodiac, then an astrological use of it for a typology of people is immediately obvious and understandable.

Ouspensky's pupil Rodney Collin is the most likely link between Gurdjieff's enneagram and the contemporary 'enneagram of person-ality' (see **appendix 1**). Collin relates Ouspensky's planetary enneagram (*Search*: 378) to Gurdjieff's notion of **types** (see Collin 1993: 143–55, 221–6). Collin suggests the possibility for each individual to develop from the type he is born into the next type on the enneagram. Thus a Lunar type needs to develop the warmth of the Venusian, the lazy Venusian needs to develop the speed of the Mercurial type, the Mercurial needs to develop the wisdom of the Saturnine type, who himself needs the courage of the Martial type; the destructive Martial type needs the attraction of the Jovial type, who in turn needs to develop the instinctive Lunar on a higher level (Collin 1993: 223). This notion of personal development via the 'points' or

TO KNOW–TO UNDERSTAND–TO BE

The Science of the Harmonious Development of Man according to the method of G.I.GURDJIEFF.

Figure 12 Enneagram: Bull, lion, man and eagle

numbers of the enneagram is central to the functioning of the 'enneagram of personality', though authors define differently types represented by each number (see Figure 13).

The path of enneagram studies probably went from Collin or Collin's pupils to Oscar Ichazu, Claudio Naranjo (see **appendix 2**) and then the Eslan Institute, from where the enneagram was taken up by Jesuit

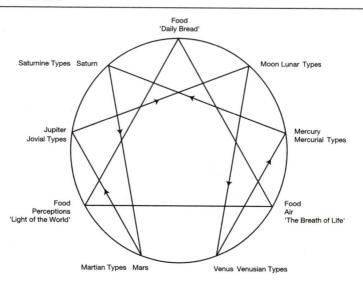

Figure 13 Enneagram: Rodney Collin, planets and types

theological centres (see Levine 1999: 12, 8) and became a tool for personal development (see Collin 1993 [1954a]). Palmer (1995), Riso (1995 [1987]) and other popular enneagram books usually suggest **Sufi** origins for the enneagram, but there is no direct evidence for this.

Gurdjieff called the enneagram a universal symbol, 'the fundamental hieroglyph of a universal language which has as many different meanings as there are levels of men'. It is a diagram of perpetual motion; if a person knows how to use it he can have great power, but to understand it a man needs instruction from 'a man who knows' (*Search*: 294; see also **alchemy** and the **zodiac**, which, like the enneagram, is a diagram of perpetual motion).

In order to give pupils the necessary experience of the enneagram through movement Gurdjieff planned to include dances based on the enneagram in his *Struggle of the Magicians*. Later, while the pupils were studying Dervish dances, the pupils gained this experience through moving around a large enneagram drawn on the floor at the **Institute** (*Search*: 294–5). The turning nature of these movements in relation to the enneagram may have suggested Dervish and thus Sufi origins for the enneagram (see **dance/dancing**).

Although Gurdjieff told his pupils that the enneagram had been kept secret and could not be met with elsewhere, Webb (1980: 499–542) shows possible Western European occult origins for the enneagram in the work of Ramon Lull (*The Great Art of Raymon Lull*, *c*.1305–8) and the *Arithmologia* (1665) of Athanasius Kircher. There are similarities between Lull's search for a geometric form of symbolic universal language and Gurdjieff's presentation of the enneagram as the hieroglyph of a universal language (see Figure 14). Webb establishes clear connections between Kircher's enneagram, the Kabbala's Tree of Life and Gurdjieff's enneagram (see Figures 15 and 16).

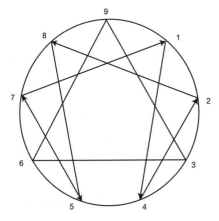

i. Gurdjieff's Enneagram: shows a circle equally divided into nine, the 9, 3, 6 triangle represents the law of three, the 1, 4, 2, 8, 5, 7 figure represents the law of seven

ii. Lull's 'T' Diagram shows a circle equally divided into nine, the points connected to form three triangles: BCD, EFG, and HIK

Lull's 'A' Diagram shows all possible lines drawn between these nine points. From these both Gurdjieff's and Kircher's Enneagrams can be drawn. Gurdjieff's Enneagram shown in heavy line

Figure 14 Enneagram: Enneagram and Lull

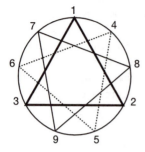

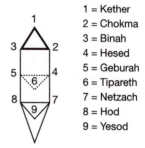

Kircher's Enneagram with the
numbers of the Tree

1 = Kether
2 = Chokma
3 = Binah
4 = Hesed
5 = Geburah
6 = Tipareth
7 = Netzach
8 = Hod
9 = Yesod

The numbers related to the
sephiroth of the Tree

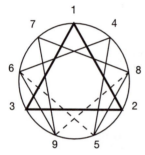

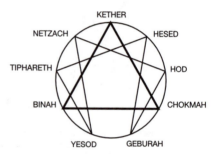

Diagrams showing the numbers and sephiroth from the Tree transferred to
Gurdjieff's Enneagram

Figure 15 Enneagram: Enneagram and Tree of Life

The three realms of Kether, Binah and Chokma, and the seven realms
of Geburah, Hesed, Tipareth, Hod, Netzach, Yesod and Malkuth of
the Tree of Life, are also related to Gurdjieff's Laws of Three and
Seven (see Figure 17). This similarity is also noted by Speeth (1977:
18).

Ouspensky's definition of the points of the enneagram according
to different microcosms (i.e. planetary, digestive) and also macrocosmos planetary 'codes' makes use of the enneagram in the same
way that the realms of the Tree of Life have been used as a decoding
key to interpret the relationship between macrocosm and microcosm.

Thus although Gurdjieff may have found the enneagram and his

i Kircher's Enneagram

ii Gurdjieff's Enneagram

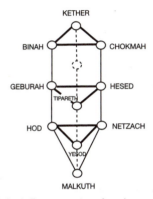

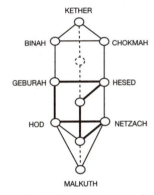

iii Kircher's Enneagram transferred
onto the tree of life

iv Gurdjieff's Enneagram transferred
onto the tree of life

Figure 16 Enneagram: Enneagram and Tree of Life: from data in Webb, 1980:
507–8

Laws of Three and Seven in the East, it is difficult to imagine that he did not also know of these Western sources. (See also Wellbeloved 2001a, 2001b; **laws: an overview; occult/occult revival**).

A prayer practice, newly termed 'Kything', that aims for a spiritual entering into another person for the purpose of establishing a communion between people, either alive or dead (see Savary and Berne 1988), is in use in relation to the enneagram (see Metz and Burchill 1987). Texts for and against the enneagram, the 'Christianising' of the enneagram and a questioning of Kything can be found on websites, among others, on that of the Anglican Renewal Ministries of Canada.

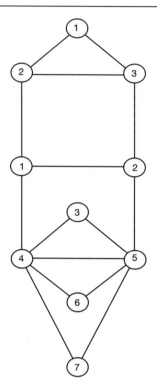

Figure 17 Enneagram: Tree of Life related to Laws of Three and Seven

Further reading

See Bennett 1983 [1974]; Nicoll 1952: vol.2; Mouravieff 1993; Work-influenced writer Vollmar 1997; and Blake 1996, who explores the enneagram in Work terms. For the enneagram of personality, see Riso 1995 [1987] and Palmer 1995; see also Almaas 1998. For a brief history of the enneagram in America, see Levine 1999 and Patterson 1998: 21–46.

ENTITY

Although in general everything either involves or evolves, an entity is something that remains for a certain time without involving (*Views*, 1924: 205).

ESCAPE

Gurdjieff often referred to the inability of man to escape from the 'prison' of his mechanicality (see **machine/mechanicality**). In order to escape a man must be aware of being imprisoned; only a **group** of such people can receive the help of those who have already escaped (*Search*: 30).

ESOTERIC/ESOTERICISM

There are many pseudo-esoteric schools of **alchemy**, the **occult** and **Theosophy** that are imitations of real esoteric **schools**. There may be real esoteric schools in the East, but a person would have no access to them because they are hidden in the inner courts of some monasteries (*Search*: 314). According to the theory of esotericism, mankind is divided into two circles: the outer circle contains everyone who is not in the small inner esoteric centre containing instructed and under-standing people, who alone can help mankind to change. The **aim** of the **Work** is to prepare pupils to receive instruction from this centre (*Views*, 1922: 78: see also **conscious circle of humanity**). Earlier Gurdjieff defined the esoteric and the exoteric as two parallel lines of civilisations. Teachings, such as Christianity, arise when external conditions are favourable to esotericism (*Views*, 1918: 211).

See also: **religion/s, new religions**

Further reading

For links between 'Esoteric Buddhism' and Christianity influential in Theoso-phical circles after 1894, see Webb 1980: 525–7; Faivre and Needleman 1992; and Faivre 1994.

ESSENCE

The term 'essence' needs to be considered along with the term **personality**. A man is divided into essence and personality. Essence is what is a person's own, what is real and true, the tastes and preferences he was born with and that cannot be taken from him. Unless a person works on themselves they are unlikely to develop their essence, which usually remains at an infantile level, although people who live in conditions of danger, nearer to nature, have more chance of developing their essence. Personality is all that is not a person's own, that is false and has been added since childhood by education and culture, and that can be removed from him. In order for essence to develop it must become active, while personality must become passive. A person in the **Work** needs to be able to distinguish essence from personality; he needs both because the only part of him that can develop is his essence, but the **buffers** and **rolls**, which function to support his personality, provide the struggle through which a person can grow. Without some experience of his own mechanicality (see **machine/mechanicality**) a person will have no reason to work on himself. For work to proceed well, both essence and personality need to be equally developed. Unfortunately, both are subject to abnormal development, and in many people whom we see in the street the essence has died before the personality; in such cases these people are already dead (*Search*: 161–4). Gurdjieff showed his 1916 group an experiment in the separation of essence from personality in which one man 'woke up' and revealed a strong essence, while another 'went to sleep' and revealed little essence (*Search*: 251–4).

Essence is referred to as one of the three independent **machines** that man is born with, and which continues to form till his death. The others are **body** and personality. Each machine may develop differently (i.e. a man may have brave personality but a timid essence). The thinking centre is the **centre of gravity** for the personality (see **intellectual/thinking centre, intelligence**); essence is purely emotional, its centre of gravity or **soul** is the **emotional centre**:

> it consists of what is received from heredity before the formation of personality, and later, only those sensations and feelings among which a man lives.

> (*Views*, 1922: 136–7)

Elsewhere Gurdjieff mentions that essence and personality are untied by **conscience** when under conditions of great shock or sorrow (*Views*, 1924: 239).

'Our essence consists of many centers, but our personality has only one center, the formatory apparatus' (*Views*, 1924: 144). Here Gurdjieff refers to the **formatory apparatus** in terms of a centre, though elsewhere he says it is not a centre. It is necessary to learn to discriminate between essence and personality. Then what has been lost can be re-established. This is the purpose of development, rather than the acquisition of anything new. Later a pupil can see what to change and how to change (*Views*, 1924: 143–7; see also **habits**). The desire for change must come from the essence, not the personality (*Views*, 1924: 239–40).

Essence and mind have nothing in common, no interdependence; however, the mind can become identified with the essence. Essence is weak, and being dependent on changing influences (e.g. food or weather) can change at any moment. It takes great power to give direction to the essence, thus the essence must be separated from the mind, which, having few influences, can be better kept in a direction (*Views*, 1923: 148–54). However, Gurdjieff also said that essence belongs to **type** and does not change (*Views*, 1924: 143; see also **mind**; **work, lines of**).

Both essence and personality have mechanically acquired prejudices and partialities. Our essence absorbs almost nothing from the time we are born. Personality picks up perhaps twenty or thirty ideas (*Views*, 1924: 241, see also **considering**).

ETERNAL, THE *see* **time/the eternal**

EVIL *see* **good and evil**

EVOLUTION/INVOLUTION

There are both evolutionary and involutionary processes. These are always in motion, and both have limits. Involution is the process through which the worlds are created from above, in the **Ray of Creation**, from the **Absolute** to the **Moon**. In contrast, evolution proceeds from the lower to the higher (*Views*, 1924: 187; see also **impressions**).

Involutionary processes are distinguished from evolutionary processes. Involutionary processes are conscious in their origins in the Absolute, but become more mechanical the further they travel from the Absolute: this expresses a downward flow of energy from above to below, from the one to the many, a Creation and then a Fall.

Evolutionary processes start half consciously, but become more conscious as they proceed. The evolutionary processes must struggle against unconscious mechanical forces and occasionally against split-off parts of the evolutionary force itself (*Search*: 306–9). This expresses an upward movement towards the Absolute, from the many towards the one, a redemption or re-creation (see also **entity**).

The evolution of man cannot occur separately from surrounding **Nature**, nor can it result from the conquest of nature. **Humanity**, as part of **organic life**, exists to serve the needs of the Earth and to provide food for the Moon. Therefore humanity neither progresses nor evolves: to do so would be harmful for the planetary world. The evolution of mankind corresponds to the evolution of the planets, but this takes place over such long cycles of time that no essential change can take place in the life of mankind. There are planetary forces that inhibit the evolution of humanity as a whole and of individual humans. However, individual men do have the possibility of evolving. For them the opposing forces are useful, because it is by overcoming obstacles that a man can develop the qualities he needs. The evolution of man is the evolution of his **consciousness**, of his **will** and of his power of **doing**; these do not evolve unconsciously (*Search*: 56–9).

However, we may compare the above with Gurdjieff's statement that although there is no way of assessing what stage of evolution the Ray of Creation has reached now, organic life has to evolve in order to supply the needs of the evolving Earth and Moon. The evolutionary part of organic life on earth is humanity, which also has a specifically evolving part. Humanity as a whole is now at a standstill; changes can only be made at moments of 'cross-roads', representing the 'intervals' in the **Law of Seven**. If the Ray of Creation does not continue to evolve, then part of it may die. If organic life – and specifically humanity – does not evolve to fulfil its purpose, it may be destroyed.

> The evolution of humanity can only proceed through the evolution of a certain group, which, in its turn will influence and lead the rest of humanity.

> (*Search*: 305–15)

There is a possibility, for a limited time, for the Moon to evolve, to become a planet like the Earth, and for the Earth to become like the Sun (*Search*: 25–6). Gurdjieff's ideas of planetary and psychological evolution echo those of Blavatsky. Both extend Darwinian evolution to a Nietzschean evolution of man into a super-race.

Arising from Gurdjieff's views, and because of contemporary ecological concerns, the evolution of man is seen by some people in the Work as a road whereby the Earth might be 'saved' (see George 1995), while other people focus on the need for self-perfection and the formation of an elite.

See also: **conscious circle of humanity; Gnosticism**

Further reading

Blavatsky 1988 [1888]; for Blavatsky's transformation of Darwin's theory of evolution into a theory of the cosmic spiritual evolution of individual man and of an evolution of race, see Webb 1971b: 52–4. See Kingsford (in Weigel 1886 [1694]: 45–6) on the 'two great wheels of Evolution and Involution', the outer of which is the macrocosm, the inner the microcosm; for evolutionary psychiatry, see Ellenberger 1970.

EXERCISES

In Essentuki in 1917 exercises were given to pupils to enable them to relax unnecessary tensions and gain control over their muscles, so that they could take up postures adopted in **schools** for praying or contemplation. These exercises always began with the muscles of the face. Sensing exercises in which **attention** is transferred from one part of the body to another, exercises in which movements were made in conjunction with moving the attention internally in the body, these exercises could be further complicated through repetition of words and through breathing patterns. Extreme fatigue could enable the handing over of the activities engaged in from the intellectual to the moving centre (*Search*: 358–9).

Exercises given in the second period of work in Essentuki in March 1918 were more complex and difficult than those of the preceding year. 'These included rhythmic exercises to music, dervish dances, different kinds of mental exercises, the study of different ways of breathing', as well as the study of imitation psychic phenomena – the study of 'tricks' prepared pupils to discriminate between fake and real phenomena (*Search*: 372).

In the exercises saying the words 'I am, I can, I wish' (*Life*: 134–6), the changes in the order of these verbs indicate a change of triad, as each phrase represents the affirming, denying or reconciling force of Gurdjieff's **Law of Three**.

Gurdjieff gave individual exercises to pupils, according to their specific needs, and also to **groups** (see also **prayer/praying**).

Among others, Gurdjieff gave exercises for thinking (see *Views*, 1923: 106); for putting oneself in the position of others (see *Views*,

1924: 146); to increase physical, psychical and moral power (see *Views*, 1923: 159–63); and for attitude (see *Views*, 1924: 244–5).

There are a number of exercises mentioned in *Voices*. Not all are defined, though many are generally comprehensible from the discussions about them, some are for a specific person only. Gurdjieff stresses the need for constant repetition of the exercises he gives. Nothing will be achieved at once: exercises must be done thousands and thousands of times. Gurdjieff explores the first exercise that he gives to everyone to allow them to have a collected state. For this one must not allow the **atmosphere** to go further than it should. When the pupil says 'I am':

> you will sense that you are in yourself, you will sense in the whole of the body – the echo of 'I' – and when you say 'am' you will have the sensation, completely, that you are you.

There are also exercises for reading; and for helping to self-remember. In order that results gained through exercises may accumulate and not be lost, pupils should be compelled to think at both the beginning and the end of exercises, so that what is gained remains until the next time. Care should be taken not to do anything that will cause a lot of **emanations**. It would be useful for a pupil to offer a subjective prayer and ask his **ideal** to help him to guard what he has until next time (*Voices*: 160, 232, 28, 76, 280).

Work pupils have a daily exercise to develop attention.

See also: **New Work**

EXPERIMENTS

In common with other anti-enlightenment occult 'sciences' (e.g. alchemy) and with the 'new science' of psychology, Gurdjieff presented the Work as a 'science', and refers in his texts to experiments he made in order to understand the functioning of man's body and psyche.

In *Tales* the advice Gurdjieff gives his reader is the result of:

> numerous deductions and conclusions made [...] during experimental elucidations concerning the productivity of the

perception by contemporary people of new impressions from what is heard and read.

(*Tales*: vi)

In *Meetings* Gurdjieff describes a series of actions carried out under hypnotism (see **hypnosis/hypnotism**), and a number of experiments made on his own or with the 'Seekers of Truth'. In *Herald of Coming Good* Gurdjieff refers to early experiments and observations of man's subconscious mentation carried out, while he was a hypnotist/healer and teacher of the supernatural, on people who were the 'guinea-pigs' allocated to him by 'Destiny'. The need for prolonged contact with a wide group of types for these experiments led him to form his **Institutes**.

The methods used in the Institute in France were based on the 'so-called "experimental material" handed down from the past'. Pupils can be initiated as a result of his special researches. Gurdjieff describes experiments, carried out around 1932, to find out why the kinder he was to people the more hostile they became towards him. This led to a further experiment, which Gurdjieff recounts in order to shock his pupils into thinking and feeling in a way 'more proper' to man (*Herald*: 20–5, 35–40, 68–77; see also **faith**).

The harshness of Gurdjieff's reference to pupils as 'rats for my experiments', reported by Nott (*Journey*: 38; *Teachings*: 71), may be softened if related to the fact that Gurdjieff, having been told of Nott's terror of rats, told Nott that from nature's point of view some animals, 'even rats', are better than man. However, Gurdjieff referred to his neighbours in Paris, who loved him, as 'mice', saying that if he lived elsewhere he would have other 'mice' (*Voices*: 142).

FACTORY *see* **three-storey factory/digestion of three foods**

FAITH

Gurdjieff's character Ashiata Shiemash defines three kinds of faith: 'Faith of consciousness is freedom, Faith of feelings is weakness, Faith of body is stupidity' (*Tales*: 361). Gurdjieff emphasised that no faith is required in properly organised groups. A small amount of trust is necessary, but only until a man begins to verify what is said for himself

(*Search*: 228). However, compare this with Gurdjieff's statement that if pupils in a group begin to mistrust or criticise the teacher they cannot work with that teacher. When a man distrusts his teacher, his teacher is unnecessary to him and he is unnecessary to his teacher (*Search*: 225; see also **groups**).

> Believe nothing, not even yourself. I believe only if I have statistical proof, that is, only if I have obtained the same result over and over again. I study, I work for guidance, not for belief.

> (*Views*, 1924: 201)

The injunctions against faith do not seem to be compatible with the demand for **obedience**. Gurdjieff held that faith is necessary for Christians (*Views*, 1924: 191; see also **ways/fourth way**).

Gurdjieff gave his pupils new understanding of words such as 'man' or 'world' within the context of his own teaching. He shows pupils' usual understanding of these words to be incomplete and offers his own definitions from within the context of his teaching. He insists that the pupils must verify his definitions through their own experience (*Views*, 1924: 60–74). However, the terminology of their discourse has already been fixed and so a person's findings can only fall within the already accepted Gurdjieffian terminology. For example, an experience of self-fragmentation will be explained and expressed by the pupil according to Gurdjieff's theories, and then understood as 'proof' that his theories are correct. However, it is possible to explain the experience of self-fragmentation according to other terms and discourses, including those (e.g. philosophical or religious) that Gurdjieff has already described as limited.

In the 1920s faith in the institutions of church and state and in the inevitability of progress had been eroded in Europe by the experiences of World War I. This detachment from traditional sources of faith left a need that was met by the acceptance of the many guru figures of that time.

Further reading

For the nineteenth-century factors that prepared the way for twentieth-century gurus, see Washington 1993: 5–25; for Western gurus, see Rawlinson 1997.

FALL

The **Work** teaching itself, and man's need of such a teaching, is based on the assumption that man is Fallen. This has many similarities to Christian thinking. However, while in Christianity man has been redeemed through the death of Christ, the Fall may only be redeemed in the Work through the individual's struggle against his situation.

Tales is a Fall myth that contains within it many Fall stories, and this theme is restated in Gurdjieff's other texts. In *Tales*, a high birth rate is connected with poor quality and lack of the **emanations** needed by 'Great Nature'. Beelzebub values higher quality emanations, which ensure a longer life-span and a lower birth rate; this notion suggests a reversal of the Biblical Fall, which brought about the begetting of children and a diminishing life-span.

In *Life* (22, 127–8), Gurdjieff affirms that he is a man and 'as such, in contrast to all other outer forms of animal life, is created by Him in His image'. His writing expresses the Fall, saying that man ought to justify his existence by doing the will of 'our COMMON FATHER', and that in the beginning they did so, but through laziness and a desire for peace, generation by generation, man became separated 'from the general life proceeding on Earth'.

See also: **Gnosticism**

Further reading

Milton's heroic fallen angel Satan is the literary precursor of the fallen romantic heroes of Goethe, Blake, Shelley, Coleridge and Byron, who represent aspects of the internalised myth of the Fall. Gurdjieff's Beelzebub can be seen to belong to this group of fallen heroes.

FALSE PERSONALITY *see* personality

FASTS/FASTING

At the beginning of a fast, the substances the body uses for digestion must be used up by an excess of physical exercise, otherwise they will poison the organism (*Search*: 358–9; see also **stop exercise**). Food at Gurdjieff's Institute was 'meagre and unpalatable, except on Saturday nights when there was a rich feast'. Fasts of various kinds and degrees were also carried out at the Institute (Bennett 1962: 117).

FATE

Fate is the result of planetary **influences** that correspond to a man's **type**. Fate may be good or bad; it is better than accident because it can be foreseen and evaded if necessary. However, fate only affects essence, so a person without a developed essence will not receive his fate. Fate is both collective and individual; collective fate is governed by general laws, from which a man who wishes to have individuality must free himself (*Search*: 161, 164–5).

FEAR

In 1917 Gurdjieff told his pupils that a man leading a cultured life does not realise the role fear plays in his life, he is afraid of everything and everybody, and they are afraid of him. This all-pervading fear was then especially visible, and a greater part of what had happened the previous year (1916–17, during the Russian Revolution) was based on fear and the results of fear. Unconscious fear is a characteristic feature of sleep. People have no idea how much they are carried away by fear, which becomes almost a mania (*Views*, 1917: 252–3). Only consciousness of our nothingness can overcome the fear of submission to the teacher's will (*Search*: 161). However, in 1922 Gurdjieff said that 'all emotions are rudimentary organs of something higher'; fear, for example, may be an organ off future clairvoyance (*Views*, 1922: 194; see also **emotional centre**; **terror of the situation**). Gurdjieff writes in *Meetings* (44–5) of his father teaching him to overcome timidity, fear or revulsion of mice, worms and snakes.

FOOD/EATING

Man takes in three kinds of food: the food he eats, the **air** he breathes and the **impressions** he receives. Each of these foods is transformed within the **body** (see also **three-storey factory/digestion of three foods**).

There are three excrements. The first is the result of ordinary food and must be eliminated each day. The second is sexual and must be eliminated in the bathroom, for some every day, for others every week or month or six months. The third excrement is formed in the head from the food of impressions, 'the waste accumulates in the brain';

doctors ignore it, as they ignore the role of the appendix in digestion (*Voices*, 46).

See also: **bodies**

FOOD DIAGRAM *see* **three-storey factory/digestion of three foods**

FORCES

The three forces in Gurdjieff's **Law of Three** are termed the first, second and third forces, and are also called positive, negative and reconciling forces or active, passive and neutralising forces. They are related to the three astrological modes (cardinal, fixed and mutable) and function in the same way.

See also: **astrology**

Further reading

For Hegelian triads, see Tarnas 1991: 379 and Taylor 2001: 215.

FORMATORY APPARATUS

The formatory apparatus is the only part of the **intellectual centre** that functions. New knowledge will not be received by the intellectual but by the **emotional centre** (*Search*: 235).

The formatory apparatus is not a centre, it receives and transmits impressions from the outside world to the **centres**, as well as information between centres, analogous to a typist in an office who takes and passes on messages from, for example, a set of directors (the centres), all of whom speak a different language. The typist decodes and recodes the messages, sometimes correctly and sometimes with mistakes, and transmits them through labels. What we call 'thoughts' are in reality those labels. Thoughts in various centres may never be transmitted; the centre best connected to the formatory apparatus is the moving centre, the next best is the sex centre, after that the emotional centre, and the least connected is the thinking centre. Most people live their entire lives connected only through the first two centres, few ever connect with the fourth. The formatory apparatus differs from centres in that its matter is inanimate and all its properties are organic, while the matter of the centres is animate and their properties are psychical (*Views*, 1923: 128, 135).

FOUNDATIONS *see* **Appendix 2**

FOURTH WAY *see* **ways/Fourth Way**

FRICTION

Crystallisation of inner unity can only be obtained through the friction caused by the struggle between 'yes' and 'no'. However, friction must have the right foundation. Friction arising from a fanatical belief will crystallise a man in such a way that he cannot develop further without a painful de-crystallisation process (*Search*: 32). In relation to the **Law of Three**, there must be friction between the positive and negative principles; friction/suffering leads to the third principle (*Views*, 1924: 98).

The willingness to experience friction was a necessary part of the **Work** teaching. Gurdjieff provided friction of differing kinds for his pupils, especially at the **Institute**, through the conditions of communal living and through his own treatment of pupils (*Search*: 367, 370; see also Peters 1976 [1964, 1965]: 295–7; Taylor 2001: 63–89).

See also: **conscience**

GENDER

Gurdjieff expresses the following (sometimes conflicting) views about the differing natures of men and women, and the consequent differences in their roles in life and in the Work. While he sometimes focuses on the passive and emotional nature of women in relation to the active and intellectual nature of men, he also states that both men and women contain passive and active elements.

Peters recalls Gurdjieff stating that man is active, positive and good in nature. Woman is passive, negative and evil, though in the sense of 'necessary evil' rather than 'wrong'. Women's passivity is necessary to help men: both elements are needed, as in electricity. The roles of men and women in life ought to reflect the differences in their natures, but this is not so. Men have aspiration, which women never have, and this compels men, for example, to climb mountains or to fly. Men also try to find heaven through creativity: writing, music, painting. When challenged by the fact that women scientists and artists do exist, Gurdjieff said that the (contemporary) world is 'mixed up'. Although there are also women artists and scientists, this is because women try to do men's work, which is wrong for women.

The roles of men and women in the Work are also different. Men could use their aspiration to develop themselves, but as this is not possible in today's world they achieve a kind of immortality through having children.

Women need neither the Work, nor psychological or religious teachings; they cannot achieve self-development in the way that Gurdjieff understands the phrase. Women already 'know everything', but this knowledge can be 'almost a poison' for them. Women are from the ground; their only hope to rise to another state of development is through men. If a woman finds a real man then she can become a real woman without the necessity to work, but there are now no real men. However, true human beings are both male and female (Peters 1976 [1964, 1965]: 109, 112–13).

These statements seem at variance with the fact that Gurdjieff's chosen successor was a woman and that his women pupils have played a significant role in transmitting his teaching (see **appendix 1**; **appendix 2**).

In *Views* Gurdjieff is recalled as saying that men are more developed intellectually and women are more developed emotionally; intellectual work is easier for men and emotional work easier for women, but both men and women have equal chances to work towards a fusion of the intellect and emotions so as to produce a force (*Views*, 1924: 87).

Gurdjieff identifies some men and women as belonging to a third intermediate sex, neither male nor female, due to education, society and customs (*Voices*: 261).

Further reading

For a story relating to Gurdjieff's description of woman as a necessary evil, which may remind the reader of the function of Socrates' wife, see Peters 1976 [1964, 1965]: 107–10; for positive and negative roles, see **elements**.

GNOSTICISM

Gnosticism has formed part of the European occult underground since the establishment of the Christian church. It became influential through the occult revival of the late nineteenth century. Webb (1980: 524–5) suggests Anna Kingsford's 'esoteric Christianity', a mix of alchemy and Gnosticism, as a possible route through which Gurdjieff might have encountered Gnosticism.

Gurdjieff's pupils recognised similarities between Gnostic teachings and the Work: the helpless and lost state of man; his inhabiting a difficult and remote place in the universe, far from the Absolute; man's sleep; his need for divine messengers; the failure of all divine messengers in their mission to awaken man. Anderson (1962: 42) suggests Gnosticism as coming from the same 'initiate source' as Gurdjieff's teaching, and Ouspensky recognises some of Gurdjieff's ideas about time as similar to those in Gnostic and Indian thought (*Search*: 339). Orage relates man's state with the Gnostic 'Hymn of the Robe of Glory' (*Teachings*: 129; see also **difficulties**).

During World War II, Gurdjieff stressed the need for self-hatred (see **body**; **group meetings during world war ii (1940–4)**).

Further reading

Jonas 1959; Raschke 1980. For an account of the Gnostic 'ascent of the soul', based on the idea (which Gurdjieff echoes) that we live in the most difficult part of the universe, remote from its source and subject to planetary forces (or Archons) from which we must free ourselves, see Rudolph 1983: 171–94. Mauraviev suggests a Christian Gnostic origin for the Work, see Mouravieff 1989, 1992, 1993.

GOOD AND EVIL

All evil lies in the involuntary unconscious manifestation of men-machines (*Search*: 52; see also **sin**). People act in the interests of good, even when they kill each other. Ideas of good and evil are only permanent in connection with a permanent aim. If a person knows they are asleep and has the aim to awaken, everything that helps this aim is good, everything that hinders it is evil (*Search*: 158–9). Actions are 'good' if done in accordance with conscience and 'bad' if later a man feels 'remorse' (*Tales*: 342; see also **conscience**).

In *Herald of Coming Good*, the 'good' referred to is the good that will result from the publication of Gurdjieff's writings. The text raises questions about the nature of the 'good'. Although Gurdjieff opens *Herald* with his 'good' wish to instil in people the 'psychic-initiative', which will enable them to recognise the moral obligation to help their neighbour, later Gurdjieff confesses that his automatic influence on people paralyses their initiative. This is contradictory to his nature and, the reader must assume, contrary to his wishes for their good. Later, Gurdjieff recounts an **experiment** he made to shock his pupils. The 'shocking factor' in this account might be that Gurdjieff vows vindictively to inflict lasting moral suffering on people he is angry with. This promises 'coming ill', rather than 'coming good'. In this light the reader must re-evaluate Gurdjieff and his aim in this text.

Gurdjieff's presentation of himself in his texts as both 'good' and 'evil' accords with his statement about 'real man'. Peters (1976 [1964, 1965]: 40, 115) writes that real man is neither 'good' nor 'evil' but conscious: real man always has two sides, one good and one evil, but so that one side does not destroy the other a man needs to develop **conscience**. However, the capacity for both good and evil develop together, and the struggle to find a reconciling force between good and evil was never-ending, the more one learned, the more difficult life would be.

Gurdjieff refers to a pupil as a source of evil in the world, for his family and for everyone; either the pupil will cease to be this source of evil, and acquire a real individuality, or else he will perish (*Voices*: 176).

Further reading

Nietzsche 1998 [1886].

GOOD HOUSEHOLDER *see* obyvatel

GRACE

The central focus of Gurdjieff's oral and written teaching was on the demand that the pupil worked actively on himself, rather than on the pupil's passive ability to receive help that might be termed 'grace'. However, pupil memoirs testify to the help they received from Gurdjieff's **presence**, with Bennett writing of Sufi *baraka*, an enabling energy analogous to Christian grace, as the 'key' to making the teaching work (see Wellbeloved 1998: 321–32; Bennett 1976: 219).

There are references to grace in Gurdjieff's writings. In *Tales* (54), Beelzebub is redeemed not by his labours alone but also through the intercession of a divine messenger and the grace of His Endlessness. Gurdjieff defined his own powers of telepathy and hypnotism as a 'grace' of his inherency (*Life*: 25), and writes that 'man receives all his possibilities from On High' (*Life*: 173).

Orage says, in relation to *Tales*, that because man can no longer fulfil his cosmic function, his life on earth exists now 'only by Grace' (*Teachings*: 195).

Bennett (1979 [1975]: 109–18) defines grace as 'waking up' that is never deserved, and comments that to shock people into waking destroys something 'irreplaceably precious'. However, this is at variance with earlier Bennett writings and so may be in accordance with **New Work** ideas.

Michel de Salzmann rejects the notions of charisma or psycho-analytic 'transference' as explanations for the power to awaken others that emanated from Gurdjieff's presence (Driscoll 1985: xxiii).

GROUPS

A man is unable to wake up by himself. However, if a group is formed he can be helped by his **teacher** and the group members. The teacher decides which **types** should work together. The group must have an a **aim**. In the beginning the aim is self-study, in which group members act as mirrors for each other: they share their observations and do not allow one another to sleep peacefully (see *Search*: 30, 223).

Ouspensky was told that there were no conditions he must adhere to in joining a group. This was because man cannot as he is make or assume obligations (*Search*: 14). This is in contradiction with later statements about groups, in which conditions are set out. For example, group members must obey the teacher and the rules he sets out for the group. They must keep what happens in the group secret forever. This is partly because group members are incapable of transmitting to people outside the group what is happening within the group, and partly because a man needs to learn to keep silent about things that interest him (see **secrecy/silence**). A group member must never lie, either directly or by omission, to his teacher. He must continue to treat the teacher with trust and respect, remembering that he came to learn and not to teach. The group must remember its aim, to work, and not become merely a social gathering. The rules given to groups act as **alarm clocks** to help the members to wake up: they ought to be difficult and unpleasant. General rules are given to the group as a whole; individual rules are given to help members of the group see their chief fault (see **chief feature**). However, there are false teachers and false groups. The true teacher does not demand faith, but only a little trust (*Search*: 221–6). This is at variance with the idea of obedience, which is also strongly stressed. It is difficult to see how the pupil, who is asleep and cannot 'do', will be able to discriminate between the true teacher and the false.

The efforts that a pupil makes can never be set against mistakes; if he lies about a small thing this may ruin years of **Work**. Group members are co-responsible and so the mistake of one member may destroy the whole group. If a member leaves a group, no other group member may contact him. For this reason, if a husband or wife leaves a group, their partner must also leave. The group is only useful if it produces results (*Search*: 230–1, 271).

Gurdjieff wrote that pupils at the 1922 Institute in France progressed, according to their degree of comprehension, from an Exoteric to a Mesoteric (presumably an intermediate group) and finally an Esoteric group (*Herald*: 39).

Today Work groups are given exercises, which focus on one or other line of work (see **work, lines of**), or on a specific aspect of the teaching. These are explored individually in everyday life, and during days or longer periods of time while working with others in the Work. The findings and questions arising from these may be brought to group meetings.

GROUP MEETINGS DURING WORLD WAR II (1940–4)

Notes from thirty-two Gurdjieff group meetings in wartime Paris are given in *Voices*. Gurdjieff did not usually allow notes to be taken during meetings, and notes taken in Nazi-occupied Paris must surely have been a risk to him and his pupils. Yet here he acknowledges the note-taker directly (*Voices*: 75, 108). The records of the meetings are believed by the Foundations to be authentic. However, the reader should be aware that the names of note-takers and/or translators are not given, nor are the meetings dated.

In Gurdjieff's early teaching, as recorded by Ouspensky (1915–22), pupils were rendered helpless by their acknowledgement of the intricacies of their own mechanical functioning expressed in terms of complex cosmic theory (see **difficulties**). In the World War II meetings the central demand was for pupils to exercise **will** and gain control of their emotional relations to themselves, their families and others. The pupils are engaged in a paradox through which they are exhorted to be good **egoists**, but at the same time they have to constantly experience and acknowledge their own nothingness. Although they are defined as powerless and worthless, pupils must outwardly play a role and inwardly must not identify (see **identifica-tion; roles**). They must have no feelings for people other than their own blood relations (*Voices*: 116, 104, 51). Gurdjieff taught the necessity, first, of acknowledging the debt to one's parents and **Nature**, and, second, of **suffering** brought about by recalling the wrongs done to parents in the past. This intense suffering engenders **remorse**, which can connect the pupil to **conscience** and repair the past (*Voices*: 162, 164). The struggle between the needs of the physical **body**, which must be subdued and made to obey, and the psychical body, which has other desires, leads to the formation of a **master**, independent 'I' and 'real love' (see **'i'/identity; love**). The Work is expressed in terms of no compromise, all or nothing, succeed or die (*Voices*: 164, 176).

Pupils are given **exercises** (only some of which are described in the text) to do with sensing, feeling and breathing. Gurdjieff focuses on Work in relation to the family. There are contradictions here: pupils must hate and love, trust and mistrust their family members (*Voices*: 198, 73, 269–70). Parents must sacrifice everything for their children: once children arrive, the parents' life is over. They relate as brother and sister, and they must do everything for their children, even kill or commit crimes. As adults, children must in turn do everything for their parents, because they are under an obligation to pay for their births. Regardless of their own evaluation of their parents, they must give them everything they want, including becoming a good thief if that is what the parents like. Unless the children incarnate the ideal of the parents, the parents cannot love them. Should a mother ask something horrible of the child, it must be done; the child would hate the mother inwardly, but outwardly he must comply. Asked by the pupil if outwardly means in front of her, but not in reality, Gurdjieff agrees and says it is criminal advice to create such things in a child. When the pupil enquires how he can love his parent if he must hate her, Gurdjieff replies that it is the pupil's duty and he must do it (*Voices*: 155–6, 193, 270). Sometimes these behavioural demands are given as absolute and sometimes as operating only for a short period of time. Gurdjieff defines his own relation to others: his neighbours are 'mice' for his experiments, he is indifferent to pupils until they make progress, in which case they may be redefined, in terms of familial relationship, as brother or sister (*Voices*: 142, 49, 88).

It is impossible to know what, if anything, the note-takers have edited out of the records of the meetings, but as they are given in *Voices* there is only one reference to the war, about the difficulty of replacing kitchen breakages, and none to the German occupation of Paris. However, there are more than ten references to killing: the (inner) enemy, weaknesses, sacred impulses, religious faith (*Voices*: 94, 197, 139, 152).

Gurdjieff says to a pupil, who is a teacher, that if he thinks 'I am' and at the same time wishes to help while he teaches, the children will love him – he can tell the children to go and kill their parents and they will do it. This warns of the danger of influencing children. In the same meeting, Gurdjieff tells a pupil to do a task he has been given or go and 'open a vein', that he, Gurdjieff, has a pill that will make the pupil 'sleep forever' (*Voices*: 161, 159).

Perhaps because it is also taking place during wartime, the tone of the Work in these World War II meetings is as **Gnostic**, as it was in 1915–22. Pupils are incited to self-loathing and self-punishment, to think of their physical **body** as a stranger. They are distant from God, who may be contacted only through a series of intermediaries (*Voices*: 159, 200, 164, 171–4; see also **occult/occult revival**).

Further reading

For the group as part of Sufi teaching, see Bennett 1976: 218–19; for an account of the **Rope** Group, see **appendix 2** and Patterson 1999.

GURDJIEFF SOCIETY, THE *see* **Appendix 2**

HABIT

Habits and habitual functioning take up a great deal of **energy** that could be used for **Work**: for example, the flow of inner thoughts, fantasies, daydreams and inner talking, continually talking with others, unnecessary muscular tensions, emotions, and anxieties. The attempt to alter physical habits (e.g. walking) enables a pupil to observe and study his habits. Ouspensky reports habitual talking as being the chief difficulty for many, 'this habit touched everything' and was the least noticed (*Search*: 111–12, 356).

Although man is always dependent on mechanical influences, which dictate habitual responses, it is possible to study habits and eventually to replace useless habits with more useful ones (*Views*, 1924: 145).

See also: **machine/mechanicality**

HANBLEDZOIN; SACRED-HANBLEDZOIN *see*
grace; magnetism/animal magnetism

HASNAMUSS

In *Tales*, Hasnamuss beings do not have the 'Divine impulse of Objective-Conscience' (*Tales*: 235). Beelzebub describes Hasnamuss beings as having 'something' in them that produces destructive impulses. Their attributes, which may be compared to the five strivings (see **duty/striving**), are:

1 Every kind of depravity, conscious as well as unconscious.
2 The feeling of satisfaction in leading others astray.
3 The irresistible inclination to destroy the existence of other breathing creatures.
4 The urge to become free from the necessity of actualising the being-efforts demanded by **Nature**.
5 The attempt to conceal from others by every kind of artificiality what in their opinion are one's physical defects.
6 Calm self-contentment in the use of what is not personally deserved.
7 The striving to be not what one is.

(*Tales*: 406)

Hasnamuss beings with only planetary bodies die and decompose. Those with astral bodies must re-enter life in the body of a one- or two-brained being in order to try to eliminate the 'something'. A Hasnamuss with the highest being body cannot decompose anywhere in the universe and can only eliminate the 'something' through conscious labours and intentional suffering (see **bodies; conscious labour and intentional/voluntary suffering**). As lunatics and tramps are the negative defined in relation to the positive obyvatel (see **lunatic/tramp; obyvatel**), so Gurdjieff's anti-hero Lentro-hamsanin (an Eternal-Hasnamuss) is defined in relation to the heroic Very Saintly Ashiata Shiemash, whose labours he destroys. However, there is no possibility of him destroying the 'something' within himself, and so he experiences unending and unendable suffering (*Tales*: 390–410).

HARMONY/HARMONIOUS/HARMONIC

Concerning harmonious development, Gurdjieff's ideas of a congruence between macrocosm and microcosm belong to the Pythagorean world-view of the universe as composed of harmonic vibrations. This had become part of Western European thinking, and the notion of the 'harmony of the spheres' entered both Christian and occult teaching, becoming a strong influence during the Renaissance and Reformation. An octave of angels, Seraphim, Cherubim, Thrones, Dominations, Principalities, Powers and Virtues, descends from the Creator to man and 'the heavenly spheres of the planets could be manipulated into order' (Webb 1980: 510–12). Webb goes on to suggest Francesco Giorgi's *De Harmonia Mundi* as the probable indirect source of Gurdjieff's cosmology: '*De Harmonia Mundi* is written in three "songs" each divided into eight notes'. Giorgi (with Plato as his authority) said that, as man is made in the image of the greater world and the same laws apply to both, the octave can be used to scrutinise the human soul. Man can use the downward stairway of angels to ascend back towards the Supreme Creator. There were, however, inexplicable discords in the harmonious universe. Webb connects the disharmonies with the deliberate inexactitudes in Gurdjieff's idea of the **legomonism**. (See also Lovejoy 1936; his *The Great Chain of Being: A Study in the History of the Idea* examines the conflict in notions of good and evil arising from the essential disharmonies within the idea of a continuous chain of being.)

Gurdjieff's Institute for the Harmonious Development of Man (see **institute**) advocated the necessity for mechanical man to work on himself, so that he might function harmoniously and become 'real' man, possessed of will, identity and consciousness (see **consciousness**; **'I'/identity**; **will/free will**). Paradoxically, Gurdjieff created chaotic conditions in the Institute that were designed to allow pupils to experience the actuality of their malfunctioning disharmonies (see **ways/fourth way**; **work, to**).

HEAD

The head is like an apparatus: it plays the role of policeman who watches the functions of the body. It can 'constate' only if you put **attention** on something. The head is alien to the body, it is not part of the organism. 'The body can die, the head also. But the head can die and the rest go on living' (*Voices*: 93).

See also: **intellectual/thinking centre, intelligence; reason**

HERALD OF COMING GOOD

Although Gurdjieff withdrew this text (published in 1933) and repudiated it, his injunctions to readers of *Life* not to read *Herald* draw attention to the text and suggest that it be considered as part of his writings (*Life*: 49–50, 80–1). *Herald* is divided into nine sections, four before the main body of the text and four after. It is related to Gurdjieff's other texts by its emphasis on a specific period of time, which reflects the numerology of his **Law of Three** and **Law of Seven**.

The start of the text is dated Tuesday 13 September 1932 and the supplementary announcement is dated Tuesday 7 March 1933, giving a period of twenty-five weeks. Thus the significant period of time in *Herald* is the week. Unusually, the date of printing ([Saturday] 26 August 1933) is also included, which is probably significant too. The days Tuesday and Saturday are the third and seventh days of the week, ruled respectively by Mars and Saturn (see *all and everything*; **number/numerology; writings**).

Herald has a complex, often ambiguous, syntax that makes the text difficult to unravel. The summary of *Herald* below gives a factual content of the text, but not its emotional tone and content. This text focuses on occult interests, the interrelations of contemporary man, and the malfunction of the psyche. It creates two central paradoxes for the reader:

1   Gurdjieff blames the occult interests of his pupils for causing prejudice against his Institute. Paradoxically, he described his own immersion in the occult, and his plans for additions to his Institute (which was shortly to be reopened) were also expressed in occult terms that seem closer to fantasy than reality.
2   Gurdjieff refers to his own search in terms of mania and psychosis. He expresses and denies both good and ill will towards others. He describes his use of pupils as 'guinea-pigs' for his experiments and the psychic malfunctions of contemporary man that cause good intentions towards others to bear ill results. The reader must

therefore assess Gurdjieff's good intentions towards him and their likely results.

Webb (1980: 428) points out that *Herald* reveals Gurdjieff's three 'techniques of manipulation . . . for one man a carrot, for another the stick for a third hidden persuasion', and that had pupils wished to read the book they might have found 'the keys to a dozen puzzling experiences'; however, because it is frightening to think one has been under the influence of a 'skillful puppet master' most did not wish to look at what was there.

Thus the text was either rejected or ignored by pupils; the second course of action seemed to be sanctioned by Gurdjieff's apparent repudiation of the text (see above).

Herald: An outline

Gurdjieff intends his writings to make readers aware of the necessity to help one's neighbour. He explains why he led an 'artificial' life for twenty-one years while questioning the significance and aim of life on Earth, especially human life. In 1892 he decided that what he sought might be found in man's subconscious, and so he studied and practised hypnosis and taught 'supernatural' sciences. Needing all of the twenty-eight **types** of person to study he founded his own Institute, later known as the Institute for the Harmonious Development of Man.

Part of the 1921 Prospectus for the Institute at Fontainebleau is quoted, giving information about Gurdjieff's teaching and how it is implemented. Earlier plans to spread his teaching failed, so Gurdjieff turned to writing. He hopes his writings will help humanity and gives instructions about how the Three Series of these are to be made available. He warns against reading them out of the prescribed order.

Gurdjieff had observed that the kinder he was, the more hostile people became towards him. He explored this strange fact in a series of experiments in which he sought either not to influence people or to influence them through one of three methods: kindness, threats or hypnotism. He also opposed people's vanity.

He recounts a further experiment that aimed to shock those people who had met his ideas into a form of thinking and feeling 'more proper to man'. This experiment, in which he tried to raise a mortgage, confirmed his earlier findings about the results of people's altruistic intentions, but it cost him a lot, both personally and financially.

He concluded that men's inner impulses no longer affect the inner worlds of those around them. This is because men lack the upbringing and education for establishing psychic factors such as conscience. Spiritual-instructors are needed to instil these. If Gurdjieff succeeds in the aims connected with his writings, he will promote the spread of institutes to train spiritual-instructors. However, false knowledge would result from this, because Gurdjieff also vows to recover money lost in his mortgage experiment by creating lasting suffering in the former teachers who should have instilled conscience into the people he dealt with.

Gurdjieff writes that he will now renew relations with people he knew eight years ago, before he began his writing. He can be contacted via his secretary at the Institute which, thanks to his foresight, is still in good order and to which he will make improvements.

Gurdjieff adds a Circular Letter to his past pupils: this is described as like a 'prayer' to protect *Herald* – his 'first-born', which is small and weak – from destructive people. He will make his writings more available than he had previously decided. Readers of *Herald* should fill in the attached blank registration forms in order to receive these writings. He asks pupils to understand and explain his books to others. He thanks the people he studied during his twenty years of artificial life: he had neither egotistical nor altruistic impulses towards them, but desired solely to prepare a science of 'Objective Truth and Reality for future generations'. Money from the sale of *Herald* will go towards spreading Gurdjieff's writings.

In a Supplementary Announcement, dated Tuesday 7 March 1933, Gurdjieff writes that economic, political and social events of the previous days have convinced him of the wide circulation of *Herald*. As well as proclaiming his forthcoming writings, Gurdjieff also proclaims the reopening of his Institute to be established on new foundations, under a new name and with additional buildings and equipment. The foundation stone for this will be laid on 23 April, St George's Day. Gurdjieff ends with a prayer for this new beginning.

Herald may be regarded as representing a third or reconciling force in relation to the *Tales* (negative) and *Meetings* (positive). *Herald*, which deals in temporal terms with the 'unreal' future ('the coming good'), can be regarded as an involutionary third force, while *Life*, which deals with the eternal present ('life is only real when "I am" '), can be regarded in relation to *Tales* and *Meetings* as an evolutionary third force. *Life* gives a message from above, *Herald* a message from below.

See also: **writings**

HERMETICISM

'Learn to separate the fine from the coarse' refers to the work of the
three-storey factory. The saying 'as above, so below' refers to the
analogy between man as microcosm and the universe as macrocosm.
Both are from the Emerald Tablets of Hermes Trismegistus (*Search*:
180, 280; see also *Views*, 1914: 14). There are many references to
hermetically sealed places and things in *Tales*, which can be read as
indirect references to Hermeticism (see **occult/occult revival**).

The three main branches of Hermeticism are **alchemy**, **astrology**
and **magic** (see Taylor 2001: 231–2).

Further reading

For Russian Hermeticism, see Carlson in Rosenthal 1997: 150–2; for Renaissance
Hermeticism, see Yates 1964.

HORSE, CARRIAGE AND DRIVER *see* carriage, horse, driver and master

HOPE

Gurdjieff's Ashiata Shiemash defines hope as 'hope of consciousness is
strength, hope of feeling is slavery, hope of body is disease' (*Tales*: 361).

'Hope is there . . . there is a way out of this maze' (Tracol, *Parabola*,
VII: 59; quoted in Thring 1998: 132).

See also: **toast of/to the idiots, the Science of Idiotism**

HUMANITY

Humanity is not evolving: acquisition in one section is balanced by loss
in another. In general, men do not take into account the small part man
plays in organic life and in cosmic processes, his nothingness. Men are
becoming automatons, willing slaves. The constant conflict between
differing man-centred theories keeps man as he is. Ideas of welfare and
equality cannot benefit man, who needs both inequality and **suffering**.
Inequality is a necessary concomitant of **evolution**, and the perception
of suffering is a necessary part of man's function. To destroy suffering
would be to destroy the shock that that is the only thing that bring a man
to change. However, just as a few cells can begin the process of physical

change, so a small group of men can begin the process of change in humanity (*Search*: 308–9). This contradicts Gurdjieff's statements that the **Work** cannot change anything in the world (see **conscious circle of humanity**; **evolution**).

HUMOUR

Gurdjieff's jokes and humorous stories range in tone from absurd through witty to sharp, cutting and extremely dark. Gurdjieff used humour, not always kind, in his teaching. Bennett (1962: 118–19) recounts the comic, and sometimes painful, results for pupils who took Gurdjieff literally. Taylor (1998: 182) recalls Gurdjieff's use of humour as a teaching strategy: 'everything he said could be taken as a joke, an absurdity or a profound observation in disguise.'

In the song contests of Kars where Gurdjieff grew up, humour was used to subvert and distract opponents (see **oral tradition, Turkic**). Gurdjieff knew the value of jokes when used to disrupt and subvert his pupil's mental and emotional flow, and to enliven efforts to understand his oral and written teachings. In this Gurdjieff also echoes the form of Sufi teaching tales, which were often humorous and could be interpreted on many levels (see Challenger 1990). Gurdjieff's invention of the sayings of the Mullah Nassr Eddin (in *Tales*) seems to belong to this tradition. Jokes and puns, by virtue of their metaphoric and polysemic qualities, encourage questioning, an important aspect of Gurdjieff's teaching (see **questions/questioning**).

Gurdjieff's reader may well question which bits of texts are jokes. For example, in *Tales* Gurdjieff names our solar system as Ors. This word derives from the Greek *ouros*, a word for buttocks/arse. Thus, according to Gurdjieff, our solar system is the buttocks of the universe (Clairborne 1989: 181). Is the whole of *Tales* a joke? If it were, would that make it less valuable than if it were not? The Surrealist André Breton wished to include quotations from *Tales* in an anthology of black humour (see Duit's writings, first published in Waldberg 1989 [1973]: 20).

See also: **writings**

Further reading

Erdener 1995. Freud's connection of jokes and the unconscious aroused Breton's interest in humour, see Breton 1997.

'HYDROGEN'

'Hydrogen' is the term used to refer to a substance without relation to the force passing through it (see **elements**; Webb 1980: 510).

HYDROGENS, TABLE OF

In Gurdjieff's cosmology, everything from the **Absolute** to the **Moon** is material. Gurdjieff relates the descending notes of his **Ray of Creation** to the **forces** (active, passive and neutralising) and to the **matter** ('carbon', 'oxygen' and 'nitrogen') through which they pass. The Absolute has the finest matter and the highest number of vibrations, while the Moon has the most dense matter and the lowest rate of vibrations.

All the notes in the Ray of Creation conduct forces. 'Carbon' conducts the active force, 'oxygen' the passive force and 'nitrogen' the neutralising force. A triad of these forces acting together through matter form a 'hydrogen'. The triads are interrelated so that the note, which conducts the neutralising force of the first triad, becomes the active force of the second triad. See the note La in Figure 18A. La is a neutralising third force in relation to the notes Do and Si in the first triad, but becomes the active force in the second triad of La, Sol and Fa; this pattern of how the notes relate to each other is repeated throughout the three descending octaves of the Ray of Creation.

The notes also relate to each other in terms of density: in the first triad of Do, Si and La, Do (as conducting the active force through 'carbon') is the least dense; La (as conductor of the neutralising force in matter termed 'nitrogen') is the next most dense; and Si is the most dense (see Figure 18B). In the second triad, La (as conductor of the first force) is less dense than Sol or Fa. This pattern replicates throughout the three octaves.

Gurdjieff allocates numbers to each of the matters ('carbon', 'oxygen' and 'nitrogen'). Put together these triads produce 'hydrogens' of increasing density (see Figure 18C). The full table of hydrogens ranges from hydrogen 6 to hydrogen 12,288; however, the first two hydrogens are considered 'irresolvable' for us and the table is reduced (see Figure 18D; for the full table and reductions, see *Search*: 174).

The chemistry of hydrogens is an **alchemy** that allows us to relate all the substances of the human organism to their places in the Ray of Creation. A hydrogen may represent a simple element or group of

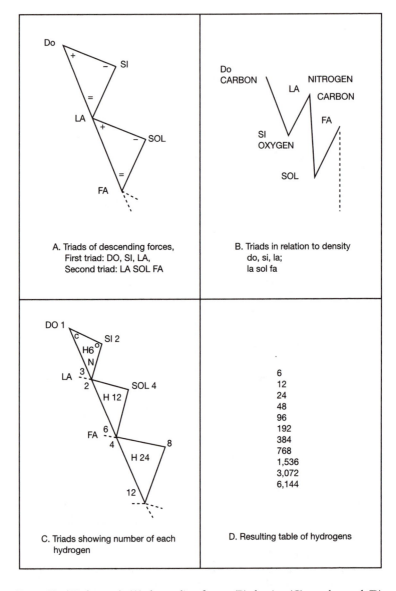

A. Triads of descending forces,
First triad: DO, SI, LA,
Second triad: LA SOL FA

B. Triads in relation to density
do, si, la;
la sol fa

C. Triads showing number of each
hydrogen

D. Resulting table of hydrogens

Figure 18 'Hydrogens': (A) descending forces, (B) density, (C) number and (D) table of hydrogens

Figure 19 Table of hydrogens related to Ray of Creation, human functioning and
some chemical elements

Triads of notes in the Ray of Creation	'Hydrogens'	Corresponds to matter related to human functioning	'Hydrogens'	'Hydrogens' in relation to some chemical elements
Do, si, la	6		6	
La, sol, fa	12	Unknown to physics and chemistry; corresponding to our psychic and spiritual life	12	Hydrogen Carbon Nitrogen Oxygen
Fa, shock, mi	24		24	Fluorine
Mi, re, do	48		48	Chlorine
Do, si, la	96	Air, gases, animal magnetism, emanations	96	Bromine
La, sol, fa	192	Air	192	Iodine
Fa, shock, mi	384	Water, liquid, food	384	
Mi, re, do	768	Edible	768	
Do, si, la	1,536	Inedible (i.e. wood)	1,536	
La, sol, fa	3,072	Iron	3,072	
Fa, shock, mi	6,144		6,144	
Mi, re, do	12,288		12,288	

elements that have a specific function in the world or in man. All the
hydrogens from 6 to 3,072, which includes a large group of chemicals,
can be found functioning in man's organism. Some of the hydrogens
defined by Gurdjieff in relation to the Ray of Creation are shown in
Figure 19 (see *Search*: 170–4). Later, Gurdjieff expanded his table of
hydrogens from the three octaves (as in Figure 19) to twelve scales,
which Ouspensky found incomprehensible until he understood the
diagram as a 'moving diagram' that represented a mystical dance
(*Search*: 274–7, Table 4).

See also: **enneagram; Law of Reciprocal Maintenance/Reciprocal Feeding; three-storey factory/digestion of three foods**

HYPNOSIS/HYPNOTISM

Hypnotism has an extremely important place in Gurdjieff's ideas, and is seen in his texts to function both creatively and destructively. The references to hypnotism within his texts should be understood in relation to the specific function of that specific text. These functions relate to his **Law of Three** (see **writings**).

Gurdjieff saw humanity as a whole as highly susceptible to falling under 'mass-hypnosis', which induces war and other ills. He saw the individual's usual state of 'waking sleep', not as normal but as 'hypnotic sleep'. He told a story about a rich magician with many sheep that he controlled by hypnotism. The sheep believed the magician's suggestions that they were immortal, that skinning them would do them good, that he was a 'good master' who loved them, that they were not sheep but lions, eagles, men and magicians (*Search*: 219; see also **enneagram** and Figure 12).

However, Gurdjieff also states that he saw hypnotism as a means by which he could study people, with the aim 'neither egotistic nor altruistic' of preparing a science for the benefit of future generations. Gurdjieff writes that he collected oral and written information about Asian hypnotism, studied for two years, acquiring considerable powers, and then practised as a hypnotist–healer for five years. Gurdjieff's **Institutes** were founded to provide him with 'guinea-pigs' for his experiments, and he used hypnotism as one means of artificially influencing students (*Herald*: 83–4, 20–2; see also **aim; influence**). Gurdjieff connected **schools** with hypnotism and explained the ability of a Benares fakir to lie on a bed of nails as the result of hypnotic experiments carried out on him in a school (*Search*: 61–2).

Gurdjieff vowed not to use his hypnotic powers for his own needs, but only as a source of study, and bound himself to live 'in some ways' an artificial life in order to avoid the destruction of himself and his works for general human welfare, and also to avoid enslaving others (*Life*: 25; *Herald*: 11–13).

However, in *Meetings* he does give examples of his own use of hypnotism in conflicting terms of abusive egoism and altruism. For example, he writes of using hypnotism for his own ends to make money through demonstrations. He presents himself as ruthlessly unconcerned with the well being of men hypnotised, so that:

one could stick a large pin into their chests, sew up their mouths, and placing them between two chairs with the head on one and the feet on another, put enormous weights on their stomachs; after which anyone in the audience who wished could come and pull a hair out of their heads, and so on and so forth.

He also records acting as a hypnotist–physician, curing addicts to drink and drugs, and curing his friend Soloviev (*Meetings*: 177–98, 146–7; on Gurdjieff as hypnotist and healer, see also Peters 1976 [1964, 1965]: 132–3, 213–15, 219–25, 246–53). Gurdjieff continued this practice for the rest of his life (Webb 1980: 473).

Gurdjieff's hero Beelzebub echoes his profession of hypnotist in *Tales*: Chapter 32 ('Hypnotism') and Chapter 33 ('Beelzebub as Professional Hypnotist') deal with hypnotism and the action of hypnotism on a man's atmosphere. Beelzebub describes a new form of hypnotism that alters the functioning of consciousness. This enabled contact to be made with the conscience, usually buried in the subconscious and uncontactable. Thus, in relationship to man's sleep, hypnotism was both the cause and the cure (see **atmosphere**; **magnetism/animal magnetism**).

The process of Gurdjieff's teaching as a whole can be regarded as an alternative form of hypnotism that disrupts and counters the hypnotism of the pupil's conventional views, his sleep. The teaching provides an alternative world, the escape from which is a painful but necessary initiatory experience for the pupil (Webb 1980: 549). The fact that Gurdjieff found ways of sending even his most devoted pupils away from him supports this understanding of the **Work**. Gurdjieff used the usual attributes of the magician/hypnotist to influence his pupils; through the 'magnetism' of his presence, through his mode of speaking and through the theatrical atmosphere, isolated from the 'outside world', in which he taught at the Institute and later at his apartments in Paris, where the curtains were permanently drawn:

[Gurdjieff's] gestures, his manner of expressing himself, the incredible range of tone and dynamics in his voice, and his use of emotion, all seemed calculated to spell-bind his auditors; perhaps to mesmerize them to such an extent that they were unable to argue with him at the time.

(Peters 1976 [1964, 1965]: 112)

Gurdjieff gives an account of how, when needing money, he went and sat by an antipathetic man: 'I sit like poor simple man and look at him'. The man takes out all the money he has, puts it on the table and goes away. Gurdjieff says that the man will remember nothing; 'such power I have but not often wish to use' (Taylor 1998: 140–1).

Mesmer (1734–1815) is one of the few people held in respect in *Tales*. Indeed Gurdjieff can be seen as belonging (as do Freud and Jung) to that set of psychological thinkers who were influenced by theories of double consciousness arising out of Mesmer's work on animal magnetism and magnetic sleep. Puysegur (1751–1825), who developed Mesmer's work, concluded that there are two independent existences in man, each of which has its own memory and one of which can only be reached through hypnotism (Crabtree 1993).

See also: **occult/occult revival; New Work**

Further reading

For Mesmerism in relation to Spiritualism and to Christian Science, see Webb 1971b; for Gurdjieff as hypnotist, see Webb 1980: 75–93.

'I AM' *see* exercises; 'I'/identity

IDEAL

This term was used in the group meetings held during World War II. If a person does not have an ideal, if they do not believe in God, then their father, mother or teacher can serve them as an ideal. The ideal (person) serves as an intermediary between the pupil and God, and can be called upon to help bear the burden of **suffering** caused by **remorse** of **conscience**. Gurdjieff also refers to an 'external ideal', such as religious **faith**, and suggests that the pupil must destroy this in order to have real contact with feeling (*Voices*: 173, 198, 200).

See also: **exercises; groups; group meetings during World War II (1940–4); prayer/praying**

'I'/IDENTITY

Man has no permanent 'I', only a multiplicity of small changing 'I's, each of which takes charge for a period and then is replaced by an 'I' with quite other tastes, qualities and abilities. The Whole exists only as a physical thing or abstract concept and so is never expressed.

Changing conditions (e.g. the weather, education, religion) call up different sets of 'I's that fight one another. An Eastern teaching allegory (see **allegory/analogy**), similar to those given in the Gospels, suggests that man's situation is like a house in which there are many servants but no **master**. The house is threatened because there is no order: the only chance for salvation is for a group of servants to elect a temporary or deputy steward (see **steward/deputy steward**) who may direct the servants to their proper places and work, thus preparing for the arrival of a real steward who will prepare for the arrival of the master. Understanding his situation is not enough; in order to realise his possibilities, a man must be willing to **sacrifice** and risk everything for the sake of liberation (*Search*: 59–61; see also **exercises**; *life is real only then, when 'i am'*).

Gurdjieff led his pupils in the 1940s to experience extreme **remorse** for their past relations with parents; this aroused feelings of self-hatred and self-repugnance.

In 1978 Tracol wrote that the question 'Who am I?' is not everyone's question. However, he also said that a man finds his true identity as a seeker, and that Gurdjieff himself exemplified the seeker that each man 'is destined to re-discover in himself' (Tracol 1994: 94, 91, 95).

Gurdjieff's birthplace suffered many political, social and economic changes brought about by the successive overthrow of different ruling powers (see Bennett 1976: 17–18). Due to these circumstances Gurdjieff experienced a multiplicity of languages, religions and political ideologies, and perhaps the absence of any sense of a permanent unchanging identity, both in himself and in his surroundings.

Impermanence of the 'I' was also reflected in psychological theories – first, of double consciousness and, later, of multiple personalities – that arose out of the work of Mesmer (1734–1815) and Puysegur (1751–1825) (see **hypnosis/hypnotism**; Crabtree 1993).

IDENTIFICATION

Man is constantly identified with whatever has attracted his **attention**, and particularly identified with what he is most interested in, including work on himself. The struggle against identification is difficult because man wrongly defines it as, for example, 'enthusiasm', 'passion' or 'zeal'. An identified man is a thing, unable to **self-remember** or do anything sensible. A specific form of identification is **considering** (*Search*: 150–1). Unconscious **fears** cause identification: a man is afraid of other people and they are afraid of him, he is afraid of future loss, illness and unpleasantness (*Views*, 1917: 252–3).

IDIOTISM, TOASTS OF THE IDIOTS *see* **toast of/to the idiots, idiotism**

IMAGINATION

Wrong work in centres is principally caused by imagination. Each centre has its own form of imagination. It is important to observe this. If imagination is decreased, personality is decreased (*Search*: 111, 165). However, exercises were given for the development of imagination (*Life*: 132–6) because it can be helpful in forming a connection between the conscious and subconscious. In this sense imagination is seen as a positive attribute; more usually in the Work it is regarded as negative, i.e. man has an imaginary idea of himself as conscious and awake.

See also: **kundalini**

IMMORTALITY *see* **bodies; mortality**

IMPRESSIONS

Impressions are the most important **food** for man. Although a man can live without eating for several days, or without breathing for a few minutes, he can not live for even a single moment without impressions. The chief source of impressions is **Nature**, which transmits through impressions the '**energy** by which we live and move and have our being' (*Search*: 181). The quality of impressions can be improved through the practice of **self-remembering**, which is the only possible way for a man to evolve (*Search*: 188, 321; see also **three-storey factory/digestion of three foods**).

Our inner impulses do not make any impression on the inner worlds of the people around us (*Herald*: 72).

In 1984 Tracol (1994: 99) wrote that even though we do not recognise that they are there, the higher centres do receive the food of impressions, especially when we are asleep.

INFLUENCES

Two kinds of influences are governed by the **Law of Accident**: 'A' influences created in everyday life and 'B' influences that originate outside ordinary life, from an esoteric centre or school, but may have become distorted. A man needs to be able to discriminate between 'A' and 'B' influences, so that gradually he remembers all the 'B' influences and together these form in him a magnetic centre that attracts help for him via contact with 'C' influences – those that come directly from an esoteric centre or from a person who knows the Way (see **ways/fourth way**). Such a meeting is called the 'first step' on the 'stairway' that connects ordinary life with a Way. A person will be completely dependent on his guide while he ascends the stairway; after this, he is on the Way and may even be independent. In the Fourth Way a person can only ascend to a higher step if he puts another person on his own step (see **conscious circle of humanity**; **stairway**). Men are also under planetary influences that act mechanically on individuals and on masses (*Search*: 310; see **astrology**).

Two kinds of influences arise near us: chemico-physical and associative. Influences from chemico-physical causes are the result of a mixture of a man's emanations (which vary from centre to centre) with the emanations of another person. This gives rise to feelings of ease or ill-ease in their presence. There are three kinds of associative influences, which are the result of our conditioning. The first is mechanical: e.g. when a person pushes me or weeps, it has a mechanical effect. Associations are also activated by forms (i.e. beauty): we can influence or be influenced by clothes, which might be called a person's 'mask'. The second kind of associative influence is by feelings (i.e. relationship): here we are responsible for our own inner and outer attitudes to others and also for their attitudes towards us, because their attitudes reflect ours. If 'you love, she loves [. . .] you receive what you give', although sometimes (due to chemico-physical influences) if you like her, she does not like you. The third kind of associative influence is by persuasion or suggestion, and by notions of superiority or inferiority. These are powerful influences and arise due to the fact that information is generally received by one centre only. None of the **centres** on their own have the capacity for critical evaluation or consciousness, and so influences are not challenged.

Critical perception of new material, including influences, is possible if it is received by more than one centre. Therefore it is necessary when thinking to try to feel, and when feeling to try to direct thought onto the feelings (*Views*, 1924: 254–65).

Chemico-physical influences can be resisted by passivity. Emanations can be received where there is calm and an empty place. However, emanations will rebound if I am full, so in both cases 'I am ensured'. Freedom from associative influences requires 'an artificial struggle'. If we are completely under the influence of these small things, we cannot receive the influence on us from the planets, the sun and more distant **entities**. In one sense, inner influences are enemies because they prevent our reception of outer influences. However, in another sense they are helpful because outer influences can be bad as well as good. But we need to live in the outside world as well as in the inner world, and so it is necessary to be free of internal influences. Of the many methods to free oneself from these inner enemies Gurdjieff suggests active reasoning (see **reason**). For example, if self-love is wounded by an insult from another person, who thinks I am a fool, it is possible to have self-love in another sense, to reason that he has formed his own opinion, but I know I am not as he thinks and so I am not hurt. However, if his insult has truth in it, I can be grateful to him for showing me my foolishness (*Views*, 1924: 254–65; 1923: 266–70; see also **love**).

Gurdjieff writes (*Herald*: 64, 68) that, although he sought to keep his undesirable manifestations under control, his hypnotic powers induced an automatic influence over others, in both waking and hypnotic states, which caused him **remorse**. He also writes that he experimentally used three methods to artificially influence pupils: through kindness, threats and hypnotism. We can see that the text itself echoes these methods, having encouraging, threatening and spellbinding stories (see **experiments**).

Through their influence, wise tutors can repair the psyche of those who have been miseducated, if they watch over them for two years. Gurdjieff planned to train spiritual-instructors to help in this task (*Herald*: 73–6).

Orage held that the only three ways of influencing people are by magnetisation, competition and example (Anderson 1962: 96).

See also: **planetary influence**

INITIATES/INITIATION

While Gurdjieff seems to repudiate the notion of initiation (see below), he refers to it in his writings in a way that gives it value. These definitions should be understood in the context of the specific texts in which they occur.

Gurdjieff said that transitions from one level of being to another may be marked by initiation ceremonies or rites. These do not in themselves effect change, nor do the methods taught by schools effect initiation. This can only come from the person himself; inner growth can only come from the man himself (*Search*: 314–15). Initiation cannot be gained through a ceremony: a person initiates himself through his own understanding (*Views*, 1914: 27–8). However, though we can make modifications, we cannot change ourselves without help from outside (*Views*, 1922: 78).

The above statements seem in contradiction to Gurdjieff's saying that Great Knowledge is passed on orally through initiates and that, when the centres of initiation die out, ancient knowledge goes underground (*Views*, 1918: 56–7).

In *Tales*, references to initiates occurs principally, though not exclusively, in Chapters 25 and 27 in connection with Gurdjieff's character, Ashiata Shiemash. In them, initiates are defined as 'meritorious beings, who have themselves received their information from similar meritorious beings' (*Tales*: 351).

In *Life*, Gurdjieff refers to plans for the esoteric group of students at his Institute to be initiated theoretically and practically, but only after a long period of having been experimentally tried and verified (*Life*: 77). Later, he writes of **exercises** that he plans to initiate pupils into and from which they will learn secret notions. He defines the 'being' of initiates on earth, in almost all epochs, as divided into Saint, Learned and Sage (*Life*: 132–6).

In *Herald*, Gurdjieff plans to promote his writings and to give access to his Third Series (*Life*) to people who have been assessed by those who have been admitted to the 'so-called rights-of-initiates', according to a code established by Gurdjieff, which is a modification of regulations that have always existed on earth (*Herald*: 57).

For an improbable story about initiation that Gurdjieff tells his pupils, see the introduction to this book. The term 'initiation' does not seem to hold an important place in current Work practice.

Further reading

For an account of ancient initiate tests and their relation to early Christianity, see Welburn 1994. For an account of how Steiner drew on this tradition, see Welburn 1997.

INNER ANIMAL

Gurdjieff defined the 'inner animal' of each member of his group the **Rope**, and used descriptions of the specific qualities and nature of these 'animals' to teach his pupils. The inner animal had to be contended with, but must remain a friend, for without its help the pupil could not obtain a **soul** (Patterson 1999: 92; see also **appendix 1**). Gurdjieff does not seem to have used this method with other groups, though he did use nicknames (see Zuber 1990 [1977]: 8).

See also: **chief feature**

INNER/INTERNAL CONSIDERING *see* **considering**

INSTINCTIVE CENTRE *see* **moving/instinctive centre**

INSTITUTES

Although Gurdjieff mentions teaching workshops in Tashkent before he began his groups in Russia around 1912, his institute under the title 'The Institute for the Harmonious Development of Man' (generally referred to as 'the Institute') began in Tiblisi in 1919. Ouspensky gives part of the prospectus for this Institute, which declared, wrongly, that branches of the Institute were already established in other major cities (*Search*: 380–1). The Tiblisi Institute was dissolved in May 1920 due to unsettled political conditions in Georgia; it was restarted in October of that year in Constantinople, and closed again in May 1921. After preliminary attempts to establish his institute in Germany (in Hellerau) and in England (in London), Gurdjieff established his Institute at Le Prieuré des Basses Loges at Avon near Fontainebleau, about forty miles from Paris. It was fully functional for two years, until 1924 when, after a car accident, Gurdjieff began to put his teaching into a written form. Though he originally asked pupils to leave, many drifted back to the Institute, but it did not function at the same pitch of intensity as it had done over those first two years. Gurdjieff left the Prieuré in 1933 (dates from Moore 1991: 326–32; Taylor 1998: 76 gives 1933–4 as the leaving date). Gurdjieff wrote in 1933 that his Institute was still in good order (*Herald*: 78). This was not the case: he had lost the Institute when the mortgage was foreclosed. His hope in 1934 of opening a new Institute in Taos in the United States was not fulfilled (Webb 1980: 340). At the end of his life, Gurdjieff was still suggesting that he wished to secure a building in order to restart his institute (Webb 1980: 471).

Aims

Gurdjieff writes that he was led to found his institutes in order to provide himself with a wide variety of people to study (see **type**). His first institutes in Russia and other countries were disrupted by war (*Herald*: 25). Gurdjieff described the people studying with him as 'guinea-pigs' (*Herald*: 22) and 'rats' needed for his experiments (*Journey*: 38). A brochure for the French Institute presents it as a continuation of the **Seekers of Truth**, a society founded in 1895 with the aim of studying 'so-called supernatural phenomena'; the brochure outlines the 'theoretical base and pedagogical principles' of the Institute, mentioning medical and psychological specialists, laboratories and a medical centre, 'the extent of these facilities seems to represent more a goal than a reality' (Taylor 1998: 73–5). The reader can compare this with the quite different psychological terms in which the teaching of the Institute was presented in 1922–3 ('by means of psychoanalysis' – Webb 1980: 234), and also with an extract from the prospectus for the Institute given in *Herald* (pp.32–40).

In brief, the aim of the Institute, from the pupil's perspective, was to provide conditions under which they might work on themselves, through a variety of methods, to develop an harmonious functioning of the intellectual, emotional and instinctive centres (see **centres; friction; harmony/harmonious/harmonic; work, to**).

Conditions, teaching and methods

Although the mundane tasks of everyday living were part of Institute life, it provided extreme conditions that were quite different from the everyday life in which, Gurdjieff stressed, work must be carried out. The Institute might perhaps be regarded as a **school**. Gurdjieff taught through a variety of themes, in connection with which there were fasts, mental exercises combined with hard physical labour, **movements**, and psychological tests, 'so penetrating that everyone seemed to be stripped spiritually naked' (Bennett 1962: 113–30). There are a number of pupils' memoirs that give accounts of life at the Institute (see *Journey*; *Teachings*; Peters 1976 [1964, 1965]; see also Taylor 1998, 2001).

Ouspensky visited Gurdjieff at the Institute in 1922 and 1923. During this time Gurdjieff continued the work on his ballet and on

Dervish **dances**, together with exercises for the development of memory, **attention** and the **imagination**, as well as of 'imitation psychic phenomena' and a lot of strenuous work connected with the household (*Search*: 385–6).

The Institute provided special conditions for work, but to gain from being there people needed to remember why they had come. All the pupils, good or bad, stupid or clever, are damaged in one way or another; each pupil must accept that he is as damaged as the others, and that he can see the condition of others clearly only because it has been artificially shown to him. In order for his work to be worthwhile, a pupil must become an **egoist**, must regard everyone at the Institute (including Gurdjieff) as a means of helping him. The Institute can only help an adult pupil 'to be able' to achieve a desire once the pupil himself has separated his **mind** from his **essence** and formed a primary wish that he remembers (*Views*, 1923: 107–11).

Gurdjieff writes (*Life*: 77–8) that there were three groups of students in the Institute: exoteric, mesoteric and esoteric; these were given teachings according to the **group** in which they belonged.

Further reading

For pupils' memoirs of the Institute, see the second section of the bibliography (*Works by Gurdjieff's pupils*) and Moore 1980.

INTELLECTUAL/THINKING CENTRE; INTELLIGENCE

Gurdjieff spoke of the intelligence of the Moon, Earth, planets and the Sun. The intelligence of the Sun in relation to the Earth is divine. In relation to the table of hydrogens (see **hydrogens, table of**), he said that all matter has consciousness and intelligence, and that the speed of vibrations shows the level of intelligence (*Search*: 25, 317). Ouspensky notes that Gurdjieff gave his ideas little by little, giving only general principles and holding back the most essential ones, often himself pointing out the apparent discrepancies caused by his suppressions. Gurdjieff said that the thinking centre is too slow to do the work of the emotional or instinctive **centres**; if it interferes, it brings wrong results (*Search*: 55–6, 109).

Our mind does not have any connection with our **essence**; it depends on few influences and so even a weak man can give direction to his mind. However, Gurdjieff also said that the power of changing ourselves does not lie in the mind. Although only the mind cares about the future, only the body and feelings can 'do'. But even if a person desires with his mind, it will not change him: his desires must be in his emotions (*Views*, 1923: 148, 222–3).

In order to gain a critical awareness of new material when you have a thought, try to feel; when you feel, try to direct your thoughts (*Views*, 1924: 264–5). The mind must always remember what it wishes. The only difference between a child and an adult is the mind: the adult mind has more material. Being 'grown-up' does not depend on age, nor on essence, but on the acquisition of independent logic of the mind. A child of eight may be grown up and a man of sixty a child (*Views*, 1923: 151–2).

INTENTIONAL SUFFERING *see* conscience; suffering/ pleasure

INTERVALS

Intervals are the points in the musical scale where the speed of vibration changes (see **law of seven; ray of creation**). In relation to events, the intervals are moments of deviation from the original direction. Changes in direction at the interval can be seen in all individual, social, political and religious human activities. These changes go unrecognised, but eventually they bring about the opposite of the original direction. So, for example, Christianity has retained its name but changed into something diametrically opposed to the Christianity of the Gospels. Intervals can be filled accidentally by shocks arising from other octaves, or a man can learn to recognise moments of interval and create an additional shock consciously by **self-remembering** (*Search*: 129, 124–35).

See also: **enneagram; Law of Octaves; shocks; three-storey factory/ digestion of three foods**

INVOLUTION *see* evolution/involution

JUSTICE

Gurdjieff warned pupils that they might be treated by their teacher in such a way as to fully justify their grievances against him. However, this would be a test to see whether or not the pupil behaves decently (*Search*: 228–9; see also **knowledge**).

All people are different in preferences and in race, and so subjective laws will be different. However, our differences could be united by a small number of objective laws – then our lives would be neither lonely nor unhappy (*Views*, 1922: 173).

Mankind's 'maleficent idea of "Good and Evil" ' is castigated by Beelzebub in Chapter 44 of *Tales*: 'In the Opinion of Beelzebub, Man's Understanding of Justice Is for Him in the Objective Sense an Accursed Mirage'. In order to be really just and good, a person must first become 'an out and out egoist' (*Tales*: 1236).

'Only he can be just who is able to put himself in the position of others' (*Views*: 275, aphorism 26). Similar words are found over the main entrance to Purgatory (*Tales*: 1164). At the end of *Tales*, Hassein has feelings of compassion for humanity. These show that he has been able to put himself in the position of others (*Tales*: 1162–4).

'As you sow so shall you reap' is an expression of objective justice. Not only individuals but also families and nations reap the result of past actions. Sometimes the results converge on us: as sons or grandsons, we must regulate them – this is not injustice but a great honour. Misfortunes suffered in youth have been brought by someone: he is dead; you are on earth and must reap; you must not be egotistical, it is an honour to be a link in the chain of your blood (see also **remorse**). You are responsible to your family to repair the past. Justice is not concerned with little things, but all the same nothing is done on earth without justice (*Voices*: 174–5).

KNOWLEDGE

In St Petersburg in 1914, with Russia at war, Gurdjieff taught that knowledge, like everything else in the world, is material; as such, it is limited. Thus esoteric knowledge, preserved from ancient times and distinct from our science and philosophy, cannot be given to everyone. If each person were given his small share of the knowledge available, it would not change his life in any way. However, a large amount of knowledge taken by a small group can produce good results. Although this seems unjust, it is not, because most people do not want any knowledge and refuse even the amount allotted to them.

In times of **war** and 'mass madness', especially during the fall of cultures, geological cataclysms and climatic changes, people lose even their common sense and the instinct for self-preservation. At such times there is a great deal of rejected knowledge, which may be collected by those who want it. Knowledge is not hidden from anyone, but it takes much labour to transmit and to receive. The person who wants knowledge must make the effort to find 'a man who knows' to teach him, and be prepared to work for it (*Search*: 36–40).

The level of knowledge a man has depends on his level of **being**. Knowledge is not the same as understanding, and so increase of knowledge does not lead to increase of understanding. 'Understanding is the resultant of knowledge and being'. While knowledge is the function of one **centre**, understanding is the function of three centres: it is when a man also feels and senses what is connected to what he knows. One of the difficulties in transmitting knowledge is the lack of an exact **language** (*Search*: 67–8).

However, compare this with Gurdjieff's answer when Ouspensky complained that Gurdjieff gave ideas in 'riddles'. Gurdjieff said that knowledge was never transmitted in a complete form in a **school**: the pupil must learn from jokes or stories, must be clever in how he approaches his teacher, and if necessary be ready to 'steal' knowledge (*Search*: 277).

Gurdjieff distinguished between subjective and objective knowledge. He referred to all ordinary knowledge (i.e. knowledge acquired through scientific observation and accessible in subjective states of consciousness) as subjective knowledge. Objective knowledge was based on ancient methods of observation and accessible in a state of objective consciousness. The idea of 'the **unity** of everything, unity in diversity' is one of the key ideas in objective knowledge. There have been religious and philosophical methods to prepare students to achieve the state of objective consciousness necessary for the transmission of this knowledge to them (*Search*: 278–80; see also **myth**; **symbols/symbolism**).

All our knowledge, whether valuable or worthless, is information that has been poured into us and can easily be taken from us. Great Knowledge is handed on from centres of initiation (in India, Assyria, Egypt and Greece) by means of symbolic writings and legends, and preserved through the oral tradition, through customs, rituals, memorials and sacred art (*Views*, 1918: 55–7; see also **art**; **legomonism**; **religion/s, new religions**).

KUNDABUFFER

This term is used by Beelzebub in *Tales* to refer to an organ placed in men, at the base of their spines, by the Archangel Loosisos. The function of the organ is to prevent men from seeing the reality of their situation. It is feared that if men knew that, as part of organic life on Earth, their sole purpose is to feed the **Moon** they might kill themselves. Kundabuffer enables men to see reality upside down, and to put the satisfaction of their own pleasure before everything else. Although the organ was removed, its effects continue to manifest themselves so that men cannot perfect their being (see *Tales*: 88–9, 695–6). The word seems to combine the functions of **buffers** and **kundalini** as defined by Gurdjieff.

See also: **religion/s, new religions**

KUNDALINI

'Kundalini' is wrongly defined in 'occult' literature as a sexual force. Kundalini is actually the power of **imagination** that can act in any **centre** to replace real function. It is the result of hypnotic suggestion and allows man to **dream** that he is awake (*Search*: 220).

LANGUAGE

Examples are given of the different definitions people give to the word **world** in terms of their interest in astronomy, physics, many-dimensioned space, religion or Theosophy. The correct definition would be one that encompassed all the above and indicated the point of view of the speaker. The word **man** is then defined in Work terms (*Views*, 1924: 63–8).

People believe that they understand one another, but this conviction is false. Apart from information of a practical character, people are unable to communicate with others because, due to vague and inaccurate thinking, each word used may have thousands of different meanings. Each person speaks a language of his own, dependent on the material available and on his own complex associations. For example, when the word 'man' is used in conversation it will have specific associations and definitions for each listener and speaker according to his general interests or profession. Man may be thought of in relation to gender, to relations between the sexes, to religion, to health and sickness, to the astral body – man may be defined in terms of zoological type, criminality or morality. There is no universal language and, as new sciences bring new terminologies and nomenclatures, people understand each other less and less. The circle of life to which we belong is sometimes known as the 'confusion of tongues'.

The study of the systems of ancient knowledge begins with the study of an exact language, based on the new principle of **relativity**. 'It introduces relativity into all concepts and thus makes possible an accurate determination of the angle of thought.' All ideas in this language are related to conscious and volitional **evolution**. Everything is examined in terms of the evolution possible to it, its place in the evolutionary ladder. In this language the word 'man' can be referred to in seven ways, as man number one through to man number seven.

It is then possible to define, for example, **knowledge** in relation to a specific man. The knowledge of man number seven, which is 'the complete and practical knowledge of All', is different from the knowledge of men on other levels. The same division into seven categories must be made in relation to being, to art, to religion, to everything relating to man (see also **law of seven**).

Three universal languages exist. The first exists within the limits of one's own written or spoken language. In the second language, people speak their own language, yet understand each other through written language (e.g. figures or mathematical formulæ). The third language is on a level where all differences disappear; both spoken and written language are the same for all (*Search*: 68–74, 96; see also **enneagram**; **myth**; **symbols/symbolism**).

The form in which ancient or Great Knowledge is expressed and transmitted changes from epoch to epoch. Thus the language that expressed Great Knowledge several hundred years ago is incomprehensible to us. Our language will be incomprehensible and the content lost for future generations (*Views*, 1918: 210–11). Objective knowledge overcomes the weakness of ordinary language by transmitting ideas via myths and symbols (*Search*: 279).

Further reading

See *Tales*: 332–8 (the story of Hamolinadir and the Tower of Babel); Wittgenstein 1995 [1922] (see also **lies/lying**).

LAW OF ACCIDENT

What happens to **man** number one, two or three is determined either by the Law of Accident or by **fate** or by his own **will**. The Law of Accident, which may be either good or bad, affects a man's **personality**; the Law of Fate affects a man's **essence**. If his essence and will remain undeveloped, then a man is ruled mainly by the Law of Accident, which cannot be foretold (*Search*: 100–1; see **influences**; **magnetic centre**; **type**). However, Gurdjieff also stated that people who hunger can be brought by accident to begin a way (*Search*: 360).

LAW OF DUALITY/TWO

When he begins to study phenomena, man sees the Law of Duality, one principle opposed to another, operating in the cosmos and in himself. He can only observe the cosmos, but he can express his understanding of the laws of duality in himself by confining the manifestation of the law to the permanent line of struggle with himself (*Search*: 180–1; see **will/free will**).

The duality of affirmation and negation operates everywhere, on every scale – what is affirmed in science is denied in religion, what is affirmed in one **centre** of a man is denied in another centre – but it is possible, 'if we try slowly, gradually, but steadily', to stand in the middle of this law and be free (*Views*, 1924: 199). For example, if two people argue, this brings a third force into operation and something new is created. However, this result is outside, we can also bring this law inside us (*Views*, 1924: 208; see also **astrology**).

Other dualities in the teaching are expressed as passive/active, involution/evolution, objective/subjective. Thus, 'passive man serves involution; and active man evolution' (*Views*, 1924: 199).

LAW OF OCTAVES

Octaves must either ascend (evolutionary octaves) or descend (creative octaves). Thus energy is constantly fluctuating as vibrations speed up or slow down (see **law of seven**). It is important to observe this in daily life, rather than becoming too theoretical. Octaves constantly interrupt each other and so are diverted from their original direction. In a man's life, the orderly ascent or descent of an octave can only come about by accident (see **law of accident**), but in a **school** he can learn to create the additional **shocks** needed to allow the octave to flow on to its desired conclusion.

There are fundamental and subordinate octaves. The fundamental octave is like the trunk of a tree; its branches are like subordinate octaves; in turn, the branches have smaller branches, which have leaves, and each represents a subordinate octave.

The seven fundamental notes of the octave and the two 'intervals,' *the bearers of new directions*, give altogether nine links of a chain, three groups of three links each.

(*Search*: 134, original emphasis)

Gurdjieff expanded his teaching on octaves to include 'inner octaves' and 'lateral octaves'. Just as each level of vibration is penetrated by all other levels of energy, so each note contains a complete inner octave and each note of the inner octave also contains an inner octave (see also **world/s, all worlds**). 'Each note of an octave may at the same time be any note of any other octave passing through it' (*Search*: 139).

Only cosmic octaves, such as the **Ray of Creation**, ascend and descend in an orderly way. The Ray of Creation is the first complete example of the Law of Octaves. Figure 20 shows how a lateral octave fills the **interval** of the Ray of Creation, allowing it to flow on to completion.

The lateral octave, which starts at the Sun and ends at the Moon, has three notes (La, Sol and Fa) that constitute organic life on earth and fill the interval between Fa and Mi of the Ray of Creation. The last two notes of the lateral octave (Mi and Re) blend with the Mi and Re of the Ray of Creation, the cosmic octave.

The Ray of Creation is also expressed as three octaves of radiations (see Figure 21), so as to show the relation of **matters** and **forces** of

Figure 20 Law of Octaves: Cosmic and lateral octaves

	Cosmic octave (Ray of Creation)	Lateral octave (Sun/Moon)	
Do	The Absolute		
Si	All Worlds		
La	All Suns		
Sol	Our Sun	Do	
Fa	The Planets	Si	
Interval	*Interval*	La, Sol, Fa	These notes constitute organic life
Mi	The Earth	Mi	Cosmic Mi and lateral Mi blend
Re	The Moon	Re	Cosmic Re and lateral Re blend

Figure 21 Law of Octaves: Three octaves: Absolute–Moon

	Octaves	Intervals filled by	Matter	Force
	Do		'Carbon' (C)	Acts as first force
The Absolute	Interval	Filled by the will of the Absolute		
	Si		'Oxygen' (O)	Acts as second force
	La		'Nitrogen' (N)	Acts as third force
	Sol			
	Fa			
	Interval	Filled by unknown shock		
	Mi			
	Re			
	Do			
The Sun	Interval	Filled by radiations in the Sun's atmosphere		
	Si			
	La			
	Sol			
	Fa			
	Interval	Filled by unknown shock		
	Mi			
	Re			
	Do			
The Earth	Interval	Filled by radiations in the Earth's atmosphere		
	Si			
	La			
	Sol			
	Fa			
	Interval	Filled by unknown shock		
	Mi			
	Re			
Moon	Do			

different planes of the **world** to our own life. Gurdjieff develops this diagram to show how he obtained his table of hydrogens (*Search*: 133–6; see **hydrogens, table of**). The symbol that unifies all knowledge of the structure of the octave is the **enneagram** (*Search*: 285).

LAW OF RECIPROCAL MAINTENANCE/ RECIPROCAL FEEDING

This law is defined in *Tales*. When His Endlessness (God) realises that his dwelling place, the Sun Absolute, is vulnerable to time, he creates the universe into which he expels **time**. The Law of Reciprocal Maintenance (called by Beelzebub 'the Trogoautoegocrat') functions so that the universe is nourished by an exchange of substances, and this protects the Sun Absolute from the destructive results of time: i.e. change, decay and death. The fundamental purpose for the existence of men and the other three-brained beings of the universe is to serve as apparatuses through which cosmic substances are transmuted for the purpose of reciprocal maintenance. Organic life, including human beings, was allowed to form on the Earth for the specific purpose of sending emanations to feed the Moon (*Tales*: 136–7, 775, 780–1; Anonymous 1973: 630–3; for further references to this law, see also **brains**; **food**).

Bennett expresses this concept as the world brought into existence because '"being" and "time" are mutually destructive'. Nothing separate and closed can continue to exist without renewal from outside itself. 'Full renewal requires full mutuality.' Cosmic harmony is maintained by universal giving and receiving of energy by the interaction of different classes of being. He connects this law with the Diagram of Everything Living, also known as the Step Diagram, which Gurdjieff gave his pupils in Essentuki around 1917. In this diagram, classes of being are defined by what they eat and what they are eaten by. He equates the 'Eternal Unchanging' on this diagram with the Trogoautoegocrat (Bennett 1976 [1961]: 204–13; see Figure 22).

This diagram (Figure 22) is adapted from information from and the Step Diagram in *Search* (p.323). As we do not know the classes of creatures above us on this ladder, Gurdjieff called them 'angels' and 'archangels'. Later, Ouspensky's group agreed to regard the 'angels' as planets and the 'archangels' as suns. We can see that man eats invertebrates, but is eaten by archangels. The numbers refer to the

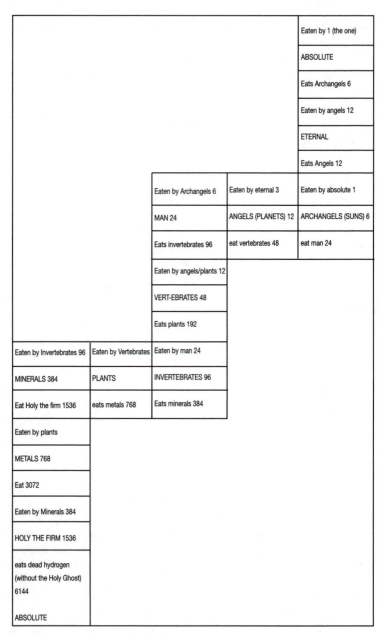

						Eaten by 1 (the one)
						ABSOLUTE
						Eats Archangels 6
						Eaten by angels 12
						ETERNAL
						Eats Angels 12
			Eaten by Archangels 6	Eaten by eternal 3	Eaten by absolute 1
			MAN 24	ANGELS (PLANETS) 12	ARCHANGELS (SUNS) 6
			Eats invertebrates 96	eat vertebrates 48	eat man 24
			Eaten by angels/plants 12		
			VERT-EBRATES 48		
			Eats plants 192		
Eaten by Invertebrates 96	Eaten by Vertebrates	Eaten by man 24		
MINERALS 384	PLANTS	INVERTEBRATES 96		
Eat Holy the firm 1536	eats metals 768	Eats minerals 384		
Eaten by plants				
METALS 768				
Eat 3072				
Eaten by Minerals 384				
HOLY THE FIRM 1536				
eats dead hydrogen (without the Holy Ghost) 6144				
ABSOLUTE				

Figure 22 Law of Reciprocal Maintenance/Reciprocal Feeding

Source: From information in *Search*: 322–4.

Note: See also the Step Diagram in *Search*: 323.

average 'hydrogen' of each class of creature. Gurdjieff noted that this diagram contradicts information about hydrogens he has given elsewhere, but that nonetheless both give the right information and, after a long time, it will become clear to pupils. The lowest hydrogen, 6144, is in fact an incomplete 'nitrogen' that, lacking a corresponding 'carbon', cannot transform into an 'oxygen' for the next lowest triad: thus it becomes a 'hydrogen' without any possibility for further development (*Search*: 322–4).

Orage relates this law to the three foods we eat, including the nourishment we receive from others (e.g. from talking with them), and suggests that as the food I eat becomes the cells of my body therefore 'I am what I have eaten and digested – literally, I have eaten myself'. The universe also eats to live: each part of it is the product of the eating of the Great 'I', ' "the Great I AM", which is God'. He connects this idea with the eating of Christ's flesh in the Eucharist, and in other rites of cannibalism (*Teachings*: 143).

See also: **food/eating; vampirism**

LAW OF SEVEN

The Law of Seven is also sometimes referred to as 'the octave'. There is a separate entry here for the **Law of Octaves**, but the terms do overlap. The Law of Seven is one of the fundamental laws of the universe (the other being the **Law of Three**) and describes the universe in terms of vibrations that proceed through all existing kinds and densities of **matter**. However, unlike scientific thinking contemporary with Gurdjieff's formulation of the Law of Seven (*c*.1912), which regarded vibrations as proceeding uninterruptedly, Gurdjieff regarded vibrations as discontinuous. His law explains the speeding up or slowing down of vibrations as analogous to a musical octave.

The rate of vibrations doubles between the Do of one octave and the Do of the next higher octave. But the rate of increase is not constant from note to note throughout the octave. At two places in the octave the rate of increase is retarded. These are the places in the scale where the semi-tone is missing, creating what Gurdjieff terms an interval (see Figure 21 in **Law of Octaves**). In terms of human life experience, for example, when having an **aim** to do something, the intervals are the places where direction is changed unconsciously, where energy does not continue to flow in the planned direction unless what Gurdjieff terms a **shock** is given (see **interval**). The seven-tone scale is the formula of a cosmic law that was worked out by an ancient school and applied to music. The Law of Octaves manifests itself in all kinds of vibrations, including light, heat, chemical and magnetic vibrations (*Search*: 122–5; see also **cosmoses**; **ray of creation**).

This law is known as the Law of Heptaparaparshinokh in *Tales* and is the principal subject matter of Chapters 30, 39 and 40, as well as 41 where Pythagoras's monochord is adapted for further experiments (*Tales*: 888–92). The synthesis of ideas that relates the seven notes of the musical scale, the seven colours of the spectrum, and the ratio of distances between the seven known planets of antiquity, derived from Pythagoras, occurs in Western European occultism, especially during the Renaissance and the late nineteenth-century occult revival. Some of these probable sources for Gurdjieff's Laws of Seven and Three are explored by Webb (1980: 499–542). Blavatsky's eternal law, which unfolds everything manifested in nature on a sevenfold principle, has affinities to Gurdjieff's Law of Seven (Blavatsky 1988 [1888]: vol.1, p.152).

See also: **enneagram; harmony/harmonious/harmonic; number/ numerology; Theosophy**

Further reading

For a detailed study of the Law of Seven, see Smith 1993.

LAW OF SOLIOONENSIUS

Gurdjieff wrote (*Life*: 47) that this law was learned from an ancient Armenian papyrus, and that 'periodic tension in suns and planets acts on the common presences of all three-brained beings'. This ought to provoke religious feelings, but instead provokes **war** (see *Tales*, Anonymous 1973: 561).

See also: **astrology; influences**

LAW OF THREE

The Law of Three is one of the two fundamental laws on which Gurdjieff's cosmology is based; the other is the **Law of Seven**. Taken together, they are an expression of how creative, destructive and redemptive processes function in the universe. While the Law of Seven controls substance, the Law of Three controls process: it creates all phenomena in the diversity or unity of all universes.

The Law of Three states that every event or action, on whatever scale, from the molecular to the cosmic, is the result of three interacting forces. The first force is an 'active' force that expresses the desire or impulse towards action. The second force is 'passive', representing resistance or opposition to the impulse to act. The third force is that which reconciles the first and second forces: a 'reconciling' force. These are also known as 'positive', 'negative' and 'neutralising' forces. All three forces are equally active, only being named as 'active', 'passive' or 'neutralising' in relation to one another at a given moment. The duality of the first and second forces is recognised in science (e.g. the positive and negative forces in electricity); however, the third force is not recognised and is more difficult to observe. For example, a person may desire to work (active/ first force), but this is opposed by inertia (passive/second force), thus nothing happens. However, a reconciling third force, perhaps in the form of new knowledge, may appear and enable the person to begin work. When the law has been observed internally, it becomes easier to observe it externally. Our understanding of the world in relation to only two forces is the reason we do not see the 'real world'. This can only be seen when we can see the manifestation of the third force. The only place where the three forces constitute a whole is in the **Absolute**, and this notion of an indivisible trinity can be seen in various ancient religions, including Christianity and Hinduism (*Search*: 77–9).

This law is known in *Tales* as the Law of Triamazikamno, and is referred to especially in Chapters 17 and 39. For the triadic form of Gurdjieff's writings, see **number/numerology, symbols/symbolism** and *Beelzebub's Tales to His Grandson*.

The order of the three forces as expressed in triads is important and determines the outcome of events or actions. For example, the triad 1,2,3 (in which the first/active force is followed by the second/passive force) is reconciled by the third force in an involutionary way. This is the order in which the forces descend from the Absolute in the Ray of Creation. However, when the order of the triad is changed to 2,1,3 (in which the second force is followed by the first force), the reconciling action of the third force makes for an evolutionary outcome. Gurdjieff's apparently arbitrary insistence on reading his texts in the correct order so as to achieve the result he desires for us may be understood in this light. When *Tales* represents his passive/second force and *Meetings* his active/first force, then reading *Life* (his reconciling/third force) will allow the reader to become reconciled in a beneficial and evolutionary state. Reading them in the order *Meetings*, *Tales* and *Life* would give an involutionary result.

This change in order of triads is shown in *Life* (110–11, 135–6), where **exercises** given by Gurdjieff use the phrases 'I can, I am, I wish'; these relate to the three forces, 1,2,3. Gurdjieff uses these phrases in two orders: first, 'I can, I wish, I am' (1,3,2) and, second, 'I am, I can, I wish' (2,1,3). Bennett (1976 [1961]: 103–28) defines the six possible expressions of the three forces as the 'triad of involution' (1,2,3), the 'triad of interaction' (1,3,2), the 'triad of evolution' (2,1,3), the 'triad of identity' (2,3,1), the 'triad of universal order' (3,1,2) and the 'triad of the spirit' (3,2,1).

The naming of forces as first, second or third in relation to their function (i.e. active, passive or reconciling) can easily be confused with their position in a specific triad: e.g. in the triad 2,3,1, where the first force is in the third or result position. Another potential area of confusion lies in regarding the position of the forces as 'higher' or 'lower'. The third force, represented by 3, is a higher number than 1 or 2, but is 'lower' in place in the Ray of Creation where a descending triad is expressed as 1,2,3.

These distinctions may go some way towards clarifying the differing expressions of the Law of Three that Moore points out. In one case, the third force is the result of the action of the other two forces: e.g. the sperm unites with the ovum to create the embryo. In another formulation, the third force is the agent of change that yields a result: e.g. flour and water become bread only when bonded by fire. The **matter** resulting from the process of the three forces can be defined as 'higher' for the preceding 'lower' (i.e. bread is 'higher' than flour and water), but 'lower' than the preceding 'higher' (i.e. bread is 'lower' than fire) (Moore 1991: 44; see Figures 23 and 24).

Campion (1994: 81–2) gives two versions of Sumerian divine trinities: a trio of male sky gods and a trinity of the first male god and female god with their divine child. These may be regarded as influential on later Christian and occult expressions of trinities. Both forms of trinity are recognisable in Christianity: the indivisible Trinity of God the Father, God the Son and God the Holy Spirit (corresponding to the three forces in Gurdjieff's Absolute) and the trinity of Jesus and his 'parents' Mary and the Holy Spirit. Other trinities expressed in the Western European occult tradition can be found: in the fusion of sulphur and mercury to produce gold in **alchemy**; in the Kabbala's three sets of trinities; and in the synthesis of

Figure 23 Law of Three: Triad shown vertically

Ascending Triad 2-3-1		Expressed in relation to the higher and lower in the ray of creation
3	Fire	
1	Bread	Higher than flour and water, lower than fire
2	Flour, Water	

Note: This shows how the triad 2-3-1 is visually expressed in terms of higher and lower substances. But because this is a static diagram it is easier to read it incorrectly as ascending, i.e. 2-1-3, or descending 3-1-2

Figure 24 Law of Three: Triad shown horizontally

2	3	1
Passive matter	Higher reconciling matter	Resultant active matter
Flour and water	Fire	Bread
Second force	Third force	First force

Note: This shows the triad 2-3-1 set out horizontally

trinities expressed by Blavatsky (1988 [1888]: vol.1, pp.2,14; vol.2, pp.181,446). Gurdjieff's active, passive and neutralising forces can be related to the astrological modes of action: the cardinal, fixed and mutable (see **astrology**; see also **enneagram**).

In relation to Freud: 'Orage said that Freud's triadic consciousness – ego, super ego, and mediating id – correspond to Gurdjieff's positive, negative and mediating forces' (Taylor 2001: 218).

LAWS: AN OVERVIEW

Gurdjieff's cosmological laws have their origins in Mesopotamian astronomy/astrology, echoes of which are also found in Judaism, Christianity, Hinduism and Islam, and in the occult and esoteric thinking derived from Pythagoras, 'the father of a long tradition of number symbolism' (Webb 1980: 503; see **astrology**; **number/ numerology**).

The laws defined here are the **Law of Accident**, which is applied only to humanity, and the cosmological laws that apply throughout the universe: the **Laws of Three** and **Seven**, the **Law of Octaves** and the **Law of Reciprocal Maintenance/Reciprocal Feeding**. Although infrequently used in the Work, the **Law of Duality/Two** is a useful heading under which to give Gurdjieff's teaching about opposing forces (for the Law of Two as used in relation to astrology, see West 1991 [1970]). These and other second-degree cosmic laws are defined in *Tales* (see Anonymous 1973: 349–51). The only second-degree law defined here is the **Law of Solioonensius**.

Gurdjieff gave the origins of his teachings as the hidden esoteric schools in the East. However, Webb (1980: 542) suggests that **Theosophy** and Blavatsky's *The Secret Doctrine* were the immediate origin of much of Gurdjieff's cosmology. He traces the probable Western European origins of the **enneagram** (the geometric figure that symbolises the Laws of Three and Seven) from sources that include the *Great Art* of Ramon Lull (*c*.1305–8) and the *Arithmologia* (1665) of Athanasius Kircher.

According to Gurdjieff, although laws themselves do not vary, the way they are manifested does vary in relation to different levels and different planes of the universe (*Search*: 206).

LEGOMINISM

'Legomonism' is the name Gurdjieff's hero Beelzebub gives in *Tales* to a method, devised by the Atlantians, of transmitting information from initiate to initiate from the remote past to the present. A Legominism is a conscious work of art, based on the **Law of Seven**, that contains a purposely made 'mistake' or 'lawful inexactitude'. The inexactitude will contain the information to be transmitted (*Tales*: 349–50; see also Chapter 26 for the Legominism 'The Terror-of-the-Situation' and Chapter 30 on 'Art'). Gurdjieff's *Tales* is regarded by pupils as a conscious work of art, and so pupils have looked for its inexactitude. However, there are many 'inexactitudes' to be found in the text (see **art**).

Webb (1980: 500–1) connects Gurdjieff's Legominism with the concept of traditional knowledge 'transmitted . . . by personal contact . . . from generation to generation'. Moses, Pythagoras, Christ and Leonardo da Vinci, among others, are considered teachers linked in the chain of the Tradition or Perennial Tradition.

Further reading

Gettings 1987 explores an astrological 'Legominism' in the church of San Miniato al Monte in Florence.

LEVELS OF BEING

In Western culture being is not valued: its meaning is regarded as the same as existence. It means more than non-existence. Although people may seem the same, they may have different levels and categories of being. A man's **knowledge** depends on his level of being (*Search*: 65, 26; see **being**; **man**).

Cosmic levels of being are defined according to three 'traits of being': by what a creature eats, by what he breathes and by the medium in which he lives. While no creature can make changes to the **food** it eats or to the **air** it breathes, man can improve the quality of his **impressions**. This will introduce higher **'hydrogens'** into his system, and in this way **evolution** becomes possible. Levels of being can also be classified by the food that each being eats and by the being for which he himself serves as food (*Search*: 320–1).

See also: **bodies; cosmoses; Law of Octaves; Law of Reciprocal Maintenance/Reciprocal Feeding**

LEVERS/POSTURES

Man's body, essence and personality are activated by levers, which are formed in the **centres** by the age of sixteen or seventeen. They are set into motion by external shocks. One lever touches another: these are termed **associations**, either of body, essence or personality. In abnormal life, man also forms levers outside the centres (e.g. in the flesh); these 'provoke movement independently of the soul' (*Views*, 1922: 136–42).

LIBERATION

In order to be effective a man's desire for liberation must be so strong that he is prepared to sacrifice everything for it (*Search*: 61). It is possible for a man to become free from some of the forty-eight laws he is under (see **ray of creation**), but this requires great knowledge and experience of struggle against these laws (*Search*: 84–5). The lesser liberation from **influences** within us must be achieved in order to obtain the great liberation, which is from the influences outside us (*Views*, 1923: 266).

LIES/LYING

Truth and falsehood do not exist for a person whose identity is formed of multiple 'I's and whose buffers protect him from inner contradictions (see **buffers**; **'I'/identity**); such a person tells incessant lies (*Search*: 159). Lying plays a big part in a man's life, even if it is by suppression of truth. He lies both to himself and others. His first effort must be to conquer lying in relation to his teacher; if he does lie, he must confess it to himself, to others and to the teacher (see **group**). When pupils no longer lie so well, friends not in the **Work** find them dull (*Search*: 224, 229–31, 245). It is difficult to tell the truth about ourselves, because we do not know the truth (*Search*: 249). People lie mechanically, just as they tell the truth mechanically. Truth and lies can only have value if a man can control them; for this he needs a certain level of **being** (*Views*, 1922: 76). Gurdjieff said that sometimes truth could only be given in the form of lies (*Search*: 314; see **schools**).

Further reading

To compare Kierkegaard's views on deception and illusion with Gurdjieff's views on sleep, see Kierkegaard 1962 [1939]. Kierkegaard (1813–55) was influential from the early twentieth century and much read in Europe in the 1920s in the fields of literature, philosophy, psychology and theology.

LIFE IS REAL ONLY THEN, WHEN 'I AM'

The Third Series is defined as having four books under the common title *Life is Real Only Then, When 'I Am'*, but is divided into eight unnumbered sections. Gurdjieff's aim for the text is to:

> assist the arising, in the mentation and in the feelings of the reader, of a veritable, nonfantastic representation not of that illusory world which he now perceives, but of the world existing in reality.

> (*Tales*: v)

Through this Gurdjieff is looking to share with his readers the possibilities he has discovered of touching and even (if so desired) of merging with reality (*Life*: 4). Thus in the Third Series Gurdjieff represents a third world distinct from either the inner or outer worlds that are the mechanisms controlling a man who has not worked on himself. The 'real' world represents a state more awake than 'waking consciousness' (see **consciousness**).

The narrative of *Life* traces seven-year periods and triads of events that reflect the **Laws of Three** and **Seven**. This suggests a numerologically symbolic use of dating. Dates given for events between 1927 and 1935 sometimes refer to events that did occur but on other dates than those given, and sometimes refer to events that did not occur at all. Thus it is not possible to regard the narrative or the dates as an historical record. Gurdjieff does remind his reader to take the narrative as allegory that needs interpretation. The text breaks off in mid-sentence: this is seen by some as an intentional device and by others as evidence that *Life* is unfinished (see Taylor 1998: 178–205).

The theme of suffering in *Life* is related to the theme of exile, and intentional suffering is related to intentional exile. Thus, echoing God's exile of Beelzebub, Gurdjieff exiles his own hypnotic powers and his own writings (*Herald*). We can see Gurdjieff's attempt to 'exile' Orage in terms of creating a **reminding factor** to help himself in his aim, which is to remember his real 'I' and the third (or real) world that this 'I' inhabits (see **suffering/pleasure**; for the relation of *Life* to Gurdjieff's other texts, see also Taylor 1998; **astrology**; **number/ numerology**; **zodiac**).

Life: *An outline*

Gurdjieff's 'Prologue' focuses on themes of suffering, which relate the inner to the outer world, and to the relations between people. Gurdjieff defines the Three Series of his writings, through which he wishes to transmit his teaching. He describes how his original plans were thwarted, his early dissatisfaction with himself, his later dissatisfaction with his writings, and his understanding of how both conscious and unconscious **suffering** can help his **aims**.

He outlines a series of plans for writing, for study and for strengthening his health. These include 'treading on the **corns** of everyone he meets' so as to see into their inner world. He completed *Life*, but finds it needs to be rewritten. He mentions the purpose for which *Herald* was written and that it should not be read now.

In the 'Introduction' Gurdjieff writes of finding his New York pupils wrongly focused on observation. He details how this has come about and seeks to remedy the situation by asking pupils to sever their connections with Orage, whom Gurdjieff had sent to run the group.

Gurdjieff says his readers should take his accounts in *Life* as allegories and learn from them (see **allegory/analogy**).

In his 'First Talk' Gurdjieff explains that misunderstandings about his teaching arose due to the teaching of pupils who were not fully qualified, and because after his accident he had focused on his writings. Now he begins to correct these mistakes and to teach the **group**.

In the 'Second Talk' Gurdjieff recounts how he sent Orage to look after the New York group. Gurdjieff now demands that pupils sever connections with Orage.

In the 'Third Talk' Gurdjieff teaches about three impulses that must arise and be manifested in real man. These are expressed as 'I can', 'I wish' and 'I am'. He gives an **exercise** for the division of **attention**.

In the 'Fourth Talk' Gurdjieff first recounts what happened after his demand that the pupils sign an agreement to sever connections with Orage. He describes his reactions when Orage also signs the agreement, and his fining of tardy pupils. The talk itself focuses on the importance of air, its involutionary and evolutionary elements. The text breaks off before revealing a secret about air.

In the 'Fifth Talk' Gurdjieff gives two exercises in attention. Gurdjieff's reception of air and **impressions** during his demonstration of divided attention helped him, because he already has an 'I'. As yet his pupils do not, so they must do the exercise without expectations.

In 'The Outer and Inner World of Man' Gurdjieff writes of the active and passive forces that form the inner worlds of people and of attention through which the inner parts of man may be connected.

He narrates two coincidences. These are related to intentional suffering, to the subject matter of his writing, and to the death of Orage seven years to the day after Gurdjieff had written to advise him about his health. Gurdjieff implies that Orage died because he did not accept the intentional suffering that 'exile' from Gurdjieff would have caused him.

Gurdjieff writes about contemporary worthless expressions of mourning. He reaffirms that all deaths can remind us of our own. Only this realisation can bring faith, hope and love to birth again.

Through the medium of a Persian song Gurdjieff introduces the subject of the soul. Its presence is 'I am'. It is part of 'All-Being'.

Gurdjieff recounts another coincidence in which an article in a Russian newspaper expresses exactly what he wished to write about the prolongation of human life, in the context of contemporary science; he includes this article in his chapter.

Gurdjieff states that all men have two worlds that are formed automatically. If a man works on himself, by an intentional blending of the two worlds he gains a third world. In a man with only two worlds, the 'I' is missing. The 'I' results from contact between inner and outer worlds. This third function of man represents the third or real inner world of man.

Gurdjieff ends *Life* by writing of a paradox concerning friends and enemies. He describes the radiations given off by people and how these blend mechanically. Gurdjieff's text breaks off as he is about to explain the way in which the people he comes in contact with form psychic factors that express 'attitudes diametrically opposed to me' (see **psyche/psychic/psychology**).

Exercises given by Gurdjieff (*Life*: 110–11, 135–6) use the phrases 'I can, I am, I wish'; these relate to the three forces: 1,2,3. Gurdjieff uses these phrases in two orders: first, 'I can, I wish, I am' (1,3,2), this triad represents the world as process; second, 'I am, I can, I wish' (2,1,3), the triad of evolution (for a full definition of triads, see Bennett 1976 [1961]: pp.91–9; see also **law of three**).

The Russian article referred to above was not an invention of Gurdjieff's (see Taylor 1998: 198, 204).

LINES OF WORK *see* work, lines of

LITERAL UNDERSTANDING *see* **understanding, literal**

LOVE

Ouspensky refers to people's negative attitude to the Work because of its 'absence of love' (*Search*: 165). Gurdjieff explains that 'mechanical man cannot love – with *him it loves or it does not love*' (*Search*: 254, original emphasis). Mechanical love can be misdirected and has no value. Real love, Christian religious love, must be learned. Where there is life, there is love. Each plant, animal and person is a representative of God, each is sensitive to love and functions better when loved. If a person wishes to love his neighbour, he must begin by trying to love plants and animals. No change can take place in a man who does not change his attitude to the outside world, but he must learn what to love and what not to love, leaving aside the 'most clear-cut things which are undeniably bad'. A man can make **experiments** with his attitudes to what he likes and dislikes (e.g. if he likes certain flowers, he might try to dislike them and vice versa). Everything living is interdependent: 'whoever does not love life does not love God' (*Views*, 1923: 243–5). God said whoever loves their parents loves him; we can ask ourselves if we loved our parents as they deserved or mechanically. If we do not love them, we cannot love God (*Views*, 1922: 173).

There are two kinds of self-love that are outwardly alike but inwardly opposite to one another. True self-love, which we do not have, is desirable and necessary and is an attribute of the soul; the possession of it leads to freedom: a person with self-love 'is a particle of heaven. Self-love is I – I is God'. However, we possess false self-love in which we are ruled solely by internal influences and this self-love is the principal weapon of the devil. To distinguish between the two we need to practise 'active reasoning' (*Views*, 1923: 269–70; see **influences; understanding**).

Gurdjieff refers to love as a sacred feeling,

> [the] possibility of its manifestation [...] given to us by our Creator for the salvation of our souls and for the mutual support necessary for a more or less happy life together.

In contemporary weak, will-less people love has degenerated into a vice (*Meetings*: 9).

Gurdjieff cited 'Philadelphia', that is, in translation from Greek, 'the city of brotherly love', as the common destination for seekers of all religions, saying that after reaching 'Philadelphia' the road is the same for everyone (*Views*, 1924: 191).

Gurdjieff taught that people need to love one another in order to work together, and all the component parts of a human being should also love each other. Peters paraphrases Gurdjieff's definition of 'real love' as:

> understanding another human being so that you can help him, even if the assistance goes temporarily against the person's nature. Caring for the person exceeds any personal desire or gratification.

(Peters 1976 [1964, 1965]: 163–5)

There are two different strands of Gurdjieff's 1940s teaching on love. One echoes his past teachings: that sex and love need not be mingled, that love is internal and can be felt for a person of the same sex or an animal. He urged love of neighbour as the '*Way*' (emphasis in the text) to bring what is felt for parents to everyone, and the ability to enter the situation of another. He taught that Jesus performed his miracles through the power of real love joined with magnetism; that accumulated vibrations cause a current that brings the cosmic force of love, the greatest power in the world. He suggested that with love and a study of magnetism pupils may cure paralytics and blindness (*Voices*: 23, 163). However, on many other occasions he advocated a complete lack of feeling for anyone other than blood relations. All love and respect must be liquidated, transformed into indifference. The pupil must neither love, nor esteem internally, nor have sympathy or antipathy, with anyone except people of the same **blood**; all others must be rejected. Our contact with parents must not be changed, only the form of contact, since they are of the same blood. Strangers are of another blood: we must be free of them (*Voices*: 150–1). Gurdjieff urged an intense involvement of his pupils with their parents, whether the parents are dead or alive (see **remorse**; **role**).

In 1982 Tracol (1994: 137) expressed his experience of Gurdjieff as a being with 'unbounded love, neither left to chance or without price, a love of extreme exactingness', born of his witnessing his pupils' suffering.

Further reading

Orage *On Love* (1998 [1957]) professes to be a translation, but was written after an all-night conversation with Gurdjieff; see also Taylor 1998, 2001: 242–6; Wellbeloved 1998: 321–32.

LUNATIC/TRAMP

Lunatics and tramps are defined in relation to the **obyvatel**, who looks on patriots as psychopaths and pacifists as lunatics. Tramps are members of the intelligentsia, artists, poets and bohemians who despise obyvatels, but could not exist without them (*Search*: 363).

See also: **Hasnamuss**

MACHINE/MECHANICALITY

Man is a machine and functions mechanically. All his actions, words, thoughts, feelings, convictions, opinions and habits function under the power of external influences. There is no difference between 'savages' and 'intellectuals'. Just as everything internal 'happens' to a man, so his external life (e.g. popular movements and **wars**) also 'happen'. Machines cannot 'do' anything and are not responsible for their actions (see **doing**). It is possible to stop being a machine, but first a person must know his machine. He must understand that he is a machine, not just with his mind, but convinced of it with his 'whole mass', never to forget it (*Search*: 19–21; see also *Search*: 58–9). The majority of people 'are diseased, broken machines' with whom nothing can be done: the level of their **being** is too low to allow them to receive **knowledge** (*Search*: 66).

Everything in the machine is interconnected and counterbalanced. It is impossible for a man to change just one thing in himself without the machine making other changes in order to maintain balance (*Search*: 108).

The machine is 'clogged with dirt' and must be cleaned before a man can develop himself, but he needs help to do this (*Views*, 1918: 50).

Gurdjieff refers to three inner machines, **body**, **essence** and **personality**, that need to be developed in each person and to the deformation caused by one-sided development. The lack of connection between machines causes an inability to express oneself fully (*Views*, 1922: 82–3). However, compare this with the difficulties caused by the connections between **centres** (*Search*: 347–8). Thus, both the connection and the disconnection of machines/centres causes problems.

The data on which the development of the body depends are 'heredity, geographical conditions, food, and movement'. The personality is formed by what a man hears and reads. Essence is emotional and is formed from heredity before personality is formed. All three machines develop independently. A man may therefore be brave in his essence but cowardly in his personality. We may also compare this with the statements about connectedness above.

Each machine is activated by postures or levers (see **levers/postures**). In order to define a person we must distinguish between his body, essence and personality, and evaluate the whole man as the sum of these parts. By analogy (see **allegory/analogy**) bread/a man is composed of the right proportions of flour/physical postures, water/emotional postures and fire/intellectual postures. Without all three ingredients in the right proportions, there is no bread or individual man (*Views*, 1922: 136–42).

MAGIC/MAGICIAN

Magic is the ability to do (see **doing**). A magician is a person who can 'do'; ordinary men cannot 'do', with them things happen. Magicians are people who understand the laws of nature and know how to use them, to transform substances and to oppose mechanical influences. Christ was a magician, a man who had this knowledge. White magic uses knowledge for good, and black magic for its own selfish ends. Black magic does not necessarily imply evil. Black magicians can be altruistic. However, their identifying trait is that, without acquainting people with what they are doing, they use people for their own aims, either through inducing **faith** and infatuation or through **fear**. A black magician will at least have attended a 'school'. More dangerous are 'occult' and 'Theosophical groups' whose work on themselves is an illusion (*Search*: 226–7; *Views*, 1918: 210–11). The definition of a black magician raises questions about Gurdjieff's demand for unswerving obedience to group teachers. If the pupil must obey, even if he does not understand the teacher's aim (see **group**), how can he discriminate between a true teacher and a black magician?

In 1918 Gurdjieff taught pupils how to do 'tricks', such as mind reading. This was to enable them to tell true from false psychic phenomena and to develop their ability to observe and be shrewd (*Search*: 372). Within months of setting up his Institute in 1922, Gurdjieff had gained the reputation of magician and charlatan (Taylor 1998: 9). In 1923 Gurdjieff offered 'tricks, half tricks and real phenomena observed in religious ceremonies of the ancient East' in a performance in Paris (advertisement in *L'Echo des Champs-Elysees*, reprinted in Moore 1991: 194).

In relation to Buddhist magic, Gurdjieff explained that a bone (which Ouspensky had been shown) was part of a particular bone formation, 'Buddha's necklace'. This was developed through exercises and connects the astral and physical bodies. A man can contact the astral body of a dead person if he has one of these bones (*Search*: 62–3). In relation to the Christian church, Gurdjieff spoke of the liturgy being carried out and witnessed by people who 'take the sacraments for magic', not knowing that these were originally demonstrations given by a **school** that is now forgotten (*Search*: 302; see also **blood**; for *The Struggle of the Magicians*, see **dance**).

Further reading

For the influential Hermitic Order of the Golden Dawn (founded 1888), see Macgregor *et al.* 1987 and Gilbert 1997; see also Melton's 'Modern Alternative Religions in the West' (in Hinnells 1998).

MAGNETIC CENTRE

A magnetic centre is formed in a person who distinguishes between ideas coming from an exoteric centre and those in everyday life (see **influences**). The centre draws him towards help in the form of a teacher. However, this centre may be wrongly formed, in which case the man will make contact with someone who, although seeming to be one, is not a teacher from an esoteric centre (*Search*: 200–4).

MAGNETISM/ANIMAL MAGNETISM

In *Tales* animal magnetism, termed 'Hanbledzoin', is the 'blood' of the Kesdjan (astral) body and nourishes this body as blood nourishes the planetary body. Hanbledzoin substances are transformed elements from the other planets and the sun of a being's home solar system. Sacred-Hanbledzoin serves the **soul** and comes from emanations of the Sun Absolute.

The active substance from the physical body together with active matter from the astral body mix to form a third magnetic substance that forms an **atmosphere** around a man analogous to atmospheres around planets. Men's atmospheres (like all other things) have electricity, of which the negative and positive parts can be controlled.

> One part can be increased and made to flow like a current. [. . .] In man, wishes and non-wishes may be positive and negative. Astral material always opposes physical material.

People lack this mixed substance that, as Mesmer rediscovered, priests used to use for healing. Magnetism is acquired only through 'conscious labor and intentional suffering, through doing small things voluntarily'. This is an example of the **Law of Three**. The **friction** between the positive and negative causes **suffering**, and this leads to the third substance (*Views*, 1930: 92–3; 1924: 98; see also **aim**). Gurdjieff refers to the power, based on 'strength in the field of "hanbledzoin" ', as telepathy and hypnotism (see **hypnosis/**

hypnotism), which he had developed within himself. He renounces this **grace** in order to refrain from the vices arising from it, and also to serve him as a constant **reminding factor** (*Life*: 25). Gurdjieff tells how he used this power in a letter to Edith Taylor (Taylor 1998: 140–1).

Mesmer's doctoral thesis expounded:

> his belief that there must be tides in the human body emanating from the stars. This generalised influence of celestial bodies on the human organism he labelled 'animal gravity'.

> (Mesmer in Crabtree 1993: 4)

MAN

The word 'man' is used by Gurdjieff to refer to both men and women. Man is an image of the **world**, created by the same laws as those that created the whole of the world. By studying the world he will know himself and by studying himself he will know the world; these studies should run parallel to each other.

There are seven distinct levels of man, each designated by a number. All men are born as man number one, two or three, and are undeveloped mechanical men. Man number one has the centre of gravity of his psychic life in the **moving centre**; in man number two this lies in the **emotional centre**; in man number three it lies in the **intellectual centre**.

Man number four was born as man number one, two or three, but has developed as a result of work in a **school**. He possesses a permanent **centre of gravity** in his valuation of his school, his psychic centres are becoming balanced, and he is beginning to know himself and his direction. Man number five is a man who has obtained unity. In rare cases a man becomes number five without having been number four and, as man number five has crystallised and cannot change (see **crystallisation**), he cannot develop further without terrible suffering. Man number six differs from man number seven only in the fact that all his properties are not yet permanent. Man number seven means a fully developed man who possesses, among other properties, **will**, **consciousness**, a permanent and unchangeable 'I', individuality and immortality (*Search*: 71–4).

Gurdjieff referred to 'real man', who possesses will, and 'man in **quotation marks**', with 'man' signifying unreal man. Although all men have two sides, real man is neither 'good' nor 'evil' (see **good and evil**), he simply wishes to acquire a **soul** for proper development. In order to make good and evil work together, a third thing is needed: **conscience**.

Man's place in the universe, distant from the Absolute and under forty-eight laws, gives a **Gnostic** sense of man's alienation and exile (see **ray of creation**).

MASTER

The concept of the internal master in charge of the house is analogous to a permanent 'I' that is in control of the machine. Man as a machine has no master; **Work** consists of preparing for the arrival of the master (*Search*: 60–1; *Views*, 1924: 88; see also **self-observation**). Every religion understands that the master is not there and seeks him; this is an aim, not a fact. A man's centres realise that when there is a master they will have to submit to him. If there is no master, there is no soul and no will (*Views*: 203, 214, 246; see also **carriage, horse, driver and master**).

Gurdjieff is defined by de Salzmann as a master (*Views*: xii). According to Bennett (1976 [1973]: 218), Gurdjieff was not a guru or a sheikh because his work with groups was preparatory to work on a much larger scale.

In 1967 Tracol wrote that the function of the master is to awaken and he is an embodiment of his role: the Bodhidharma. It is not important that a master himself be permanently awake: a man who is still searching may be more able to help others. However, while a master can profit from dialogue with anyone, we cannot. A master is a necessity, but only for a time (Tracol 1994: 111, 119–20, 122). The right attitude towards Gurdjieff, as a master, was never to forget he was both man and master, to be open without surrendering and to know how to extract the Word from him (Tracol 1994, undated: 124).

By 1924 Gurdjieff had the reputation of being a prophet, a visionary, a great philosopher and something close to 'a second coming of Christ' (Peters 1976 [1964, 1965]: 3, 7).

Further reading

For Blavatsky and Theosophical masters, see Johnson 1987 and 1994; see also Rawlinson 1997. For a personal account, see Collin-Smith 1988.

MATTER

Everything in the universe, taken in the form of the **Ray of Creation** from the **Absolute** to the **Moon**, is material and can be weighed and measured. Although matter is the same everywhere, the materiality in each of the worlds in the Ray of Creation corresponds to the qualities and properties of the energy that is manifested there. Matter or substance presupposes the existence of energy. For the purpose of observation of matter through our physical senses, the 'constant' is taken as matter, while the 'changes' in the 'constant' are called 'manifestations of energy'. The changes are the result of vibrations, which issue from the Absolute and travel in all directions, colliding and merging until they stop at the end of the Ray of Creation. The world can be seen as vibrating matter. The matter of the Absolute is the least dense and has the highest rate of vibrations; with each world that descends from the Ray of Creation, the matter becomes denser and the vibrations slower (see also **atom**).

The matters belonging to these different worlds are not separated but exist together, interpenetrating one another. Everything on earth, including a man's own body, has within it the matter of other worlds. Thus man is a miniature universe; in studying the laws and forces that govern the universe we learn about ourselves, and vice versa. However, mechanical man is an unfinished world, and the study of both man and universe must go on together (*Search*: 86–7).

The degree of intelligence and consciousness of any matter is in relation to the speed of vibrations within it: the higher the rate of vibration, the greater the intelligence. Thus comparisons can be made about the intelligence of matters. For this purpose an average 'hydrogen' is calculated for each being. This depends on the level of being that can be determined by its number of storeys in the **three-storey factory**. Man is defined by having three storeys; however, a sheep has two storeys, and a worm only one. Man therefore can be equated partly with 'man', partly with 'sheep' and partly with 'worm'. Man number one most closely with the 'worm', man number two with the 'sheep' and man number three with 'man'. The average 'hydrogen' is H 96, which belongs to the middle storey (the 'sheep'). This determines the intelligence of the centre of gravity of the physical body. The centre of gravity for the astral body is H 48, for the third body it will be H 24, and for the fourth body H 12. Using this method, it is possible to compare the intelligence of man number eight with the intelligence of a table (*Search*: 317–22; see also Figure 9 in **enneagram**, which shows food octaves).

All matter is alive and possesses a degree of consciousness and intelligence (see **hydrogens, table of**). There is usually no dead matter on earth. In a diagram relating to 'hydrogens', Gurdjieff referred to H 6144 as 'a dead hydrogen, without any possibility of passing into anything further, a hydrogen without the holy ghost' (*Search*: 317–24). All substances have four states of matter (*Search*: 90; see **elements**).

Physical matter is defined as injury, sickness, treatment of sickness and disharmony. Psychical matter is defined as effect, cause, quality, state and change (*Views*, 1923: 134–5).

Further reading

The development of quantum physics and quantum philosophy led to a new attitude to matter; on love of knowledge of matter rather than control of matter, see Williams 1987.

MEETINGS WITH REMARKABLE MEN

This is the Second Series of *All and Everything*. The text aims to 'acquaint the Reader with the material required for a new creation and to prove the soundness and good quality of it'. Described as three books, it comprises ten chapters concerning the remarkable people that Gurdjieff met. Chapter 1, which is entitled 'Introduction', contains a remarkable elderly Persian; Chapter 7 has three sections, each devoted to a remarkable person; thus there are twelve remarkable men in all. These represent personifications of the signs of the **zodiac**. There is an additional section on 'The Material Question' in which Gurdjieff himself is seen as a remarkable man.

Meetings: An outline

In his 'Introduction', Gurdjieff affirms his aim for the Second Series and, via the opinions of an elderly Persian, expresses contempt for corrupt contemporary European literature, including journalism, which cannot transmit anything of value to future generations. Gurdjieff's tales about the remarkable men he has met are intended to function as autobiography, and also to answer questions he is often asked.

While contemporary writers are disparaged in the 'Introduction', the chapter on Gurdjieff's father, a bardic poet, extols the oral tradition and the transmission of ancient legends. These helped Gurdjieff to form poetic images and high ideals. His father, despite many misfortunes, never lost heart and remained inwardly free. He died during a Turkish attack on Alexandropol in 1917 and his grave is unknown.

Gurdjieff's 'second father', Dean Borsh of Kars Military Cathedral, undertook Gurdjieff's education. He held unusual views relating to the responsibilities of adulthood, sex and marriage. He outlined ten principles on which education should be based. He is buried in the Cathedral grounds.

Bogachevsky, who as Father Elvissi is now living in an Essene monastery, tutored Gurdjieff and aroused his interest in abstract questions. Unable to find answers to occult-related questions, Gurdjieff learned from Bogachevsky the difference between objective and subjective morality, and that the untrammelled conscience knows more than all the books and teachers put together.

Pogossian, the first friend of Gurdjieff's youth, shared with him an interest in supernatural phenomena. Failing to find answers in religion or science, they searched for the Sarmoung Monastery, an ancient esoteric school where they hoped to enrol. During their adventures, they found a map of pre-sand Egypt, and set off by ship. Gurdjieff went to Cairo, while Pogossian remained on board, eventually owning ships and becoming extremely rich. Pogossian was always making efforts to accustom his whole nature to love work, convinced that sooner or later work is paid for, that no conscious labour is ever wasted (see **conscious labour and intentional/voluntary suffering**).

Abram Yelov, a book pedlar, became a close friend. They shared an interest in philosophy and helped each other's business ventures. Yelov held that the conscience is the most valuable thing in man, and is formed in childhood only as the result of religious faith. Yelov, like Pogossian, had unusual notions about work. Yelov said that mental work, such as learning languages, prevented his mind from hindering his other functions with dreams and fantasies. Although he lost his fortune in the Russian Revolution, he now lives comfortably in North America.

Gurdjieff met Prince Lubovedsky in Egypt. The Prince, who became interested in occult questions after the death of his wife, was much older than Gurdjieff and extremely wealthy. He became Gurdjieff's closest friend for nearly forty years.

The Prince entrusted Vitvitskaia, a young woman he was saving from the 'white slave trade', to Gurdjieff, who escorted her to the Prince's sister in Russia. There she studied music and conducted experiments in order to understand how music affected listeners.

Vitvitskaia eventually joined in expeditions with Gurdjieff and others. On one occasion they heard music that affected them all in the same way. According to her experiments, this should not have happened; her anxiety about this caused her to bite her finger so hard that it was nearly severed. Vitvitskaia died from a cold she caught on a trip on the Volga.

Gurdjieff lost touch with the Prince and believed he was dead. Then, unexpectedly, he met him again in 'the heart of Asia' on a journey he took with Soloviev, an erstwhile petty criminal (a forger) and drunkard. Gurdjieff cured him of his drinking through hypnotism. Soloviev became a loyal friend and went with Gurdjieff to the Sarmoung Monastery, where they found Prince Lubovedsky.

The Prince came to the monastery after consciously dying to his previous life. He showed Gurdjieff priestess–dancers, and apparatus used to teach them, from which Gurdjieff learned about the Laws of Movement. Gurdjieff parts once more from the Prince, who leaves the Sarmoung for another monastery where he will subsequently die.

Soloviev journeyed with the Seekers of Truth across the Gobi desert. Gurdjieff recounts the extraordinary mode of travel that they adopted. However, on nearing their goal Soloviev died of a camel bite, and the Seekers abandoned their search for a legendary city.

Dr Ekim Bey came from a different culture than Gurdjieff; nonetheless, they were like brothers. Bey is the same age as Gurdjieff. His later life was arranged exactly like Gurdjieff's. He lives quietly in Egypt as the Great Turkish Pasha, but only his physical body is healthy. Bey met Gurdjieff, Pogossian, Yelov and Karpenko, and became part of the Seekers. During an expedition they met a Dervish who taught them about the transformation of substances from food and breath. Bey is a hypnotist; he and Gurdjieff laugh at the stupidity of people who regard Bey as a magician. Gurdjieff recounts how they hypnotised two men so that pins could be stuck into them, their mouths sewn up and their bodies made to bridge a wide space between two chairs with enormous weights on their chests.

Gurdjieff became close to Pietro Karpenko through an adolescent 'duel' in which they lay down on an artillery range and waited to see if either of them would be killed. Karpenko went with the Seekers on an expedition during which they met a saintly fakir, a man who was working for the salvation of his soul. He cured three of the Seekers of illnesses and in response to a question from Karpenko spoke about the astral body of man. Two days after this, Karpenko was shot: he died two years later in Russia.

Gurdjieff met his essence-friend, the much older Professor Skridlov, in Cairo. He disappeared during the Russian Revolution. During an expedition, they met Father Giovanni, a member of the World Brotherhood whose adepts included men from all religious traditions. Giovanni teaches them about faith, the difference between knowledge and understanding, and how a soul may be acquired. In his Third Series Gurdjieff was to write about the teachings of the Dervish concerning the body, the teachings of the fakir concerning the spirit and the teachings of Father Giovanni concerning the soul. In their last meeting, Skridlov tells Gurdjieff that since meeting Giovanni his inner and outer worlds have changed. His egoism has died and he is convinced that only real values, rather than illusory 'goods', bring men happiness.

The chapter on 'The Material Question', which finds Gurdjieff in New York, provides a narrative link between *Meetings* and *Life*. Gurdjieff recounts the answer he gave to a question about funding. This was during the whole night of 8 April 1924, after a celebration of the opening of the New York Institute. This whole night of stories reminds us of the tales in *The Thousand and One Nights*, referred to earlier in *Meetings* as a fantasy that corresponds to the truth. Gurdjieff talks about his attitude to money, and the skills in earning it that he has possessed from childhood. He recounts the heroic money-making adventure of his Universal Travelling Workshop, undertaken on account of a wager with Vitvitskaia. Later, through a mixture of dealings, he amassed the sum of a million roubles and collections of carpets, cloisonné and porcelain. However, this fortune was lost due to the Russian Revolution. He details his resourcefulness in negotiating his journey with pupils and family members through the Caucasus, his arrival in France, the purchase of the Prieuré, the difficulties he overcame, and the funding of his visit to America with his pupils. As a result of this talk, two people offer him money.

Gurdjieff is now revising this manuscript, seven years to the day after the event (so the date is now 8 April 1931). He is in Child's restaurant in New York. He remembers how his car crash upset his financial plans. At this moment Gurdjieff's business partner arrives to tell him that they have lost their money due to the Depression. Gurdjieff is exhausted from six years' struggle with debt while he was writing. Once again Gurdjieff must acquire the money to pay his debts. He now writes that the date is 10 January (1932), which contradicts the above date of 8 April 1931. In three days' time, on his birthday, he will vow to pay off his debts by March (1932) and to have money with which to return to France to write. If he fails, he will publish only his already completed writings and open a new Institute 'for instruction in hitherto undiscovered means of self-satisfaction'. The end of *Meetings* connects the reader with the narrative content of *Life*.

See also: **autobiographical writings; zodiac**

MIND

The physical body is controlled by several independent 'minds' operating in separate spheres, both consciously and unconsciously, and having separate functions. These are controlled by **centres** (*Search*: 54). Even without special powers, a grown-up man, who differs from a child only in that he has more material and logic, can wish effectively with his thinking mind, can hold on to and remember his wish, as long as he does not identify with his essence, and the wish is made his primary desire (*Views*, 1923: 148–54; see **essence; identification**).

See also: **intellectual/thinking centre, intelligence**

MIRACLE/MIRACULOUS

A miracle is the manifestation in this world of the laws of another world that are unknown or rarely experienced by man in this world (*Search*: 84). Miracles do not break laws, nor are they outside laws, they take place according to laws of another cosmos that are unknown and incomprehensible to us (*Search*: 207–8; see also **absolute; cosmoses**). Ouspensky reports pupils feeling that in Gurdjieff's groups they had come in contact with a 'miracle', something that had never existed before (*Search*: 121).

MONEY

Gurdjieff asked for a thousand roubles from each pupil in Moscow, saying that pupils should provide the money for expenses and that his teaching was not a charity. In practice he did not turn away people who could not pay and was known to support many of them financially. During the stay in Essentuki in 1919, he told Ouspensky that only two of the Moscow pupils had paid the thousand roubles asked for, and that their journey had already cost him more than that (*Search*: 12–13, 371).

People who are willing to waste money on fantasies must be able to understand that Gurdjieff's labour in teaching them must also be paid for; if they could not pass this test, they would fail all others. On the question of 'payment' in general, Gurdjieff said that man never wants to pay for anything apart from useless trifles, for which he will pay anything. Important things, however, he will not pay for, but expects them to come to him (*Search*: 165–6, 178).

Gurdjieff remained in constant need of money, in spite of an ability to make money through various means, which are mythologised in 'The Material Question' in *Meetings*. He received fees for curing drink and drug addicts, as well as from consultations about personal matters, and he also 'sheared' from pupils. His expenses were high, because of the number of people, both family and pupils, that he supported (see Bennett 1976 [1973]: 136; Taylor 1998: 78–80). He distinguished between money that he earned for his family and money that he asked for from pupils.

Gurdjieff told Peters (1976 [1964, 1965]: 259–60) that there cannot be understanding between rich and poor, because both of these understand life in terms of money and so cannot give all their energy to his Work. If the rich gave up money and the poor the desire for money, they could learn something. At the Institute Gurdjieff often struggled with money: he did not make or earn money; he did not need money for himself, and when he had too much he spent it. He asked for money and gave the givers the opportunity to study. However, if they felt he 'owed' them something, they would never learn from him. Gurdjieff also uses the numbers in sums of money symbolically (see **theosophical addition**).

MOON

The Moon is referred to in relation to the outer world, the macrocosm, in terms of the **Ray of Creation**, and also in relation to man's inner world, the microcosm, where the Moon represents a passive force equated with involution and mechanicality. Man gains liberation from his 'inner moon' through the growth of mental powers and the development of **consciousness** and **will**.

In relation to the macrocosm, the Moon is a living being evolving to become a planet. The energy for its growth comes from the Sun and the planets of our solar system. This energy is collected in a huge

accumulator that is formed by organic life on the Earth. Everything living on Earth is food for the Moon. No energy is lost in the universe; on Earth the death of each mineral, plant, animal or man sets free some energy. These 'souls' that go to the Moon may possess some consciousness and memory, but under conditions of mineral life can only be freed after immeasurably long cycles of general planetary evolution. In Christian terms, the Moon is 'outer darkness'. Man as he is cannot free himself from the Moon, which controls all his actions of every kind, including the evil, criminal, self-sacrificing and heroic.

The Moon and Earth are interdependent; the Moon is an electromagnet that 'sucks out the vitality of organic life'. If its action stopped, organic life would crumble to nothing (*Search*: 83–6). The Moon is like the weight in a clock, and organic life is like the mechanism brought into motion by that weight. If the weight were removed, the mechanism would stop (*Search*: 95; see also **law of reciprocal maintenance/reciprocal feeding**).

There are different definitions of the Moon: one as the growing tip of the Ray of Creation, and the other as its dead end. In the first definition, the Ray of Creation from Absolute to Moon is like a growing branch of a tree. If the Moon does not grow, the whole Ray of Creation will stop or find a new path for growth (*Search*: 304–6). However, Gurdjieff also said that, in the line from Absolute to Moon, 'the moon is the last point of creation on this line' (*Views*, 1924: 196).

Food that satisfies the Moon at one period may not be enough later on, so organic life must evolve to sustain the Moon (*Views*, 1924: 196). 'The moon is man's big enemy'. We are like sheep that the Moon feeds and shears. When 'she' is hungry, she kills a lot of us. Passive man serves the moon and involution. Inside us we have a moon, and if we knew what our inner moon is and does, we would understand the cosmos (*Views*, 1924: 198). 'It is possible to study the sun, the moon. But man has everything within him. I have inside me the sun, the moon, God, I am – all life in its totality' (*Views*, 1924: 102).

In *Tales* the Moon is one of two fragments split off from Earth; the other fragment is called Anulios, which meant 'never allowing-one-to-sleep-in-peace' (conscience). Anulios can be read in reverse as Soi-luna (Thring 1998: 260).

See also: **astrology**

MORALITY

The objective feeling of morality is connected with nature '(or, as is said, with God)' and with orderly immutable moral laws, established over centuries, that accord physically and chemically with human nature and circumstances. Subjective feeling of morality is based on a person's own experience, qualities and observations, and is what he lives by. People have theoretical ideas, but cannot apply them. With us, morality is automatic (*Views*: 172–3).

See also: **justice**

MORTALITY

Everything is mortal, even God, though God is mortal in a different way to man. There is the possibility for man to have existence after death (*Search*: 91; see **bodies**).

MOVEMENTS

Each physical posture corresponds with an inner state. Pupils have a limited number of habitual postures, but when they do Gurdjieff's movements they are able to experience and observe themselves in new postures and new states (*Views*, 1921: 167–70). Movements have two aims: first, to bring together the body, mind and feelings, and to manifest them together; and, second, to study the ancient knowledge contained in them (*Views*, 1923: 183; see also **music**).

The characteristics of movements in ordinary, everyday life that can be useful are those in relation to a person's present and future constitutional peculiarities; the participation of breathing in movement; of thinking in movement and in relation to old unchanging characteristics of movement. For Work, the pupil needs to acquire an additional sensation and feeling. For the movements to be useful, all of the above conditions must be present (*Views*, 1923: 174–5).

See also: **dance/dancing; levers/postures**

MOVING/INSTINCTIVE CENTRE

Inner functions, breathing, heartbeat and blood circulation are instinctive, and outer reflexes are in-born, while moving functions have to be learned through imitation but without reason. All **centres** can function automatically, but when they are observed, they are no longer automatic. The moving centre works much faster than the intellectual centre (*Search*: 114, 194; see also **'hydrogens'**).

Work on the moving centre can only be organised in a school. Usually the wrong work of the moving centre deprives the other centres of support. The moving centre follows the body, which is lazy and full of stupid habits that inhibit work (*Search*: 347–8).

MUSIC

Snake charmers use a primitive approach to objective music; the ears cannot hear the melodies of the inner octaves, but they can be felt by the **emotional centre**. Snakes obey this music and if it were more complex men would also obey it. Objective music, which depends on inner octaves, can produce psychological and physical effects, freeze water, kill a man or knock down walls, as in the Biblical legend of Jericho. Objective music can also be creative, this is suggested in the legend of Orpheus, in which knowledge is transmitted by music (*Search*: 297; see also **occult**). The use of 'objective' music in relation to plants is narrated both in *Tales* (p.892), where it withers them, and in *Meetings* (p.133), where it speeds up their growth. Webb (1980: 509–13) notes that many of Gurdjieff's references to the miraculous effects of music are discussed by Athanasius Kircher (1601–80). Gurdjieff pays tribute to Pythagorean thinking in *Tales* (pp.871–917), where the Bokharian Dervish Hadji-Asvats-Troov has adapted Pythagoras's monochord for his own investigations into sound vibrations.

Music can be used during **exercises** (external tasks) as a means of separating our mechanical automatism from our unconscious automatism, and to differentiate between them (*Views*, 1923: 220; see **attention**). In 1949 Gurdjieff told Taylor that he taught pupils to listen to and hear themselves, and that one day, after doing movements and listening to music for a long time, the music is heard without listening. Later 'you hear it from inside when no music is playing outside.' Later still, doing the same movement and listening to the same music,

> you no longer hear or feel with body but with consciousness. Then you on a higher level [. . .] outside is noise of world. Inside is music of self.

(Taylor 1998: 182–3)

Gurdjieff's musical collaborator was Thomas de Hartmann (see **appendix 1**); together they composed more than 300 pieces of music. The movements and ballet music were mostly created in the early years of their working relationship, while most programme music was created in the last two years of their collaboration, which ended in 1927 (Moore 1991: 349–51). Between 1923 and 1927 they composed more than 100 short pieces of music on Eastern religious themes, which were to be played before readings of certain chapters of *Tales* so that pupils might be emotionally tuned to the ideas in the text (Bennett 1976 [1961]: 167; for music as part of the Turkic oral tradition, see **oral tradition, Turkic**).

Pupil memoirs give accounts of Gurdjieff in later years, in Paris and also the United States, playing music on a hand-held harmonium (*Journey*: 118–19).

The music which Gurdjieff/de Hartmann were writing in the 1920s showed an Eastern influence that was in accord with contemporary musical interests. Recordings of de Hartmann/Gurdjieff are commercially available: for a list of recordings, see Driscoll 1985 or de Hartmann and de Hartmann 1992 [1964].

MYTH

Ouspensky writes that Gurdjieff defines 'myth' as a means of transmitting objective **knowledge** to the higher **emotional centre** in a form that avoids distortion and corruption. The fundamental idea of objective knowledge is unity (see also **symbols/symbolism**), and this has been transmitted through myth 'from **school** to school, often from epoch to epoch'. The idea of **unity** cannot be understood by the intellect of the subjective consciousness, nor expressed in ordinary language, because this has been 'constructed through the expression of **impressions** of plurality'. The inability of people to understand, explain or summarise myth protects the ideas of objective knowledge carried in myth from false interpretation (*Search*: 278–80).

Gurdjieff's account of his childhood confirms these ideas by telling how the experience of hearing his father (see **ashok**) recount ancient legends, including that of Gilgamesh, enabled him to 'comprehend the incomprehensible' in later life (*Meetings*: 34). Gurdjieff also recounts that in around 1913 he read a magazine article about 4,000-year-old tablets that had been discovered in the ruins of Babylon. On one of these was the twenty-first song of Gilgamesh in a form that was almost the same as the one he had heard from his father. Gurdjieff writes that this experience affirms the view that legends are handed down by Ashoks almost unchanged for thousands of years; however, the reader should note that change is an integral part of the oral tradition (Tigay 1982 shows how the myth of Gilgamesh changed over a period of about 1,500 years; see also **oral tradition, turkic**). Gurdjieff writes that he regrets 'having begun too late to give the legends of antiquity the immense significance that I now understand they really have' (*Meetings*: 36; see also **oral tradition/oral transmission**). The myth of Gilgamesh, who falls asleep and thus fails to achieve the immortality he seeks, is Gurdjieff's basic model for the seeker of hidden lore (Taylor 1998: n.187).

Russian, European and American interest in myth during the 1920s and 1930s (the period during which Gurdjieff was writing) had resulted from several sources: the archeological and anthropological exploration of ancient cultures during the nineteenth and early twentieth centuries, especially those in Mesopotamia and Egypt; the publication of Frazer's *Golden Bough* (1994 [1890–1915]); the synthetic mythology employed in Theosophical literature (e.g. Blavatsky's *The Secret Doctrine*, 1888); and the focus on myth as a means of exploring the psyche (Freud's *The Interpretation of Dreams*, 1900; Jung's *Psychology of the Unconscious*, 1916). These interests were expressed in literary form by modernist writers in such works as Bely's *Petersburg* (1916); T.S. Eliot's *The Waste Land* (1922), Joyce's *Ulysses* (1922) and *Finnegans Wake* (1939), and Yeats' *A Vision* (1925). These writers drew on Greek and Christian myth, and on Theosophically influenced versions of these myths. Gurdjieff's own writings echo these interests (see **Beelzebub's Tales To His Grandson**).

Tales is itself a myth that incorporates and subverts many other myths, among them the Biblical myths of Creation, Fall, Redemption and Revelation; the myth of Atlantis; the myth of the supremacy of Classical Greece, with its scientific and philosophical achievements; the traditional teachings of Buddha, Moses, Jesus and Muhammad, and the esoteric and occult myths connected with these teachings; and modern myths of progress that include the Enlightenment, Industrialisation, Marxism and Darwinian evolution. Together with his other writings, Gurdjieff's **Meetings with Remarkable Men** (1963) creates a myth of his life-story in a form similar to the myth that Blavatsky created of her own life-story (Johnson 1990). It also refers indirectly to other myths (see **autobiographical writings**; **writings**).

Orage (*Journey*), Tracol (1994) and Nicoll (1954, 1984) all interpret Biblical myth in **Work** terms as esoteric teachings. Although these might suggest a definitive, 'right' interpretation, this would go against Gurdjieff's insistence on multivalence.

Further reading

Teachings; *Journey*; Webb 1980; Johnson 1990; Moore 1991. For Biblical myth and literature, see Frye 1983; for Greek myth, see Kirk 1974; for Gilgamesh, see Jastrow and Clay 1920.

NARCOTICS

Narcotic substances are sometimes used by yogis and in 'schools', but the purposes of their use may differ. The right use of narcotics is for self-study: for example, to enable a pupil to see 'what can be obtained later as the result of prolonged work.' Each function of a person can be strengthened, weakened or put to sleep by the use of substances that are not merely narcotic, although many are prepared from drugs such as opium or hashish (*Search*: 8–9). Narcotics can be used to separate personality and essence: the personality can be put to sleep leaving only the essence functioning. Narcotics may also connect a man for a short period with his higher emotional centre (*Search*: 162–3, 195; see also **centres**).

Gurdjieff refers to his role as healer in *Meetings* and *Tales*, where he makes many references to drugs, especially opium, cocaine and alcohol, in the contexts of chemical analysis, and as the cause and cure of illness. Drinking alcohol, sometimes in large quantities, was part of Gurdjieff's ritual **toast of the idiots**. In a role separate from that he adopted as a teacher, Gurdjieff also earned money from time to time as a healer, treating people for drink and drug dependency (Bennett 1976: 136; Peters 1976 [1964, 1965]: 213–14).

According to Bennett, Gurdjieff used intensive methods with a specific women's group (see **rope**; **appendix 2**). Through the use of drugs, Gurdjieff opened up hidden channels of the psyche and developed their psychic experiences. These women developed their powers far more swiftly than former pupils, and have recorded their experiences in unpublished memoirs that Bennett read but was not allowed to quote from (Bennett 1976: 232).

In the 1940s Gurdjieff told a pupil to work rather than take opium to ease suffering. However, he did give each pupil in a group a bottle of medicine to take while working, during a holiday period. He said that the chemical could help to accumulate results and give the fire for revitalising the pupil's functions (*Voices*: 22, 99–100). He also remarked on the usefulness of alcohol: when a pupil drinks it helps Gurdjieff, because alcohol opens and shows aspects of the interior, 'important for knowing someone' (*Voices*: 71).

NATURE/GREAT NATURE/THE COMMON MOTHER

Nature, referred to in *Tales* as 'Great Nature' and 'the Common Mother', is female. She has dual functions in relation to involution and evolution: feeding and providing for men, and slaughtering them. Nature is sometimes constrained to kill large numbers of men in order to adapt to their forgetfulness of the higher Cosmic Purpose for which they are on Earth (see **astrology**). The development of hidden possibilities in man is against Nature and against God, the **evolution** of large masses of humanity is opposed to Nature's purposes. Nature provides the flow of **impressions** without which we would die (*Search*: 47, 181).

'Mother Nature' can be seen as representing the 'female' in Gurdjieff's teaching, and that which is forgotten or unrecognised in *Tales*. As a symbol of **death** she is the forgotten aspect of life that Gurdjieff urges his pupils to remember (see also **gender**).

There are ambivalent references to Nature in *Voices*. Sometimes she helps and sometimes hinders a person's work. We owe a debt to our Mother Nature for the food we eat. There is an obligation to pay for these cosmic substances by conscious work, not to eat like an animal but to render our work on ourselves as payment to Nature for what she has given. On the one hand, if the pupil works, Nature will be a sister of charity and will bring him what he needs, for example, money if he needs it. In another case she will cut off money if this is necessary for a pupil's work, 'Nature calls on conscious spirits' who will arrange for the conditions the pupil needs. When a pupil is unhappy, Gurdjieff says that Nature wishes the pupil well, because she brings the pupil to work by making other things distasteful. Nature must be thanked when a crisis begins that enables the pupil to see his own nothingness. On the other hand, if the pupil is on a good path, Nature will crystallise in him the exact factor to prevent him continuing. Nature puts many **dogs** in us to make us weak, perhaps having an interest in ensuring there are few men on the right path (*Voices*: 25–6, 171, 188, 153–4).

Further reading

For the female as 'forgotten' in our culture, see Tarnas 1991: 441–5; see also Neumann 1955.

NEGATIVE EMOTIONS

There is no normal centre for negative emotions. Self-study and self-observation should be accompanied by the struggle not to express unpleasant emotions such as bad moods, worry, fear and anger. These emotions, if they become intense, can consume all the substances that the organism has prepared for the next day, a man can be left inwardly empty, perhaps for ever (*Search*: 56, 112, 198).

If someone is insulted, they must try 'to prevent the reaction to the insult from spreading all over the body', 'try not to be taken by this feeling'. The thing that makes another person antipathetic is not in them but in me. We are touched deeply by things that ought not to touch us. We should be free of other people's opinions; we may have to pretend to be angry, but we should be free inwardly. Sometimes we should retaliate, sometimes not; in order to decide, we have to be free inside. If someone calls me a fool and I know I am not one, it does not offend me. But if I am called a fool when I have been one, then I am not hurt either, because I have been helped and can perhaps act differently next time (*Views*, 1923: 161–2, 249–50, 268–9; see also **emotional centre**).

Nott writes (*Journey*: 96) that after Gurdjieff's car accident he no longer used the term 'negative emotions': he used 'dabbel'/'devil' for the denying part, the negative emotions.

In one of the group meetings held by Gurdjieff during World War II, de Salzmann says that negative emotions must be separated, so they are not in the **essence** but can be used when necessary (*Voices*: 159).

NEUTRALISING FORCE *see* Law of Three

NEW WORK

Without Gurdjieff's charismatic presence, the dynamic of his teaching could not continue unchanged. During his lifetime, Gurdjieff provided conditions so that pupils could learn to work on themselves. Later they were expected to leave and work on their own. If they did not, he made life so unpleasant for them that eventually they did leave.

Thus the pupil's intense experience of Gurdjieff was limited. However, pupils now remain in the **Work** for long periods of time and are not encouraged to leave. Thus the process of change from 'ordinary life' to life with Gurdjieff, followed by a return to 'ordinary life', is no longer continued. Changes have been made that suggest the Work is now in the process of redefining itself as a Tradition.

The teaching introduced by de Salzmann in Paris in the late 1960s or early 1970s, in the context of the counter culture, emphasised the notion of reception, of 'being worked on', 'being remembered'. Although Gurdjieff may have introduced new teachings at the end of his life about which no records are available, de Salzmann's teaching differs from Gurdjieff's demands for unremitting struggle and effort that are echoed in his pupils' writings of their experience with him. Gurdjieff stressed that active man serves evolution but passive man serves involution (see **duty/striving**; **evolution**). For recognition of the change in direction of the Work made in the 1980s in London, see Moore 1994.

Bennett (1976: 119–21) writes that Ouspensky's account of Gurdjieff's teaching omits any mention of an enabling force, termed 'grace' in Christian doctrine and 'baraka' by Sufis. However, this has not been mentioned previously by Bennett and may well be in agreement with de Salzmann's new teaching. Bennett writes that Gurdjieff spoke to him about this in the Institute, but the idea did not form part of his oral teaching. In Bennett's view the enabling energy is the 'key' to making the teaching work. He concludes that Gurdjieff omitted it because the different periods of his teaching were **experiments** in which he was learning about different **types** of people in order to free them from their disease of believing 'any old tale'. Bennett's views about Gurdjieff's experimentation make sense of the differences between different periods of Gurdjieff's teaching, often brought to an abrupt end with the dismissal of pupils. Although not extant in Gurdjieff's theory, pupils do record their experience of this energy, received as **love** or **grace** (see Wellbeloved 1998: 321–32). Tracol (1994) and George (1995) reflect an awareness of receptive, or New Work, ideas.

In 1978 Tracol wrote that the Work reconnects with the methods of search of the Great Tradition (Tracol 1994: 89) and with what happens to disciples after the death of a master. He suggests that they must not 'inaugurate a cult, become sectarian or fanatical, freeze his thought and codify his slightest utterance'. He echoed Gurdjieff's warning of the dangers of any kind of crystallisation in 1967 (Tracol 1994: 109–10).

George (1995: 93), a long-term pupil of de Salzmann, refers to an article in the journal *Parabola* (no reference given) in which de Salzmann writes about objective thought. This is a look from 'Above'; without this look she does not know she exists, she is blind and driven by impulse. The look makes her responsible and free. In moments of self-awareness she feels known and blessed by the look, which embraces her. Her essence is the place where she and the one who looks may be reunited, the source of something unique and unchanging.

George writes of receiving energy through the crown of the head while participating in a Work retreat (George 1995: 97–8). He recounts the teaching he received from Christian, Islamic, Hindu, Sufi and Tibetan Buddhist teachers. He finds a unity between the esoteric teachings of these traditions and emphasises de Salzmann's interest and fellowship with spiritual teachers from other Traditions. He feels that the Work may be a new Tradition in the making. However, a new Tradition 'is not an eclectic salad of older teachings. To be valid, it must be nothing less than a new revelation' (George 1995: 94–5). He records de Salzmann's reluctant view that organisational structures and hierarchies are necessary to provide steps through which people can find their way towards the 'ultimate leap of freedom' (George 1995: 88). This seems to differ from the view that a Fourth Way School exists only for a short time (see **ways/fourth way**) and for its own purpose, rather than that of the pupil. For a detailed account of de Salzmann's teaching methods and aims from 1980–90, see Ravindra 1999.

New Work looks back to establish lineage, of a kind, with other esoteric teachings and established Traditions. In terms of science, there is a concern to show that Gurdjieff was ahead of his time and that his occult science is confirmed by contemporary scientific discoveries and theories. For discussions of these themes, see Moore (1991: 343–8).

Further research is needed to trace the origins and history of the changes brought about by new practices, and the terminology that accompanies them (see also Wellbeloved 2001b).

Further reading

For the counter culture, see Roszak 1969. For what happens after a 'prophet' or teacher dies, see Miller 1991. For accounts of pupils' experiences of this new period of the Work, inside and outside the American Foundations, see Patterson 1992, Kherdian 1998 and Ginsburg 2001. For a contemporary interpretation of the Work, focusing on psychology rather than cosmology, see Tart 1986. For a brief academic assessment of de Salzmann, see Rawlinson 1997: 313; see also Moore 1994: 11–15 and **Appendix 1**.

NEW WORK TERMINOLOGY

The exercise of the attention, which used to be referred to in English as 'morning preparation', has been changed in process and aim, and is now referred to as 'meditation' or 'sitting' (terms probably taken from the Zen practice of *zazen*). Sitting is also used to refer to groups of pupils meditating together; in London this began in the 1960s and was known as 'special work'. Ravindra (1999) refers to meditation as 'quiet work'. This receptive mode may have been part of Gurdjieff's late teaching in the 1940s, though there is no sign of it in the group meetings held during World War II (see *Voices*). Receptivity is not referred to in beneficial terms in Gurdjieff's writings, nor his pupils' memoirs, all of which emphasise the necessity for struggle and effort.

See also: **New Work**

'NITROGEN'

One of the four states of **matter** (see **elements**; **hydrogens, table of**).

NONENTITY/NOTHINGNESS/NULLITY

Everyone is a zero, a nothing. Gurdjieff urged pupils to see their nothingness in order to work to transform the nothingness into something definite. As they are, they can have no objective opinion, can do nothing (*Voices*: 51, 70, 107, 176, 188, 197, 274).

See also: **egoism/egoist**

NUMBER/NUMEROLOGY

The importance of number in Mesopotamian astronomy influenced, and was combined with, Pythagorean and Platonic number symbolism. The idea that 'mathematics could be used to synthesize knowledge' and that the proportions that underpinned Greek music were supposed to be those that underpinned the structure of the cosmos were concepts that formed the core of a tradition of thought that 'extends from Plato to the late Renaissance period' (Butler 1970 [1964]: 18–19). Western European culture reflects the enduring influence of number symbolism in philosophy, in theology and Biblical exegesis, in the occult sciences of alchemy, astrology, Kabbala and Hermeticism, and in the arts. 'In literature, music, and the visual arts numerology was the dominant compositional mode, up to and including the eighteenth century' (Brooks 1973: 2).

Gurdjieff said only numbers can serve as an exact language. Words are inexact because people use words according to their own definitions: the meanings change according to a person's thoughts, humours and associative images. No-one can be sure what is meant by a word. Contemporary philosophy understands this, but has failed to establish an exact meaning for words (see **language**). We must be able to designate 'all the qualities of things by numbers in relation to some immutable number' (*Views*, 1924: 60–74). However, this immutable number is not discussed further.

We can see that Gurdjieff's valuation of number as able to convey exact meaning contradicts his definition of numbers as multivalent symbols that 'can never be taken in a final and definite meaning'. He taught that number symbolism is connected with geometric figures, with the Kabbala's symbology of letters and words; **magic, alchemy, astrology** and the combination of these in the Tarot, all offer symbolic systems, none of which must be understood as having a single fixed meaning.

> In expressing the laws of the unity of endless diversity a symbol itself possesses an endless number of aspects from which it can be examined and it demands from a man approaching it the ability to see it simultaneously from different points of view.
>
> (*Search*: 283)

Numbers can be added, multiplied, divided and subtracted in a variety of ways, each yielding new digits, new aspects of the diversity of the whole. If we accept that the all must remain unknowable, as the all is not temporally finite and we are (in Gurdjieff's terms) mortal, even if we acquire all four bodies, then numerology as a hermeneutical practice accords well with Gurdjieff's ideas about the value of searching, of process, of making an effort to understand. Numerology evades closure on any of the subjects it addresses. It avoids the literal **understanding** that Gurdjieff says leads to delusions (*Search*: 283–4).

Understanding through numerology (i.e. through a diversity of meanings) may well be uncomfortable for those who look for the security of an absolute number value. But these values, i.e. 'the uncompromising materialism of early Victorian science' (Webb 1980: 534), had already been undermined by twentieth-century mathematics and physics (relativity and uncertainty) by the time Gurdjieff began writing *Tales* in 1924.

Gurdjieff's cosmological ideas, expressed in the symbols of number, while referring back to the Traditions, might also be understood by his pupils in relation to the new sciences, especially quantum physics. As shown in Rudhyar (1963 [1936]), the two had in common an understanding of the limitation of Greek rational thinking and of ideas of absolute time and absolute space. For the progression from three to four, see **elements**; also **language**.

See also: **enneagram; Law of Three; Theosophical addition**

Further reading

Hopper 1938. For number in theology, see Quirolo 2001; for number in scripture, theology and literature, see Fowler 1964, Butler 1970 [1964] and Brooks 1973.

OBEDIENCE

> It is necessary to obey another or to follow the direction of general work, the control of which can belong only to one person. Such submission is the most difficult thing that there can be for a man who thinks that he is capable of deciding anything or of doing anything.
>
> (*Search*: 240)

Compare with **faith**.

See also: **sacrifice**

OBSERVATION *see* **self-observation**

OBYVATEL

In addition to the 'Ways' of the fakir, yogi and monk or the 'Fourth Way', which are grouped under the term the 'Subjective Way', there is also the 'Objective Way' – the 'Way' of people in life (see **ways/ fourth way**). The obyvatel is defined as a good person living in accord with his own **conscience**, who is evolving, usually slowly, yet sometimes faster than a monk or yogi, without the need for a particular teaching. The obyvatel knows that 'things do themselves', therefore he is not deceived by people who live in fantasy, whether these fantasies are to do with politics or with 'Ways'. The Russian word *obyvatel* means 'inhabitant', but is used wrongly in a contemptuous way by people who, because they are interested in 'Ways', look down on the obyvatel. Gurdjieff stresses that not all obyvatels are people of the Objective Way, some are 'thieves, rascals and fools'; however, 'the ability to orientate oneself in life is a very useful quality from the point of view of work'. No-one can embark on a 'Way' who has not attained the level of obyvatel – i.e. someone who is able to support at least twenty people from his own labour (*Search*: 362–5).

See *also*: **lunatic/tramp**

OCCULT/OCCULT REVIVAL

Moscow and St Petersburg were centres for the late nineteenth- and early twentieth-century occult revival. From 1881 to 1918 thirty occult journals and more than 800 occult titles were published in Russia, reflecting interests in spiritualism, Theosophy, Rosicrucianism, alchemy, psycho-graphology, phrenology, hypnotism, Egyptian religions, astrology, chiromancy, animal magnetism, fakirism, telepathy, the Tarot, black and white magic, and Freemasonry (Carlson 1993: 22).

Gurdjieff took notice of contemporary interests and presented his teaching accordingly. The cosmological form of his teaching was fully outlined between 1914 and 1918 in a form that takes account of the occult revival in Russia.

Gurdjieff's early pupils told Ouspensky that their group carried out occult experiments and investigations (*Search*: 6), and in 'Glimpses of Truth' Gurdjieff explains that he is expressing his teaching in an occult form because the pupil has already studied the occult, but that 'truth speaks for itself in whatever form it is manifested' (*Views*, 1914: 14). However, Gurdjieff also warned that professional occultism – professional charlatans, spiritualists, healers and clairvoyants – were incompatible with **Work**; his group members should not tell them anything, because it might be used to make fools of others. Occult, mystical societies and spiritualism can bring no results (*Search*: 243–4, 48; see also **alchemy**; **astrology**; **kundalini**; **schools**).

Although occult studies can be helpful in training a man's mind, Gurdjieff stresses the dangers of following occult or esoteric teachings. These may reduce a man's capacity for reason and induce psychopathy and a willingness to believe what is often repeated. A pupil may be induced to use his knowledge: 'The emphasis laid on miraculous results and the concealment of their dark sides will lead men to try them.' However, a man will not know enough about his machine to avoid irreparable damage: he may end up in a lunatic asylum. People who are failures in life will try to use occult powers in order to subjugate others; bored people will use occult methods as an escape from daily life. As these pupils fail in their endeavours, it is easy for them to become charlatans (*Views*, *c.*1918: 51–5; see also **hypnosis/hypnotism**).

In relation to **prayer** Gurdjieff explained that certain substances emanate from the Earth and from the sun and planets of our solar system (see **emanations**). These make contact at **points** in the solar system that can reflect themselves in materialised images that are the inverted images of the All Highest or Absolute. Gurdjieff also spoke of forces and phenomena: cosmic phenomena may go against a pupil's work; foreign forces around a pupil may produce events when a man really wishes to struggle (*Voices*: 24, 29, 165).

See also: **love; telepathy; vampirism**

Further reading

For the political, social and economic instability underlying the occult revival in Russia and France, see Webb 1971a, 1971b, 1976. For the occult in Russia, see Rosenthal 1997 and Young 1979; for the French occult revival, see McIntosh 1975.

OCTAVES, LAW OF *see* Law of Octaves; Law of Seven

ORAL TRADITION/ORAL TRANSMISSION

Gurdjieff refers to the oral tradition in two ways: as a transmission of teaching and as story-telling. The pupil can only receive direct and conscious **influences**, which are outside the **Law of Accident**, through the oral transmission of a teaching directly from one person to another (*Search*: 201; see also **occult/occult revival**; **secrecy/ silence**). Gurdjieff writes that he collected oral information about hypnotism (*Herald*: 20).

He also refers to the oral story-telling tradition of the Middle and Far East. Here the epic or myth is retold to a group of listeners, sometimes out of sequence and often with **music**. The composition of Gurdjieff's texts embodies many aspects of the Turkic oral tradition experienced in his childhood (see **oral tradition, Turkic**). They were read aloud to groups, often out of sequence, and preceded by music written by Gurdjieff and de Hartmann. Gurdjieff later questioned the listeners and amended his text so as to make it more difficult.

Gurdjieff distinguishes between the degenerate literature of the West and the Eastern oral tradition in which story-telling still fulfils the real purpose of literature, both ancient and modern, which is the perfecting of humanity in general (*Meetings*: 10). He stresses the value of ancient legends, myths and folklore, and the necessity of understanding, for example, the *Thousand and One Nights* as a fantasy which nonetheless corresponds to the truth. Even though the episodes described are improbable, yet 'the interest of the reader or listener is awakened and enchanted by the author's fine understanding' of people's psyches (*Meetings*: 18).

Gurdjieff uses comparisons between Eastern and Western literature to distance himself from literary writers. However, his writing did reflect the literary concerns of his day, including a modernist interest in ancient legends and in the structures used in archaic epics (e.g. parataxis and ring structuring).

See also: **allegory/analogy; aphorisms/sayings; myth; writings**

Further reading

Frazer 1994 [1890–1915]; Foley 1991; Ong 1982.

ORAL TRADITION, TURKIC

Gurdjieff's birthplace, Kars, was famous for song contests during his lifetime, and still is. Gurdjieff visited song contests with his father, who was an **Ashok** (Ashik), a bardic poet. Many aspects of the Ashok tradition and the strategies they used to win contests have relevance to Gurdjieff's teaching and writing.

An Ashok was an astute observer of his audience and played directly to their interests. Gurdjieff applied this skill in the overall presentation of his teachings, which were expressed in terms of contemporary interests. Contests were judged by religious leaders, and so Ashoks 'stressed religious knowledge, spiritual and mystical beliefs, and values in [their] song duellings' (Ashok Reyhani, quoted in Erdener 1995: 119).

The contestants used music to provide a 'game-like' atmosphere in which they could cover sensitive subjects and deliver insults without causing offence (Erdener 1995: 90–2, 111–21). Gurdjieff may have absorbed the Ashoks' combatative strategies of insult, sexual innuendo and ridicule too: such strategies form part of his oral and written teachings.

Ashoks have inherited some shamanic roles from earlier epic story-tellers, including those of healer and magician (Erdener 1995: 68). Gurdjieff certainly took on these roles at times in his teaching and also in his writings.

The Turkish tradition of asking riddles to test the wisdom of an opponent exists not only in song contests but also as part of the culture (Erdener 1995: 115). Gurdjieff describes his father and tutor engaged in asking each other riddles (*Meetings*: 38; see also in *Tales*, especially the riddles of the Mullah Nassr Eddin).

Further reading

Erdener 1995; Reickl 1992.

ORGANIC LIFE

Organic life on Earth acts as a transmitting station (see **moon; ray of creation**).

OUTINGS

Gurdjieff liked to arrange outings and social occasions with his students and others. Ouspensky records Gurdjieff, in the summer of 1916, taking their group of about thirty out in the country for parties and picnics. Ouspensky writes that Gurdjieff used these occasions to observe his pupils (*Search*: 238).

Further reading

For outings from the Institute in France, see also Peters 1976 [1964, 1965]: 126–31 and Taylor 1998: 126.

'OXYGEN'

One of the four states of **matter** (see also **elements**; **hydrogens, table of**).

See also: **astrology; zodiac**

PASSIVE FORCE *see* **Law of Three**

PAYMENT

Tales contains several small stories about attitudes to payment in terms of money. Joyful payment: 'if you go on a spree then go the whole hog including the postage' (*Tales*: 35), is contrasted with the folly of consuming what has been paid for, even if this proves harmful, see the story of the Kurd who eats red peppers. Gurdjieff also referred to payment in terms of **Work**. There is the necessity for us to pay for our arising and individuality (see **duty/striving**; **money**; **suffering/ pleasure**). If a person helps their neighbour, this is a debt that Nature must repay; if we enjoy what we do when we work, we are paid with satisfaction; if we do not like what we do, we will be paid, even if this is years later. We need to repair the past, to prepare for the future and to right past wrongs; the way to do this is by conscious labour and voluntary suffering (*Teachings*: 63–4, 109; see **conscious labour and intentional/voluntary suffering**).

Bennett carried out an exercise given to him by Gurdjieff for the purpose of bringing their dead mothers into contact, so that Bennett's mother could be helped by Gurdjieff's mother (Bennett 1962: 254–5). Gurdjieff told Dorothy Caruso to work in order to help her dead father, to whom she owed her existence, and later to use the present 'to repair the past and prepare the future' (Anderson 1962: 182, 191). There are also examples of this need to repay parents in *Voices*. Gurdjieff told Taylor that he had to learn to tell stories, that these 'pay for many things' (Taylor 1998: 179, 182–3).

PERSONALITY

Personality needs to be considered as a term in relation to **essence**, which is whatever is a man's own and that cannot be taken from him. It is created by 'education' and by imitation, as well as by the person's attempts to resist those around him, to hide from them what is his own and 'real'. Everything we call 'civilisation' has been created by people's personalities. Usually the stronger personality grows, the less essence shows itself. Personality, also referred to as 'false personality', feeds on imagination and weakens when imagination weakens (*Search*: 161–2, 165, 223). Personality is an artificial mask, which can change daily depending on **influence** (*Views*, 1924: 143; refer also to the **enneagram** of personality).

PHILOSOPHY *see* **schools**.

Further reading

For the influence on Gurdjieff (and Orage) of European philosophers, see Taylor 2001: 213–44.

PHOTOGRAPHS

Mental photographs or snapshots can be taken of the self (see **self-observation**).

PLANETARY INFLUENCE

Planetary influences affect the Earth, and humanity as a whole (e.g. causing **wars**) (*Search*: 24). Individuals also receive planetary influences; those that are received at the moment of birth colour the whole of life, and we are slaves to them. Gurdjieff considers planetary influence on man to be the third force: **air** is the first force, and metals and minerals the second (*Views*, 1924: 257). However, **astrology** deals only with a man's **type**, his **essence**, and not his **personality**. Gurdjieff illustrated the difference between types by dropping his stick as he was walking, and describing the different reactions to this event by his pupils as 'astrology' (*Search*: 366–7).

See also: **Moon; Ray of Creation**

POINT

A point in the universe is always limited in space. It represents a combination of **'hydrogens'** in a specific place and fulfils a specific function. It can be designated by the number of the 'hydrogen' that predominates in it (*Search*: 169–70).

POLITICS; POLITICAL IDEOLOGY

Gurdjieff referred to Western civilisation and the destructive force of Communism together as 'a sea of mud' that would 'engulf the life of Tibetans, as it is smothering the old life of the rest of the planet' (*Teachings*: 153).

While Gurdjieff decried the value of politics in general, he had a wealth of political experience (see **wars**) and began his teaching amid the political turmoil of pre-Revolutionary Russia. Discontent with establishment values may lead to revolutionary underground movements, but can also result in adherence to underground occult groups (see **occult/occult revival**). Although his motives may have been different, the methods Gurdjieff used to teach his cosmological and psychological ideas have parallels with the recruitment and teaching of some anti-establishment political ideologies. Gurdjieff effectively destabilised the world-view of his pupils by enclosing them in an anti-establishment secret elite. Once the pupil had accepted his or her complete mechanicality, 'sleep' and inability to 'do' (see **doing; machine/mechanicality; sleep**), which all further study was framed to reinforce, it became difficult to exercise any critical faculty (see **groups; secrecy/silence**). Gurdjieff himself disrupted the intense bonding of the groups who worked with him by disbanding groups, sending away pupils and periodically changing the direction of his teaching.

The occultist's claim to higher knowledge can encourage contempt for ordinary people and democracy. However, occultism can be politicised. For the strong interrelation of Russian occultism and politics, see Rosenthal (1997: 379–418).

The Work today presents itself as apolitical.

Further reading

On the dangers of Gurdjieff's 'method', see Webb 1980: 560–73. For the occult in relation to politics, see Webb 1976. For an outline of authoritarian thinking as defined in totalitarianism, see Goodwin 1991: 159–75. For a discussion of the concept of 'brainwashing' in new religious movements, see Zablocki 1998; Zablocki and Robbins 2001.

POSTURE

In relation to ancient liturgy Gurdjieff said that there were special postures for different prayers (*Search*: 303; see **movements**). Postures are recorded from birth as though on a phonograph disc. Eventually the number of postures is fixed, either many or few, and after this no new postures are formed. In every epoch, race or class, people have physical postures that are connected with forms of thinking and feeling, and are interconnected. It is impossible to change thinking or feeling without first changing moving postures. If a person assumes a posture that is connected with a specific emotion, for example grief, he will begin to experience the feeling; thus feelings can be created through artificial physical posture. Uncomfortable postures are useful, in the beginning, to gain access to **sensation** (*Views*, 1922: 138, 156–7; 1923: 232–3).

See also: **act/actor; levers/postures; stop exercise**

POWER

Three independent powers in man are: physical power, which depends on the human machine; psychic power, which depends on the material and functioning of the thinking centre; and moral power, which depends on heredity and education. These powers can be increased by economy and right expenditure of energy. However, moral power is formed over a long time and so is the most difficult to change (*Views*, 1923: 159–60).

See also: **exercises; forces**

PRAYER/PRAYING

Prayers are of many kinds, not simply petitions. They can have results, but only if a person has learned how to pray: for mechanical man, there can only be mechanical results. Many prayers are really recapitulations, to be repeated in order to experience their content with mind and feelings. If a prayer is said so that the meaning of each word is considered and questioned (e.g. the prayer 'God have mercy upon me'), then the thoughts and questions that accompany this prayer will do for the man what he asks God to do. However, this prayer repeated mechanically can have no beneficial result.

In connection with **exercises** to bring the **attention** from one part of the body to another and to experience the sound of the word 'I' in various places within and without the body, Gurdjieff described a prayer on Mount Athos in which a monk uses a specific posture and says 'Ego' aloud, listening to where the word sounds. This exercise is to feel 'I' and to 'bring "I" from one centre to another' (*Search*: 300–4). This would suggest that the training on Mount Athos is a **school**, as it deals with more than one centre.

When his wife was dying, Gurdjieff asked Peters to make a strong wish for her, saying that a wish from the heart can help, like a prayer, when it is for someone else, though not for oneself (Peters 1976 [1964, 1965]: 76–7).

Pupils should pray with three centres. This is also an exercise. The prayers will go no further than the person's **atmosphere**: 'when your prayers can go as far as America, you will be able to pray to the President'. On finishing an exercise, pupils can pray to their **ideal** to help them guard what they have obtained (*Voices*: 186, 280).

See also: **occult/occult revival; stairway**

PREJUDICES

Man has two kinds of prejudices: those of the **essence** and those of the **personality** (*Views*, 1924: 240).

PRESENCE

'Everything that touches us does so without our presence' (*Views*, 1923: 162).

There are many pupil accounts of feeling the strength of Gurdjieff's presence, and of his ability to transmit energy and teach wordlessly through his presence. Bennett (1976 [1973]: 218–19) relates this to the methods used by Sufi sheikhs (Sobbat) and Indian teachers (Darshan) to teach through presence.

See also: **grace; New Work**

Further reading

Gurdjieff's teaching on self-remembering is about being present, living fully in the present moment. This has similarities with the Buddhist practice of mindfulness; for comparison, see Nyanaponika Thera 1983 [1962].

PSYCHE/PSYCHIC/PSYCHOLOGY

In addition to his use of occult and religious (Esoteric Christian) modes of presenting his teaching, Gurdjieff also expressed the **Work** in psychological terms. The word 'psyche' itself links these apparently disparate world-views. A 'psychic', as in someone possessing paranormal abilities, relates to the occult, while psyche (meaning soul) relates both to religion and to the new science of psychoanalysis and psychology.

The abnormality and malfunctioning of man's psyche is stressed in both *Tales* and *Herald*. In *Herald*, the term 'psychic', as used by Gurdjieff in 'psychic factor', can be understood as 'psychological factor'. In *Herald*, there are dense references to the psyche, the malfunctioning of which, in Gurdjieff, his pupils and humanity in general, is one of the text's central themes. Gurdjieff describes his own quest in terms of 'irrepressible mania', derangement and slavery; his study is of the twenty-eight **types** of psyche that exist. His workshops are 'for the perfection of psychopathism' and his pupils are 'possessed by' a 'specific psychosis'. Gurdjieff aims to help the healing of humanity's mass psychosis, but reading his books in the wrong order can provoke undesirable phenomena in the psyche. The teaching is expressed in terms of the psyche: e.g. it is divided into three. Contemporary man's chief failing is described in terms of missing psychic factors (see **astrology**; *Herald of Coming Good*; **occult/ occult revival**).

There are strong links between the occult, psychology and psychoanalysis (see Webb 1976 for Freud's early connections with the occult). While earlier Gurdjieff had used the occult as a form in which to present his teaching, a growing interest in psychology and psychoanalysis in Europe after World War I saw Gurdjieff also reformulating the teaching in 'psychological' terms. This adaptation from the occult was made by other spiritual teachers, such as Hermann Keyserling, Rudolf Steiner and Roberto Assagiolo (see Webb 1980: 534–6). Occult Theosophical astrology became less involved with divination and more involved with a therapeutic exploration of the psyche within the self (see the Jung-influenced work of Dane Rudhyar: Rudhyar 1963 [1936]).

This emphasis on the psychological is evident in the fact that Ouspensky (1951), Orage (1998 [1957]), Nicoll (1992 [1952–6]) and Daly King (1951) all expressed Work ideas through texts that include the words 'psychological' or 'psychology' in their titles (see also **'I'/ identity; unconscious/unconsciousness**).

In 1982 Tracol said that Gurdjieff distinguished between the psyche and the spiritual. The psyche belongs to the field of manifestation, but the spiritual belongs to what is 'real' (Tracol 1994: 127). This exemplifies a shift away from defining the Work as a 'psychology' and towards establishing it as a 'new spiritual tradition'.

See also: **New Work**

Further reading

Webb 1980. For an account of the occult origins of psychology, see Webb 1971 and Crabtree 1993. For the psychologising of astrology, see Curry 1992: 160–3.

PURGATORY

In *Tales*, life on the Holy Planet Purgatory can be understood as representing a mediating or third force in relation to the Sun Absolute (first force) and the rest of the Universe (second force). According to the narrative, Purgatory was formed after the separation of above from below. Initially, beings from all planets in the universe came to dwell there in order to purify themselves, after which they left to dwell on the Sun Absolute. However, after an unforeseen catastrophe in the universe, this was no longer possible, and the beings on Purgatory had to remain there forever (see *Tales*: 744–810).

The reader might relate Gurdjieff's Planet Purgatory, with its late creation and change in function, with Purgatory as a late addition to Christian dogma and perhaps also with the change in understanding of Christian Purgatory from having a symbolic to an actual purpose (see **suffering/pleasure**). The change in the nature of Gurdjieff's Purgatory also reflects the change in the Limbo of Christian theology. After Christ's descent to harrow Hell, Limbo was sealed and the souls within had to wait for the Second Coming.

QUESTIONS/QUESTIONING

In 1916 Ouspensky realised that his original questions about Gurdjieff's teaching had been naïve and based on a self-confidence from which he was now becoming free. He was thus understanding Gurdjieff better. New pupils asked the same questions that Ouspensky and his group had themselves asked. It gave them some satisfaction to realise that these questions could not be answered: one had to learn in order to understand this. However, Gurdjieff said that all questions, if they are aching questions, can lead a man to the system (**Work**) (*Search*: 238–9, 244). Each pupil should ask himself 'What am I?' He will see through asking this question that he has lived his life without asking and therefore with the assumption that he is 'something'. Asking this question will give a focal point for his search (*Views*, c.1918: 42–3).

Gurdjieff wrote that he had searched for the answers to two principal questions: about, first, the significance of human life on earth (*Herald*: 13) and, second, how to stop the disposition towards suggestibility through which men fall under forms of mass hypnosis such as **war** (*Life*: 27; see also **aim**). Gurdjieff's behaviour to his pupils provoked questioning, as do his texts (see **writings**).

In addition to the requirement for the pupil to question everything (see **faith**), the key question in the Work is asked of the pupil by himself: 'Who am I?' Ravindra (1999: 101) writes of de Salzmann using this question to begin a meditation.

Further reading

Osborn 1971; this is based on recordings from Ramana's teachings – Ramana was active in the 1920s.

QUOTATION MARKS

The highest esoteric science refers to man in quotations marks as 'man', in whom the 'I' is missing (*Life*: 172). Gurdjieff uses quotation marks in his writing to indicate differences between generally held views of, for example, 'truth' or 'love' and his own definitions or understanding of these terms (usually written without quotation marks). However, Gurdjieff's use of quotation marks is not consistent. This may be due to the number of translators and editors working on his texts (see **writings**).

RAY OF CREATION

The Ray of Creation shows, in diagram form, the chain of worlds issuing from the **Absolute** (see **world/s, all worlds**) in which humanity finds itself:

- The Absolute
- All Worlds
- All Suns
- Our Sun
- The Planets
- The Earth
- The Moon

The idea of the Ray of Creation is distorted when taken literally. It comes from ancient knowledge and is helpful for unifying many conflicting views of the world. It contradicts some of the ideas of contemporary (*c.*1915) science in that it posits a growth from the Absolute to the Moon in which the Earth is gradually heating up to become a sun. The Moon is also warming to become a planet, and thus it will be a new link in the Ray of Creation, forming a new satellite moon of its own. The energy for the development of the Moon comes from the Sun, the planets of the solar system, and from organic life on earth. For a conflicting definition of the Ray of Creation, according to which the Moon is a dead end, see **Moon**.

Understanding the Ray of Creation in relation to the **Law of Three** helps us to determine our place in the world and to know how many laws we are under (see Figure 25).

These worlds (as shown in Figure 25) are also designated by the number of laws they are subject to (i.e. the Absolute is World 1, the Earth is World 48). The will of the Absolute manifests itself directly in World 3; thereafter, it manifests itself through mechanical laws. The more the number of laws that govern each successive stage of creation increase, the further that world is from the Absolute. For example, although life on Earth is constrained by forty-eight laws, life on the Moon would be even less free because the Moon is ruled by ninety-six laws.

Man can study the forty-eight laws he is under only by observing them in himself and by becoming free of them (see also **miracle/ miraculous**). The Earth is very far from the Absolute. Cosmically, it is a bad cold place, where life is hard and everything must be fought for (*Search*: 82–3). The Ray of Creation is also expressed in terms of the **Law of Seven** or the **Law of Octaves** (see Figure 26; see also **evolution**).

Figure 25 Ray of Creation: the Ray of Creation and Law of Three

Place in ray of creation	Number of laws each place is under	Laws composed of
Absolute/all	1	Three indivisible forces
All Worlds	3	3 laws manifesting individuality
All Suns	6	3 laws of all Worlds and 3 of its own
Our Sun	12	6 laws of All Suns and 6 of its own
All Planets	24	12 laws of the Sun and 12 laws of its own
The Earth	48	24 laws of All Planets and 24 of its own
The Moon	96	48 laws of Earth and 48 of its own

Figure 26 Ray of Creation: the Ray of Creation and Law of Seven

DO	*The Absolute*
SI	All Worlds
LA	All Suns
SOL	Our Sun
FA	The Planets
MI	The Earth
RE	The Moon
DO	Absolute Nothing

REASON

Each **level of being** has its own corresponding level of reason; the highest being has objective reason.

In relation to understanding cosmic law, there is an abyss that cannot be bridged by 'ordinary human reason', although these ideas may be grasped by intuition. We need new methods of listening and studying in order to hear new thoughts. We must be able to distinguish between mind and body. When the body does not want to work, we should not let it rest, but when the mind wants to rest, we should do so. However, Gurdjieff also says that if a person reasons and thinks soundly, he will inevitably return to himself to begin to find out about himself and his place in the world around him (*Views*, 1914: 16; 1922: 40, 114, 43).

Vanity and self-love are our most fundamental enemies. They separate us from both good and bad influences entering us from the outer world. Gurdjieff advises that we free ourselves from them through simple active reasoning. He says that 'there are *many methods* and *a great number of means*' by which we may free ourselves, and also that only active reasoning can free us, that 'there are *no other means*' (my emphasis). When we are hurt or offended, vanity and self-love close us off from the outer world. But, in order to live, we need to be connected to the outer world; when we study ourselves, we are connected with the outer world. Active reasoning should be learned through long and varied practice (*Views*, 1923: 267–8).

In *Tales*, there are many references to reason – objective, pure, sacred – and to the lack of it in ordinary men. Objective reason can only be perfected in men through conscious labour and intentional suffering; Chapters 13 and 24 of *Tales* examine this lack of reason.

Orage (*Teachings*: 159–60) differentiates between verbal reasoning, which is based on experience of words, and formal reasoning, based on experience of the senses. In Gurdjieff's definition of reason, both kinds are necessary, but verbal reason, which is the intellectual centre working on its own with energy from the sex centre, is greatly overvalued. Verbal reason has defects because it is not based on actual experience.

> Objective reason cannot be understood in the light of subjective reason. Objective reason means coming to the end of subjective reason and then having a totally different experience.

See also **thinking/thoughts**.

Do not seek to distract children; use reason with analogies (see **allegory/analogy**), which children like (*Voices*: 145).

Further reading

Compare Wittgenstein in the *Tractatus Logico-Philosophicus* (1995 [1922]: 189). For Wittgenstein, as for Gurdjieff, objectivity is more than just seeing from a more detached perspective; rather, it is a radically different kind of experience, more akin to waking from a dream.

REBIRTH *see* **death/rebirth**

RECIPROCAL MAINTENANCE/RECIPROCAL FEEDING, LAW OF *see* Law of Reciprocal Maintenance/ Reciprocal Feeding

RECONCILING FORCE

The third force in Gurdjieff's **Law of Three**, also termed 'neutralising'.

RECURRENCE/REINCARNATION

The idea of reincarnation approximates to the truth, but people who believe they have eternity in front of them will not make any effort in the present moment to see how everything repeats itself in this life (*Search*: 250–1; see **death/rebirth**; **influences**; **time/the eternal**).

Although the physical body returns to dust at death, the astral and higher-being bodies, if formed, may reincarnate over a long period of time or change into another physical body identical with the one that has died. The astral body can only reincarnate unconsciously if it meets such a body; the mental body is able to choose (*Views*: 217–18; see **bodies**).

Orage suggests that our state of being at the end of life may deserve another kind of planetary existence, 'perhaps one in the animal kingdom' (*Teachings*: 163).

The Hindu doctrine of reincarnation, introduced into Europe via Theosophy, offered an attractive alternative to the gap left by declining belief in a Christian afterlife.

See also: **repetition**

Further reading

See Nietzsche's *Thus Spake Zarathustra* (1997 [1883–5]); Eliade 1989 [1954].

RELATIVITY

Gurdjieff's principle of relativity is unlike the relativity of mechanics or Einstein's principle of relativity; it is a relativity of existence (*Search*: 213). It is the principle on which the new exact **language**, which is needed to exchange exact ideas, is based. All ideas in this language are concentrated around one idea, that of conscious evolution (*Search*: 70; see also **man**; **time/the eternal**; **world/s, all worlds**).

It is necessary to understand the relativity of each thing and of each manifestation according to the place it occupies in the cosmic order (*Search*: 89; see **matter**). The principle of relativity is established through the study of the idea of the **cosmoses**; this solves many problems connected with time and space (*Search*: 207).

Interpersonal relations, like everything else in life, are relative to us, and the relativity is mechanical. If I dislike someone, he is not to blame; the important fact is not the person, but the problem (*Views*, 1923: 159–63).

Gurdjieff's ideas have their own relativity. None of them can be grasped in isolation, but can only be understood in relation to all of his other concepts and definitions, and through experience.

RELIGION/S; NEW RELIGIONS

The original basis of religions has become distorted and their essentials forgotten. The changes in direction of religions (e.g. in Christianity from the Gospel preaching on love to the Inquisition) can be understood in terms of the **Law of Seven** (*Search*: 129).

Religion corresponds to a man's level of **being**, therefore it is different for man number one, two, three or further (see **man**). Mechanical man cannot 'do', and so he is unable to 'live' the religion (e.g. to turn the other cheek). If he is trained to 'do' this mechanically, it will simply mean that he is unable not to 'do' it. Religious teachings have two parts: one teaches what must be done, and the other part teaches how to do it. The techniques of religion – breathing, posture, tensing and relaxing of groups of muscles – are the secret instruction given in religions. There is a secret part of Christianity that teaches 'how to carry out the precepts of Christ and what they really mean' (*Search*: 299–304). A Christian is a man who is able to fulfil the Commandments with mind and **essence**. A man who wishes to do so only with his mind is a pre-Christian. A man who can do nothing, 'even with his mind, is called a non-Christian' (*Views*, 1923: 154).

The mystery religions used ceremonies of initiation to mark changes in level of being (see **initiates/initiation**). By themselves, rituals cannot produce any change, but esoteric groups and religions imitate these ceremonies. In reality there is only self-initiation acquired through **Work** (*Search*: 314–15; see also **prayer/praying**).

The rituals of the early Church were not taken from the Judaic or Greek religions, nor invented by the Fathers of the Church, but taken from a **school** of repetition in prehistoric Egypt. The form of worship in Christian Churches (prayers, hymns, religious symbols and holidays) echoes the repetition by the school of their learning concerning the universe and man. The sacred **dances** that accompanied these repetitions have not been incorporated into Christian worship. Thus prehistoric Egypt was Christian, its religion composed of the same principles and ideas (*Search*: 302–3).

This may be an echo of St Augustine's declaration that 'the Christian religion has always been in the world, only after the coming of Christ was it called Christianity' (quoted in Waterfield 1987: 136).

In *Tales*, religions were brought to Earth by Sacred Individuals so that men might overcome the abnormalities formed in them by the organ **kundabuffer** (*Tales*: 696–7). However, Gurdjieff shows that, with the exception of Christ, all of them failed. Gurdjieff stated that the aim of his **Institute** was to help pupils become Christian (*Views*, 1923: 152) and also referred to his teaching as 'esoteric Christianity' (*Search*: 102), a term that would have been familiar to pupils via Theosophical absorption of Anna Kingsford's and Edward Maitland's alchemical and Gnostic Esoteric Christianity, and Bessant's *Esoteric Christianity* (see Webb 1980: 525).

In the **group meetings during World War II (1940–4)** Gurdjieff says that God created our intellect and body so we can inure the body to struggle and educate our bodies with our heads; that pupils must kill sacred compulsions; that a person who wants liberty must kill even the love of God or Our Lady, even the idea of believing in a saint. 'If you pray to God, God himself can send you to the Devil.' Objectively, parents are more than God. He emphasises that direct contact with God is impossible (see also **stairway**). There is no place for God in us, but our parents have the future place of God in us. We owe them everything, so we work first with them. For every man, up to a certain age his father must be God: 'God loves him who esteems his father. When he dies there is a place where God can enter in.' This is so even if the father is unworthy (*Voices*: 66, 152, 77, 173–5, 162, 193).

Although Gurdjieff used the vocabulary of religion (i.e. spirit, soul, God) during his lifetime, the Work was presented until around 1965–70 as an esoteric, occult teaching, as a psychology and as philosophy – it was not regarded by pupils as a religion. Since the mid-1960s it has moved towards being a Tradition. This is an aspiration for the continuity of the Work that is in contradiction with the teaching that Fourth Way schools are always impermanent (see **new work**).

Taylor (2001: 213–14) writes that Gurdjieff never claimed to have founded a religion, but cites Durkheim (1963: 47) who defines religion as 'a unified system of beliefs and practices relative to sacred things'; in this sense the Work can be defined as a religious movement.

Writing in 1982, Tracol (1994: 136) stated that there is no incompatibility between the Work and religious dogmas and ritual, which are neither imposed nor neglected, and that there are disciples of Gurdjieff who are church-goers or of a religious persuasion.

In academic terms, the Work is classified as a New Religious Movement and is regarded as being a key influence on subsequent new religious movements, as well as on New Age people 'who emphasise the mechanistic nature of the person' (Rozak 1975: 47).

Further reading

For religious experience, see James 1985 [1929]. For new religions, see Needleman 1977. For New Religious Movements, see Barker 1989; for the Work as a New Religious Movement, see Heelas 1996; for the New Age in America, see Kyle 1995; for New Age religion and esotericism, see Hanegraf 1995. For a repudiation of Gurdjieff in relation to the 'tradition', see Perry 1978; for an account and analysis of twentieth-century Western teachers, including Gurdjieff, see Rawlinson 1997; for appropriation of Gurdjieff's teaching after his death, see **Appendix 2**.

REMINDING FACTOR

In *Life*, Gurdjieff writes of his need for an unending reminding factor, because, despite his considerable telepathic and hypnotic powers, he fails to remember himself in ordinary life (*Life*: 19–25). External reminding factors only work for a while. Then he realises that the 'devil' has been sent into exile to be a continuing reminding factor for God. By analogy, he can 'exile' his own telepathic and hypnotic powers, the lack of which will serve as a continuing reminding factor of his aim. Taylor (2001: 197) suggests that Gurdjieff's 'exiling' of Orage, recounted in *Life*, was intended to act as a reminding factor for Orage.

The consequences of past actions, not only one's own but also those of one's family or nation, must be faced and repaired. This responsibility can act as a reminding factor (quoted in Thring 1998: 263).

Nott, who was given a red pepper to eat by Gurdjieff as a reminding factor, recalls Gurdjieff telling a small boy at the Institute, who was misbehaving, that he must obey his parents, and then smacking the boy hard as a reminding factor (*Journey*: 76–7).

See also: **alarm clocks**

REMORSE

In *Life*, Gurdjieff writes that he does not wish to re-experience the state of remorse for his ordinary inner and outer state of being, which alternated with other painful experience (*Life*: 19–20; see also **conscience**).

In *Tales*, remorse is a cosmic law, the sacred Aieioiuoa (*Tales*: 141, 410). There is also a planet Remorse, one of three small planets on which redemption is possible for certain beings. Orage expresses objective remorse as:

> what one should feel in the presence of a being who has developed himself into a higher state of consciousness than one's own – a wish to be what one ought to be.

When we self-remember, elements in our body experience remorse, which acts as a light in that it allows us to observe previously hidden things in ourselves (*Teachings*: 142, 146). However, having experienced one's own nothingness it is important to continue to feel remorse rather than despair or self-reproach, because these waste energy. The acknowledgement of and experience of feeling remorse of conscience for having done wrong or sinned, in itself brings forgiveness of the wrong. Remorse of conscience 'helps, in some mysterious way, to repair the past' (*Journey*: 8, 76).

In the 1940s group meetings, Gurdjieff focused on the need to experience remorse of conscience. Only this will act as a reminding factor for **self-remembering**. Remorse purifies; it also repairs the past. This can be understood simply as stopping a habit one acquired in the past, although Gurdjieff also suggests that remorse can repair wrongs done by previous generations. Voluntary **suffering**, caused by remorse, repairs the past by paying for it. Remorse must be created. Gurdjieff gave exercises to help pupils feel remorse. 'The effect of true remorse is hatred of yourself, repugnance towards yourself'. You have to feel nauseated a lot to kill your (inner) enemy; do 'I am' to take away the fear of depression (see **'I'/identity**). Rejoice that the impulse to change has awakened in you. 'One must punish oneself mercilessly against this filthy creature'; everybody must. You must come to hatred of yourself, hatred of the past, of your parents, of the upbringing you had. Curse your past, but give your parents as much help as you can. To work on remorse, revive childhood memories of when you were bad, made your parents cry; feel all your faults, suffer: 'in that suffering you can have happiness given by real love' (*Voices*: 111, 160, 162, 197–8, 200, 164).

Needleman (1994 [1992]: 168) suggests that Gurdjieff's teaching on remorse is comparable to the 'way of tears' of the Desert Fathers.

REPETITION

Ouspensky had a special interest in the idea of eternal recurrence, that a man's life might be repeated many times. Gurdjieff said that this was an approximation of the truth, but that he did not teach about repetition of lives because believing in it would lead people to passivity. A man needs to see how everything repeats in this life; if he strives for change, a man can see all laws in one lifetime. He added that if a life is repeated, conditions (e.g. planetary influences) may change and 'possibilities *for everything* (he emphasised these words) exist only for a definite time' (*Search*: 250–1).

Further reading

Ouspensky 1984 [1931].

RESPONSIBILITY

Mechanical man cannot be responsible for his actions (*Search*: 19–20; see **machine/mechanicality**). When people belong to a Work **group** they have a common responsibility for each other's successes, mistakes and failures (*Search*: 231; with reference to a pupil's responsibility for the past and future happiness of his own family, see **remorse**).

RIVER OF LIFE

Gurdjieff compares human life in general to a river and a man's life to a drop of water. The river divides in two and the drop may be in the stream that flows out to sea, where there is a possibility for the drop to evolve, or it may remain in the other stream, which goes down into the earth where the drop becomes part of involutionary construction.

In order to cross from one stream to another, a man must be prepared to die to his usual life (*Views*, 1924: 236–8; see also *Tales*: 1227–31). Gurdjieff also told of two parallel rivers. In the first, we (the drops of water) are sometimes on the surface, sometimes at the bottom; our suffering depends on our position, and is useless because it is accidental and unconscious. In the other river, the drop may suffer today because it did not suffer enough yesterday, it can also suffer in advance: 'Sooner or later everything is paid for. For the Cosmos there is no time. Suffering can be voluntary and only voluntary suffering has value' (*Views*, 1924: 85). The river of life metaphor echoes Biblical themes of the division of waters (Exodus 14: 21, II Kings 2: 8, Matthew 3: 16 [all King James Version]). The 'pure river of water of life' (which is undivided) is referred to in Revelation 22: 1 [King James Version].

ROLES

Each person has a limited number of roles, which they play in relation to their family, place of work or friends. He remains identified with his role and comfortable within it. When new circumstances arise, he has no role and so feels discomfort. However, in order to study himself, a man must endure this discomfort (*Search*: 239–40). Acting is not a helpful profession for work; 'all roles are built out of postures, it is impossible to acquire new postures by practice; practice can only strengthen old ones'. Only a man who has 'I' can act (*Views*, 1924: 176–8).

'Externally, one should play a role in everything'; this makes life easier. However, internally we must be free of **considering**, we must cease reacting inside to everything that happens outside (*Views*, 1924: 95–6).

'To play a role is not an aim but a means'. Gurdjieff gives an example of how to play a role, how to do what the other person likes. A woman likes him to kiss her hand, so he does it:

> I am kind to her. Interior I want to insult her, but I don't do it. I play my role. So then she becomes my slave. Interior I don't react.

His neighbours love him because of the role he plays, but objectively for him 'all that is *merde*, inside. It is my experimenting. For me they are mice' (emphasis in the original; see **experiment**; **slavery/slaves**). Playing a role means behaving as one ordinarily does but without inner identification. A pupil must work so as to have no close union with anyone internally, they must not love nor esteem, have sympathy or antipathy, all love and respect must be liquidated, but externally they play a role. Others must not realise that a role is being played. A person can feel free while playing a role, and fulfil their obligations better, internally they can be more patient; however, they recognise that each person objectively is a **nonentity**. Gurdjieff is different with everyone, yet for him everybody has the same stinking **emanations** (*Voices*: 187, 54, 142, 74, 151, 154–5, 259–60).

Webb (1980: 190–1, 537–9) remarks on the fluidity with which Gurdjieff himself changed role from one period of teaching to another, and that his roles encompassed the big role of Teacher, the intermediate role intended to influence a specific pupil, and 'a generalized role to ensure a relationship of *meaning*' within the milieu in which he was operating, whether in Russia, Caucasus, Tiflis, Essentuki, Hellerau or Fontainebleau. Webb connects Gurdjieff's teaching on roles with contemporary explorations of, among others, the psychodrama of Jacob L. Moreno and the method acting of Konstantin Stanislavsky (1863–1938).

Gurdjieff's 'many roles challenged the reading of a single nucleate centre beneath them' (Taylor 2001: 252). Bennett (1962: 250–1) and Georgette Leblanc (quoted in Anderson 1962: 149) both give accounts of experiencing Gurdjieff without his customary 'mask'. Gurdjieff has influenced theatre via Peter Brook.

Further reading

Brook (1988).

ROLLS

Rolls are created within the **centres** as a result of external stimuli (e.g. education or religion). The strength of a man's small 'I's depend on the strength of the rolls in centres. What is seen as individuality is the specific interconnection of rolls within centres (*Search*: 60, 163, 388). Rolls, or reels, are the mechanism, similar to a wax cylinder, on which **impressions** are recorded. Some of these are recorded before birth, sometimes recorded on more than one roll and with a chronological record. Memory is the imperfect unrolling of these impressions, although **hypnosis** shows how all impressions remain permanently stored on the rolls. This may also be seen through an accidental shock, or seeing a specific face or place. The internal life of a man is only the unrolling of these records of impressions. His individuality depends on the quality and order in which they unroll, and the interconnections between them (*Views*, 1924: 73–4).

ROPE, THE

Gurdjieff gave this name to an all-women group he taught in Paris in the 1930s (see **appendix 1**).

RULES *see* **groups**

SACRIFICE

Sacrifice is an important factor in Gurdjieff's teaching. In *Life* he relates the self-sacrifice of his hypnotic and telepathic powers, which provided him with a **reminding factor**, a means of **self-remembering** (*Life*: 19–25). Sacrifice causes **suffering**, which may be useful or useless.

A person must understand why he needs to sacrifice 'his own decision' and obey a teacher for a while. In religions this is demanded immediately, but in Fourth Way Schools subordination to a teacher's **will** is only required once a person realises his own nothingness, that he actually has nothing to sacrifice, that in fact he does not exist. A person can only acquire will through the conscious subordination to the will of another (*Search*: 160–1; see also **obedience**; **teacher**; **ways/fourth way**).

Sacrifice is necessary, but this consists in sacrificing things such as 'faith', 'tranquillity' and 'health', which in fact man does not possess. Although suffering is necessary, a man will not be able to work unless he has sacrificed his suffering. Usually people will sacrifice their pleasures before their sufferings (*Search*: 274).

It is necessary to sacrifice the illusion of freedom, to voluntarily become a **slave**, to obey inwardly and outwardly: 'he does what he is told, says what he is told and thinks what he is told.' Knowing he has nothing, he is not afraid of losing anything, and in fact he gains, but he must 'pass through the hard way of slavery and obedience'. No-one could sacrifice everything, and this is not asked. What is required is an evaluation of what is to be sacrificed and no attempt to change this later (*Search*: 365–6).

A person may have to temporarily sacrifice his own attainments (e.g. special powers) in order to raise other people to his level. If he fails, he will lose his powers (*Search*: 202).

Later, Gurdjieff said that all pleasures must be sacrificed; they are *merde* and make for slavery. Two pleasures are allowed: objective pleasure from a work result, and a voluntary relaxation necessary for an aim. All present pleasures must be sacrificed, for the sake of the future (*Voices*: 162, 194).

Gurdjieff's attitude to suffering may bring to mind the Christian theology of necessary sacrifice: Christ's sacrifice of himself redeemed the world from sin.

SAYINGS *see* aphorisms

SCHOOLS

A school, which follows esoteric traditions and is created on the principles of the **Law of Octaves**, is the only place where a man can learn to 'do' through gaining an understanding of the Law of Octaves (*Search*: 134). Such a Fourth Way school is never permanent. It always has 'some work of a definite significance and is never without some *undertaking* around which and in connection with which it can alone exist' (*Search*: 312, emphasis in original). Sometimes people who have been in a Fourth Way school that has now completed its work and closed, begin independently to work for their own aims (see **aim**; **ways/fourth way**). Sometimes people who have not understood it continue the Work in an imitated form; most **occult**, Masonic and alchemical schools that we have heard of belong to this type. But even pseudo-esoteric schools can retain some truth. Most people could not assimilate pure truth, so they need to receive the truth in the form of 'lies'. Esoteric schools may exist in the East, but in the guise of monasteries and temples, so they are difficult to find (*Search*: 312–14; see also **religion/s, new religions**). Schools were divided up a long time ago and in part these divisions still exist. There was 'philosophy' in India, 'theory' in Egypt, and in 'present-day Persia, Mesopotamia and Turkestan, "practice" '. However, philosophy, theory and practice cannot be understood in the usual way. There are no general schools, only specialist schools in which each guru is an expert in one discipline (e.g. astronomy or sculpture). Thus the pupil would need to study for a thousand years to learn what he needs (*Search*: 15). Gurdjieff mentioned 'Tibetan monasteries, the Chitral, Mount Athos, Sufi schools in Persia, in Bokhara, and eastern Turkestan' and 'dervishes of various orders' as sources of his knowledge, 'but all of them in a very indefinite way' (*Search*: 36). According to Gurdjieff, 'the ballet should become a school' (*Search*: 382).

The concept of a special 'schools' of wisdom would have been familiar to Gurdjieff's pupils via Theosophical ideas concerning the Masters of Wisdom (see **conscious circle of humanity**). Before he met Gurdjieff, Ouspensky's search for the miraculous originally led him to India to search for 'schools' (*Search*: 1–6).

See also: **dances/dancing; magic/magician; narcotics**

SECRECY/SILENCE

Gurdjieff's teaching was sometimes strictly secret and at other times more open. This was for practical reasons (conditions of war in Russia and in Paris in World War II), as well as for reasons of **school** discipline. However, overall the injunctions to secrecy concerning personal exercises, and the obligation not to write about the teaching, have delayed an appreciation of the extent of Gurdjieff's influence. Gurdjieff's teaching had a high profile during his years at the Institute (principally 1922–4 and until around 1936). Without this period of publicity, Gurdjieff would not have attracted the number of pupils that he did. Gurdjieff used publicity, good or bad, as an aid to establishing his teaching. 'As a teacher, he came to shock, not to soothe, the human conscience, and, characteristically, he prompted negative judgments' (Taylor 2001: xiii).

Ouspensky experienced the idea of self-remembering as 'being hidden by an "impenetrable veil" ' to people outside **groups** (*Search*: 122). In answer to a question about concealment of ideas, Gurdjieff relates concealment with initiation (*Views*, 'Glimpses of Truth': 27–9; see **initiates/initiation; 'sly' man**).

Different reasons for the necessity of secrecy were given. Ouspensky recounts Gurdjieff's initial injunction against pupils making written records of his teaching. This was so that the teaching would not be given in a distorted form. He writes that later on pupils disobeyed this. Another reason was that man is unable to keep a secret and so he is not told any, except maybe as a test, which is usually failed; as no serious secrets would be given to him, this does not matter

(*Search*: 14, 383–4). An additional reason given for an injunction against taking notes in groups was so that the full attention could be given to what was said. Afterwards some pupils wrote down what they remembered, the results were compared and form the basis of *Views* (*Views*: ix–x).

Gurdjieff also suggested that the teaching was secret only because, until a person had the corresponding level of **being**, they could not understand the teaching. Nott (*Journey*: 103–4) writes of the difference in attitude between Gurdjieff and Ouspensky's pupils. Ouspensky's pupils 'were constantly on the watch [...] as if the police might be expected at any time'. This secrecy was not to do with the Work, but to do with Ouspensky's experiences in Russia. However, a secretive attitude still continues in pupils of his lineage.

In a 1978 interview, Tracol (1994: 94) agrees that the Work is, in a sense, an elite, hidden teaching. This is because 'most people do not want to be bothered' with Work questions, and also because there need to be conditions that lend themselves to the attempt to wake up.

Secrecy and the formation of elite groups are common to both religious and political anti-establishment organisations. Both may demand subjugation to a higher cause, obedience, agreement to the worthlessness of some aspects of contemporary life and values, and a willingness to reframe a conventional contemporary world-view in other terms and under other ideologies (see **politics, political ideology**).

SEEKERS OF/AFTER TRUTH

The adventures of this group are recounted in *Meetings*. Though such a group may have existed, there is no evidence to support this. Gurdjieff gives a definition of the group in a brochure for his Institute in France (translated by Orage). The Society was founded in 1895 'by a group of specialists, including doctors, archaeologists, priests, painters', whose aim was to study 'so-called supernatural phenomena'. The Seekers travelled in Persia, Afghanistan, Turkestan, Tibet, India and other countries. During these journeys many of the group died and some abandoned the search, thus only a small group under Gurdjieff's leadership returned to Russia in 1913 (Taylor 1998: 73–5; see also *Meetings with Remarkable Men*).

Further reading

Research by Johnson (1994) has discovered the men who were Blavatsky's 'masters'. These had previously been regarded as either mystical or fictional, and

further research may revise our ideas about Gurdjieff's 'Seekers of Truth'. See also
Webb 1980; Johnson 1995.

SELF-OBSERVATION

Self-observation is the chief method of self-study, which is itself the
Work that leads to self-knowledge. A man needs to know the right
method, receive guidance, and give much time and effort to observe
his functions, to be aware of which **centre** is functioning and to
simply 'record' his observation of the moment. If he analyses his
observations, he ceases to observe. All of man's centres function in
habitual ways of which he is unaware, and which he needs to observe
in order to gain self-knowledge. **Imagination, daydreaming** and
habits need to be observed. Although it is not possible to change his
functioning, the struggle against habits, for example, changing the
habitual speed of walking, will help him to be free for a moment to
observe how he usually walks. Struggle against immediate expression
of unpleasant or negative emotions is one of the few aspects of a man
that can be changed without creating other habits. Self-observation
shows a man that he responds to and is controlled by external
circumstances, and allows him to feel his mechanicality. As one 'I'
succeeds another 'I', he can understand that there is nothing
permanent within him (*Search*: 111–13; see also **'I'/identity**).

Once a person can distinguish between the work of centres he must
learn to take 'mental photographs' of the whole of himself as he is in a
moment. When he has collected a number of 'photographs' he will see
that his usual idea of himself is an illusion. He must then learn to
divide the real from the invented self. When, for example, an Adam
Smith observes himself, the 'I' that observes Smith is not the 'I' that is
observed. A person must feel that there are two persons within: one
passive 'I' that can at most register what the other active Smith does.
Self-observation becomes observation of 'Smith'; the observing 'I'
recognises that this Smith is only a mask, yet he is entirely in the power
of 'Smith', becomes afraid of him. The aim must be to become the
master rather than the slave of 'Smith'. In order to achieve this, a
trustworthy helper is needed (*Search*: 145–9).

Great courage is required for self-observation. We must be sincere,
lose our illusions and accept our helplessness (*Views*, 1924: 72). It is
only possible to self-observe for short periods. We only have one
attention, but we need to know how we are for the whole day.
However, useful accidental discoveries can also be made (*Views*, 1924:

240). Objective self-observation is the function of the master and not possible as we are. However, continued attempts over several years will strengthen the attention and make self-observation and **self-remembering** possible (*Views*, 1924: 88–9). We should remember what we have observed. We must carry out self-observation in everyday life; in our rooms we cannot develop a master (*Views*, 1924: 146–7; see also *Life*: 73–88). The importance of self-remembering is stated in relation to recognising the nullity of our 'individuality', the possibility of not identifying, and with the aim of convincing 'the whole being' to work, rather than just our 'meaningless consciousness'. Americans were wrongly fixated with this aspect of the Work.

Self-observation is an instrument of awakening that in itself effects changes in man's functioning.

See also: **alchemy**

SELF-REMEMBERING

Human blindness is based on the fact that people believe that they remember themselves when in fact they do not. An understanding of this leads a man close to understanding his **being**. While carrying out **self-observation**, it is necessary to self-remember, to be conscious of the self-observing, otherwise 'it' observes. The attempt to remember the self is carried out by dividing **attention**. Usually in observation the attention is directed towards the thing observed. In self-remembering the attention is divided: part is directed towards the thing observed, and part towards the self. Self-remembering, or consciousness of one's being, is the third state of consciousness (the others are sleep and waking-sleep); we cannot create it without help (*Search*: 117–19, 145).

Self-remembering can be defined as seeing both the 'I' and the 'here' of 'I am here' (*Views*, 1922: 80). Although thinking (about Gurdjieff's lecture, for example) while working is the same as self-remembering, we cannot self-remember with the mind alone; it has too little attention. The feeling and the body do not wish to remember, therefore one should teach and learn through the feeling and body. For now, it is necessary to persuade them by 'fraudulent means'; later they may develop common sense. Mechanical self-remembering, which results from **associations**, is of great value in the beginning of work. Later, it should not be used because only conscious self-remembering results in concrete doing (*Views*, 1923: 221–2, 227).

Gurdjieff's statement about the use of 'fraudulent' means and his assertion that one should teach and learn through the feeling and body calls for a questioning reassessment of the functions that his cosmological ideas and theory might fulfil. Might these be the 'fraudulent means' to convince the feeling and body of the need to work?

If the words 'I' 'wish' 'to remember' 'myself' are said with attention paid to each word separately, so that the sensation of each word resonates in a specific place in the body, these sensations can be recalled later and help a person to self-remember. The energy needed for prolonging self-remembering can be collected in the general **accumulator** only when the accumulators in **centres** 'work one after the other in a certain definite combination' (*Views*, 1923: 233–4). For complete self-remembering, the centres must be artificially stimulated: the intellectual centre, which is interested in the future, from outside; the other two, which are interested in the present, from inside. Distinguish between sensation, emotions and thoughts, and say to each 'remind me to remember you' (*Teachings*: 37).

Two of the factors that prevent self-remembering are **identification** and **considering** (see also *Life Is Real Only Then, When 'I Am'*).

In 1967 Tracol (1994: 114, 115–16) stated that 'the practice of remembering oneself is the master key to Gurdjieff's teaching' and that 'the ability to remember oneself is our birthright', although, after twenty-five years of practice, it remains indefinable. At certain moments he becomes aware of his own presence: 'I here now'. He recognises himself, but this recognition of self is constantly lost then re-found or, rather, 'it recalls itself to me'. Here Tracol (1994: 115) refers to self-remembering in the receptive terminology of **New Work**.

Although the term ('self-re-membering') suggests the putting together of the fragmented self, the practice of self-remembering, which focuses in separate moments, on parts of the functioning, can induce a sense of fragmentation that serves to affirm the definition of a person as fragmented. The acknowledgement of this fragmentation is one of the key philosophical, psychological and spiritual concerns of the twentieth century (see **'I'/identity**; **presence**).

See also: **New Work terminology**

Further reading

Tracol's 'George Ivanovitch Gurdjieff: Man's Awakening and the Practice of Remembering Oneself' from 1967 (see Tracol 1994). Fragmentation of the self is understood differently in Buddhism: compare Nyanaponika Thera 1983 [1962]; for a Buddhist concept of no-self, see Walpola 1967.

SENSATION/SENSING

In the beginning we need artificial ways to stimulate sensation, later this will not be necessary. A good method is to take an uncomfortable posture and direct attention to parts of the body. Unpleasant sensations result. We can wish in the mind for the sensation of the body to help me remember myself. 'I say to my body: "You. You – me. You are also me. I wish" ' (*Views*, 1923: 232–3).

Gurdjieff suggests that a pupil try to keep the organic sensation of the body, without interrupting ordinary occupations, and to keep a little energy to establish the habit.

> Our aim is to have a constant sensation of oneself, of one's individuality. This sensation cannot be expressed intellectually, because it is organic. It is something which makes you independent when you are with other people.
>
> (*Voices*: 26)

SEVEN, LAW OF *see* Law of Seven

SEX

People gather together ostensibly in the name of religion, politics or entertainment, but actually they are interested in being with people of the opposite sex. Sleep, hypnosis and mechanical functioning are caused by sex. Although sex causes slavery, it also has the possibility of liberation. The energy of 'hydrogen' Si 12, which is used to create a new child, can also be used to create the birth of the astral body (see **bodies**; **'hydrogens'**). This is only possible in a normally functioning organism. If the organism is sick or perverted, transmutation is impossible.

Sometimes sexual abstinence is required throughout the process of creating an astral body, sometimes only at the start, sometimes only during the transmutation. In some cases an active sexual life is helpful to transmutation. In general, sexual abstinence can only be useful in the Work if all **centres** abstain. Sexual fantasy, for example, will not help the Work. Sexual energy should be used only for procreation or for transmutation. The problem lies not in sex itself, but in the abuse of sex for psychopathic abnormal purposes (*Search*: 254–9; see **sex centre**).

At the time of Gurdjieff's teaching, children did not receive guidance or **education** in relation to sex. The importance of sex education for children is stressed in *Meetings* (54–6), and in stories in *Tales* (1032–41) that express themes of sex and its misuse. For sexual deviation, see especially Chapter 29, 'The Fruits of Former Civilizations and the Blossoms of the Contemporary'. Beelzebub equates a rising birth rate with a short life-span and degeneration, and a fall in the birth rate with long life-span and regeneration.

Sex acts need not be mingled with sentiment. If they are mingled, this makes the impartiality that **love** demands more difficult. Originally the sex act must have been sacred, performed only for procreation; gradually it became a pleasure (*Voices*: 47).

Bennett (1976: 231–2) writes that, in relation to Gurdjieff's female pupils, with some there was a strong sexual element, with others none, and that Gurdjieff's sexual life was sometimes ascetic and abstaining, but more frequently he had sexual relations with 'almost any woman who happened to come within the sphere of his influence'. Quite a number of these women bore Gurdjieff's children and some remained closely connected to him (see also **gender**).

Taylor (2001: 246, 242) writes that Gurdjieff seemed to agree with:

> the Orphic tenet that sexual union can precede marriage or take place without it and reacted as if love can not or must not be constrained by the administrative fetters of law in the social institution of marriage. [...] Gurdjieff spoke fondly of his parents and his family life as a boy, but had no intention of duplicating that domesticity in his own carefully controlled environment.

For Gurdjieff cosmic love was a divine emanation, a force implicit in the creative word that was identical to the Apostle John's *logos*, that which the Alexandrine philosophers at the beginning of the second century AD called *spermatologos* ('seed word'), comparable to Gurdjieff's *theomertma-logos* or Word-God (see *Tales*: 756). Gurdjieff had many women pupils, including the Rope group (see **Appendix 1**), who were lesbians, so it seems unlikely that he held fully or in a literal way to the notion that transmutation of sperm was necessary for the development of his pupils.

Further reading

See Webb (1980: 532) for Paschal Beverley Randolph's teaching on sex in relation to Gurdjieff; for Reich (1897–1957) and orgone energy, see Webb (1976: 472–4) and Reich (1983).

SEX CENTRE

The sex centre can be seen as the neutralising force of the triad of instinctive, moving and sex centres, which forms the lowest storey of the seven centres (see **centres**). However, the sex centre can also be taken as a centre on its own. It should function with Si 12 (see **hydrogens, table of**), but rarely does so. It is not divided into two like the other lower centres. Things are either pleasant or indifferent for it, but if it becomes connected to the negative part of the emotional or instinctive centres unpleasant feelings can result. When a man has no will or consciousness, the sex centre, which is stronger than the other centres, is inhibited by **buffers** and its energy is stolen by other centres; their functioning is recognisable by a kind of 'fervour'. As a result the sex centre has to work with inferior energy and so cannot receive the fine food of **impressions** that it is capable of. Other centres take energy from the sex centre and give it back energy that is wrong for it. If the sex centre works with its own energy, it is on the level of the higher emotional centre and indicates a person with a high level of being. Once the sex centre functions with its own energy, the other centres will function with their own energy; this will be helpful towards producing a permanent **centre of gravity**. The functioning of the moving and instinctive centres, in relation to the sex centre, depends on **type** (*Search*: 254–9). The sex centre is important in our life: 'seventy-five percent of thoughts come from the sex centre and they color all the rest' (*Views*, 1924: 126–7).

SHOCKS

Shocks must be given to man, to help him wake up, by someone whom he 'hires' to wake him (*Search*: 221; see **alarm clocks**; **groups**; **intervals**; **law of seven**). Gurdjieff gives examples of artificial mental and physical shocks needed for primary exercises in self-remembering (*Views*, 1923: 231–2).

In 'Man's Awakening' from 1967, Tracol (1994: 113) explains that Gurdjieff shocked his pupils out of blind worship by his language and the calculated contradictions in his behaviour. This obliged students to recognise the chaos of their own reactions, preparing them to do without Gurdjieff and go forward as soon as they were capable.

See also: **Law of Octaves**

SIN

Sins do not exist for people who are not on a 'way' (see **ways/fourth way**). For a person on or approaching a way, a sin is anything that prevents him from moving or that deceives him into thinking he is working when he is in fact asleep. Sins put men to sleep; they are everything that is unnecessary (*Search*: 357). To go against nature (e.g. against the **Law of Duality/Two**) is a sin, but we can do it because God has given us another law (*Views*, 1924: 199). 'If you already know it is bad and do it, you commit a sin difficult to redress' (*Views*: 273, aphorism 8).

Further reading

Compare Gurdjieff's tone of voice with St Paul in Romans 7–8 [King James Version].

SINCERITY

In relationship with others 'sincerity' is an unwillingness to restrain oneself. Sincerity should not be confused with lack of **considering**. A man should be cleverly sincere with those who are senior to him in the **Work**, and cleverly insincere with people who do not value the Work. Pupils do not know what it means to be sincere, they are used to lying to themselves (*Search*: 153, 230, 249). Fear of seeing the truth makes it difficult for a man to be sincere with himself. Sincerity is a function of **conscience**, which has, most often, ceased to work. If a pupil is sincere, Gurdjieff can help him to see his fears (*Views*, 1924: 241). In general, sincerity is weakness, even hysteria; a man must be able to be sincere and also to know when it is necessary (*Life*: 137–8). Be sincere with yourself only, trust no-one, neither brother nor sister. If you are sincere with others, they will 'sit on your head'; sincerity is a disease (*Voices*: 188).

SITTING *see* **New Work terminology**

SLAVERY/SLAVES

Man is a slave both outwardly and inwardly, and so cannot resist the planetary forces that cause **war**. The way to outward freedom is to gain inner freedom through self-knowledge. Unless a man understands the functioning of his machine, he will remain a slave (*Search*: 103–4; see **machine/mechanicality**; **sleep**). Although the general cosmic laws that man is under cannot be changed, it is possible to change one's own position in relation to them. The power of **sex**, for example, includes both the chief cause of slavery and the chief possibility for liberation (*Search*: 255). Around 1916, culture required automatons, so men were becoming willing slaves who were proud of and fond of their slavery; this is terrible (*Search*: 309). However, a pupil must become a slave voluntarily. He must do, say and think what he is told to by a teacher, because he realises his freedom is an illusion. Through slavery and obedience he can acquire everything (*Search*: 365; see **sacrifice**). Thus Gurdjieff tells us we are inevitably enslaved, either to our mechanical nature or to a teacher. He points out this inevitability in another way as 'passive man serves involution, active man serves evolution'. In both cases we are slaves, 'for in both cases we have a master' (*Views*, 1924: 198). Gurdjieff's thinking on voluntary slavery echoes the Christian notion of submission to the will of God, and also the injunction in Islam to become a slave to God.

Gurdjieff refers to chronic physical tension as one of the causes of slavery (*Views*, 1923: 120).

A different aspect of slavery was explored in the 1940s group meetings, where Gurdjieff expressed the need for us to make slaves of others. This is achieved through playing a **role** without inward **identification**. It is impossible for everyone to be equal: if we do not have slaves, we will be the slave of others. A pupil who has changed through his work, deserves objectively to have slaves. We enslave others by doing what they like, rather than what we like. A parent, or 'even God', can become enslaved (*Voices*: 54, 194).

Further reading

Romans 6: 15–19 [King James Version].

SLEEP

Gurdjieff referred to two states of sleep: the first sleep is at night; the second is usually regarded as waking consciousness, in which men walk, write and kill each other. This sleep is abnormal, hypnotic sleep, constantly maintained. We might think that there are forces that benefit from men's inability to see the truth. There is no organic reason for this hypnotic sleep. Theoretically a man can wake up, but practically it is almost impossible; generally a shock is necessary, and long, hard work (*Search*: 219, 221). We should understand sleep 'not in a literal sense of organic sleep, but in the sense of a state of associative existence' (*Views*, 1924: 70; see also **rolls**).

The **chief feature** of modern man's **being** is that he is asleep. He is born asleep, lives asleep and dies asleep (*Search*: 66). One person cannot escape sleep on his own, and even if a **group** of people get together to help each other, all may fall asleep and dream that they are awake, so they must find someone who is already awake and hire him to help them. There are many references to sleep (e.g. in the Gospels), but people take the idea of sleep as a metaphor. But man lives in a small part of himself where reality and **dreams** are mixed, and he cannot realise his full possibilities. The way to awaken is through **self-observation** (*Search*: 144).

At night there are different depths of sleep. These depend on the number of links maintained between **centres**. The better the functioning of the machine, the less time will be wasted on moving through transitional stages of sleep, between waking and sleeping, sleeping and waking. The purpose of sleep is achieved only in deep sleep when all links between centres are disconnected and there are no dreams (*Views*, 1923: 119; see **consciousness**).

Further reading

Tracol, 'Why Sleepest Thou, O Lord?' from 1981 (see Tracol 1994: 55–9).

'SLY' MAN

'The fourth way is sometimes called *the way of the sly man*. The "sly man" knows a secret which the fakir, monk and yogi do not know.' He may have found, stolen, bought or inherited this secret. However he acquired it, he outstrips the fakir, monk and yogi (*Search*: 50, original emphasis).

SOLIOONENSIUS, LAW OF *see* Law of Solioonensius

SOUL

Gurdjieff referred to the 'brains', or **centres**, as individual entities or souls (*Views*, 1923: 134). He also referred to the energy released at death as 'souls' (*Search*: 85). However, more usually he stressed the lack of a soul, saying that man is born without a soul and most people live without a soul, without a **master**. We can, however, make one. All religions lead differently towards the same place, where man has an 'I'. After that, the way is the same for all and the aim is to develop a soul, to fulfil our higher destiny. The soul is a luxury, unnecessary for ordinary life. To form it, a man must accumulate a surfeit of fine matter in his organism that can be crystallised to form a soul (*View*, 1924: 191–2, 214–18; also *Life*: 170; see also **bodies**; **religion/s, new religions**; **ways/fourth way**).

Gurdjieff's **aphorism** 'blessed is he who has a soul, blessed is he who has none, but woe and grief to him who has it in embryo' (*Views*: 275) reminds pupils that the soul is only gained through conscious **suffering**.

STAIRWAY

The 'stairway' connects ordinary life with the 'Way'. On the Fourth Way a man depends both on those immediately above him who are his teachers and on those below him whom he teaches (see **ways/fourth way**). In order to ascend the stairway he must put another person on his own step, all steps on the stairway must be occupied. Thus those on the stairway are interdependent and in unstable conditions, due to others, a person may fall down the stairway. Once he has completed the stairway, however, he is on the 'Way' and cannot lose what he has gained (*Search*: 201–2).

A pupil as he is cannot have contact with God, but he can take as an **ideal** whoever is closest to him, and pray to that person, who will also have an ideal person to pray to. God cannot be prayed to directly, but can be reached through stages. Gurdjieff suggests Jeanne de Salzmann as a person through whom the pupil can pray (*Voices*: 174; see **prayer/praying**).

STATE *see* consciousness

STEP DIAGRAM *see* Law of Reciprocal Maintenance/Reciprocal Feeding

STEWARD/DEPUTY STEWARD

An Eastern teaching tells of man's lack of real 'I' and the chaotic multiplicity of small 'I's, through the allegory of a house with many undisciplined servants. To save the house, the servants elect a deputy steward, who can direct them and prepare the house for the arrival of the **master** (*Search*: 60–1).

Further reading

Taylor 2001: 247–51.

STOP EXERCISE

Gurdjieff introduced the 'stop' exercise to his pupils in Essentuki in 1917. This exercise is a **school** discipline. At a sign from the teacher, the pupil must immediately stop what he is doing and freeze his posture, even if this is painful or dangerous, the responsibility for his well-being must be entrusted to the teacher. The purpose of this exercise is to catch the body in the midst of its habitual postures so that a pupil can learn what these are and with which thoughts and feelings these postures are connected. This is an exercise for the **attention** for **self-remembering**, in which the will of the pupil is activated by the teacher, and also an exercise for thoughts, feelings and moving centre. A pupil who wishes to evade work will find ways to evade 'stop', for example, by being careful in their movements not to expose themselves to discomfort (*Search*: 351–6). Non-mechanical study of oneself can only take place through the stop exercise given externally by a teacher. The uncustomary postures that result reveal to the pupil the circular interaction of body, thought and feeling postures, which otherwise cannot be broken or observed (*Views*, 1922: 155–8).

The 'stop' formed part of the demonstrations given by pupils in Paris and America in 1924. It was mentioned in the programme notes that are quoted in Bennett (1976 [1973]: 227–8), who refers to the stop as a Sufi exercise (see **sufi/sufism**).

STRIVINGS

For the five strivings advocated in *Tales*, see **duty/striving**.

STRUGGLE OF THE MAGICIANS

Ouspensky saw Gurdjieff's notice in a newspaper, which referred to his 'ballet' or 'revue', *The Struggle of the Magicians* (referred to here as *Magicians*). The struggle, set in an Eastern city, was between two schools, one of a white and one of a black magician. Exercises, songs and sacred national, Eastern and Dervish dances were performed. There was also an allegorical love story (*Search*: 17).

The origin of the dances in *Magicians* was the 'sacred dances' witnessed by Gurdjieff in Eastern temples. These dances demonstrate, for example, laws of the motions of the planets in the solar system. There are three thoughts at the basis of this ballet; however, these will not be recognised by the general public, for whom Gurdjieff's aim was to provide an interesting and beautiful spectacle (*Views*, 1918: 30–1; see also *Search*: 16–17).

In Constantinople in 1920 Ouspensky worked with Gurdjieff on the scenario of *Magicians* (this version was published in 1957). Gurdjieff continued work on the 'ballet' at his Institute in 1922 (*Search*: 382–3). Although never performed, *Magicians* links the Gurdjieff of 1914 with the Gurdjieff of 1948, when he rehearsed it in New York (Moore 1997: 349).

See also: **dances/dancing**

SUBCONSCIOUS

It is an error to understand the functions of the mind as conscious functioning, or as either **unconscious** or subconscious functioning, because we have three 'minds' (see **centres**). Definitions made by others of the subconscious are misleading because they define different categories of phenomenon as subconscious (*Search*: 54, 113; see also **consciousness**).

Gurdjieff's definition of the subconscious is different from Freud's. Gurdjieff defines the subconscious as being of a higher level than everyday waking-consciousness. **Faith**, **hope**, **love** and **conscience**, all of which ought to exist in man's waking state, have been driven by his abnormalities into his subconsciousness, and these two conscious-nesses, waking and subconscious, have nothing in common (*Tales*: 559, 579, 564–8).

The understanding of truths about self-perfection, and the formation of what is necessary for this, must take place in the subconscious. However, because man cannot take anything directly from his consciousness into his subconscious, we must make use of **imagination**. This can form a link between the active and passive states of consciousness (*Life*: 133–4). In *Tales*, Beelzebub relates two circulations of the blood to conscious and subconscious functioning, and uses hypnotism to alter the relation between these functions (see **hypnosis/hypnotism**).

The Foundations advocate reading *Tales* aloud, without analysis, so that it may be received in the subconscious.

Further reading

For notions that, although expressed in terms of Sun Mystery, are strikingly similar to Gurdjieff's teaching of the sinking of the conscience into the subconscious, see a lecture on 'The Sun Mystery in the Course of Human History: The Palladian' given by Steiner in Dornam, Germany, on 6 November 1921 (Steiner 1955: 16–17). According to Moore (1991: 327), Gurdjieff was in Germany from the summer of 1921 and in Hellerau in November 1921.

SUFFERING/PLEASURE

Gurdjieff distinguished between unconscious suffering, which is without value, and conscious suffering, sometimes termed 'voluntary' or 'deliberate' suffering, through which we can self-perfect. The term 'intentional suffering' is used in *Tales* and can be equated with conscious suffering. Gurdjieff refers to the difference between voluntary and intentional suffering without defining the difference. He writes of the possibility of regulating his own health by means of intentional suffering (*Life*: 151–3). In *Herald* he also uses the phrase 'deliberate suffering and conscious labor' (*Herald*: 82), and later 'prepared suffering'. We must know what makes us suffer and then make use of it, as the fire that 'cooks, cements, crystallizes, *does*', because when a person is conscious there is no more suffering, and we must suffer to repay **Nature** for cosmic substances, that is, for the food we eat (*Voices*: 25).

Work consists of subjecting oneself voluntarily to temporary suffering in order to be free from eternal suffering. Pleasure that is not earned turns into suffering (*Search*: 357). Orage defined suffering as evil if we pass it on to others, but that if 'eaten' suffering can be transformed and used for the creation of being (*Teachings*: 94). Thus, if we belong to one stream of life, our suffering depends on what happens to us and we suffer in retribution because we are unhappy;

but it is possible to belong to another stream of life in which suffering is voluntary and takes place in advance of events. Voluntary suffering has value in that eventually 'everything is paid for'. Suffering 'pierces the crust' that forms round **conscience** and the experience of this is painful (*Views*, 1924: 84–5, 247–8; *Search*: 156). It is not possible to destroy suffering, because that would entail destroying a 'whole series of perceptions for which man exists, and also because suffering is necessary as a shock' (*Search*: 307–8).

However, unconscious suffering (e.g. suffering hunger for lack of money) will have no result: it is better to have bread and voluntarily not eat it. Unconscious suffering, in one centre only, leads to the lunatic asylum (*Views*, 1924: 101). Intentional suffering must be practised together with conscious labour in order to self-perfect (see **conscious labour and intentional/voluntary suffering**).

In the 1940s group meetings Gurdjieff urged physical suffering, not eating or subjecting the body to what it dislikes, (e.g. cold water), as a means of promoting the struggle that will create the substance needed for crystallisation of 'different factors for the real functioning of conscious associations'; and emotional suffering, through recall by pupils of their own bad actions in the past, usually in relation to their parents. He refers to 'prepared' suffering. We have to know what will make us suffer and then, when this occurs, make use of it (*Voices*: 146, 198, 274, 25).

We may wonder if the disallowing of emotional relationship with any but family members, and the forgoing of all pleasures, may also have been a cause of pupils' suffering (see **sacrifice**).

SUFI/SUFISM

Taylor (2001: 229–30) writes that much in Sufism had been shaped by earlier esoteric teachings, including those of Pythagoras, and that while Gurdjieff did not speak specifically of Sufism, he did often speak of the Dervish traditions in connection with the Work. Taylor notes that the Dervishes are considered, by most historians of religion, as distinct from the mainstream Sufi hierarchy.

Gurdjieff's character the Dervish Bogga-Eddin occurs in both *Tales* and *Meetings*. In *Tales*, he leads Beelzebub to meet the Dervish Hadji-Asvatz-Troov, the only Earth being to whom Beelzebub reveals his true identity. In *Meetings*, it is through an introduction of Bogga-Eddin's that Gurdjieff is led to the Sarmoung Brotherhood, where he learns about sacred dancing. Ouspensky recalls visiting the Mehlevi

Dervishes in Constantinople in 1920 with Gurdjieff, who explained their whirling dances as containing counting exercises similar to those he had taught his pupils (*Search*: 382–3; see also **dances**; **stop exercise**).

Gurdjieff's pupil J.G. Bennett (see **appendix 1**) spoke and read Turkish fluently, and travelled in the Middle East. His own experience of Sufism led him to perceive close connections between Sufi teaching and the Work, especially the Naqshbandi Order of Dervishes (Bennett 1963, 1976 [1973]; see also **grace**). Bennett's own views – and his involvement with Idries Shah, who claimed to come from the secret centre where Gurdjieff had been taught, led to an acceptance of the Sufi origins of the enneagram among Bennett's pupils, though not by members of the Foundations (see Washington 1993: 394–8; Moore [n.d.]: 4–8, 1992: 8–11).

Further reading

Johnson 1987, 1990, 1995; Bennett 1963. For Idries Shah, see Shah 1966, 1970.

SUN ABSOLUTE, THE

In *Tales*, the Sun Absolute is the dwelling place of His Endlessness (God)

See also: **Absolute, the**

SUNS, ALL *see* **Ray of Creation**

SUPER-EFFORT

Ordinary efforts are not enough, only super-efforts 'count'. It would be better to die from making a super-effort to wake up, than to continue to live in sleep. However, this is unlikely because men have recourse to more energy than they realise through **accumulators** (*Search*: 232–3). Pupils need a **school** where the school methods and discipline will enable pupils to carry out super-efforts: that is, to go beyond the ordinary requirement in obedience to a teacher, or to perform a task in half the time it usually takes (see **centres**; *Search*: 346–8, also in relation to **New Work** and **religion**). For an account of an impractical group super-effort, see Peters (1976 [1964, 1965]: 64–5).

SYMBOLS/SYMBOLISM

The symbols used to transmit objective knowledge to the higher intellectual centre can be understood only if a pupil has been properly prepared, in which case the symbol can also show the pupil the way to objective knowledge. Symbols are useful as a synthesis of what is already understood, but will not of themselves transmit understanding. Symbols cannot be understood literally, nor can their content be given directly, but they can be an impetus for work. The pupil must make his own effort to understand them and to relate them both to the external world and to his own interior functioning. In this way they serve as a synthesis of his knowledge. Symbols were classified as 'fundamental symbols', which include the expression of the separate domains of knowledge, and 'subordinate symbols', which express 'the essential nature of phenomenon in relation to **unity**'.

'Symbols which are transposed into the words of ordinary language become rigid in them, they grow dim and very easily become "their own opposites" '. Gurdjieff describes the 'formula' 'know thyself' as a symbol leading to the knowledge of truth (*Search*: 279–85)

See also: **analogy/analogy; enneagram; understanding, literal; myth; ways/Fourth Way**

SYSTEM/THE SYSTEM

This term was used, especially by Ouspensky and his pupils, to refer to the **Work** as a system of ideas.

TABLE OF HYDROGENS *see* **hydrogens, table of**

TALKING

Whereas total silence is an evasion of life, unnecessary talking wastes a large amount of energy. Unnecessary talking is difficult to observe, because people usually connect talking with what are seen as 'good' traits, such as being helpful or being interested in others. For those in the Work to go beyond the limit of the necessary, whether in talking, eating or sleeping is a **sin** (*Search*: 356–7).

TEACHER

The higher the level of the pupil, the higher the level of the teacher: e.g. to have a teacher of the level of Christ, a pupil would need to be of the level of the apostles; if he were of a lower level, he would not benefit. A pupil cannot see higher than his own level and therefore cannot see the level of his teacher. On the Fourth Way (see **ways/ fourth way**), there is more than one teacher (*Search*: 202–3; see also **stairway**). There are false teachers that can deceive naïve pupils, who will become infatuated and even fanatical. This is why the production of infatuation is not allowed in the Work (*Search*: 227; see also **magic/ magician**). Pupils of a teacher must trust and accept the teacher totally, they cannot work if they accept one thing and reject another (*Search*: 270). Compare this with other statements about the necessity for independent critical ability: e.g. Gurdjieff's injunction to judge everything with common sense, not to 'accept anything on faith' (*Views*, 1918: 27).

As well as 'obligatory' study, each teacher has his own specialisation (e.g. sculpture or music) through which he teaches. If a pupil finds the specialisation alien to him, he must find another teacher (*Search*: 374). However, Gurdjieff also suggested that a teacher should pay attention to the pupil's interests and accordingly teach through those interests. A pupil who is sincerely seeking will become convinced of the necessity of a teacher who can be his spiritual guide, but it is extremely difficult to recognise the person who is able to guide (*Views*, 1918: 14–15, 57–8; see **difficulties**).

Contemporary education focuses on the logical. However, a teacher, when speaking symbolically about objective knowledge, the unity of diversity, cannot be understood logically (see **symbols/ symbolism**). Objective knowledge cannot be given, but must be worked for by the pupil (*Search*: 284–5). A pupil needs constant observation and definite rules in order to remember himself and to struggle with habits; for this he needs a teacher's will and stick (*Search*: 348).

TELEPATHY

When the **group** find themselves together they can do an **exercise**; the **atmosphere** around them can help them to aspire with all their being to a common aim. They can affect a whole city; they have knowledge of different telepathic acts. The material of the atmosphere is formed like a large spider's web: if a force enters one of the meshes, it can be conducted across the whole network as if through an electrical conduit. If pupils meet accidentally, they must do an exercise with all their mass towards succeeding in their aim, through auto-suggestion and representation by subjective forms. They should imagine they are in a network; if a current enters at one point, all points will feel it. 'Picture how what happens in one place happens everywhere' (*Voices*: 206–7).

See also: **occult/occult revival**

TERROR OF THE SITUATION, THE

In Chapter 26 of *Tales*, Beelzebub tells of the teaching of Ashiata Shiemash, a Messenger from Above, who came to help humanity. Ashiata understands that humans have functions that are similar to Faith, Hope and Love (although not genuine) and that Objective Conscience is buried in their subconscious. He decides to create conditions so that their objective conscience can participate in their waking existence. Orage (*Teachings*: 195) defines 'the terror of the situation' as being man's diversion from his true purpose: he develops the outer life at the expense of the inner.

THEORY/PRACTICE

In the beginning, Gurdjieff gave pupils theoretical indications of how to work, but only as much as they could put into practice. If they did not work, he would not say more (*Views*, 1923: 105; see **schools**).

THEOSOPHICAL ADDITION

Theosophical addition is a form of numerology in which any number of more than one digit is reduced to one digit by addition.

For example, 365 becomes $3 + 6 + 5 = 14$, 14 becomes $1 + 4 = 5$.

This method resolves all diversity into the fundamental laws that govern it, expressed in the numbers from one to ten. Gurdjieff explains his own Law of Seven as being relevant to all the numbers, one to ten, because the seven notes plus two intervals make nine and the eighth note that starts the new octave is added to make ten (*Search*: 283).

Figure 27 Theosophical Addition: Theosophical addition of fines

Fines	Dollars	Theosophical Addition	Total	Total All Fines
First	3,648	=3+6+4+8=21, 2+1	=3	
Second	1,824	=1+8+2+4=15, 1+5	=6	
Third	912	=9+1+2=1 +2	=3	
Fourth	456	=4+5+6= 1+5	=6	
Fifth	228	=2+2+8=12, 1+2	=3	
Sixth	114	=1+1+4	=6	
Seventh	57	=5+7=12 1+2	=3	
Total Fines			=30	=3
Three Additional Fines				
1	10		1	
2	40		4	
3	20		2	
Total Additional Fines	70	7+0	1+4+2	=7
Gurdjieff's received fines totalling	113,000			
Half of which he kept	56,500	5+6+5=16 =1=6	=7	=7

Note: there are seven fines, adding up theosophically to three; three additional fines adding up to seven; and half the total fines that Gurdjieff received add up to seven.

Many of the numbers in Gurdjieff's texts reduce to three or seven if Theosophical addition is used: e.g. the fines given to pupils in *Life*: 126–27 (see Figure 27).

THEOSOPHY

Although Gurdjieff repudiated Helena Petrovna Blavatsky (1831–91) and Theosophy, there are many similarities between the mythology of their lives, their teachings and their writings. Both were born in southern Russia and exposed to the various races and religions of the Caucasus. Youthful rebellion was followed by years of wandering in search of ancient wisdom (Johnson 1990). Blavatsky's idea of a specially evolved group of men, 'the **Masters**', living in Tibet and in some way controlling human destiny, probably came from eighteenth-century occult Masonic theory, which proposed that there were 'Secret Chiefs' who knew ultimate secrets. This became common occult doctrine, and later the 'Secret Chiefs' were held to be supernatural (Webb 1971: 147). Gurdjieff's **conscious circle of humanity** is an echo of Blavatsky's 'Masters'.

The terms 'carbon' 'oxygen', 'nitrogen' and 'hydrogen', which Gurdjieff uses for the four **elements** and which correspond to the four alchemical/astrological elements, come from Blavatsky (1988 [1888]: 593). Ouspensky writes that:

> [the] attempts to establish the origin of these names explained to me a great deal concerning the whole of G's system as well as its history.

This shows that Ouspensky acknowledged the Theosophical origins of some of Gurdjieff's teaching (*Search*: 90).

Both Blavatsky and Gurdjieff wrote texts that were concerned with ancient cultures, myths, religions, languages, texts and symbols. Both included Atlantis and Babylon as ancient civilisations whose wisdom had been lost. Both expounded on consciousness, initiation, electricity, magnetism and hypnosis. Webb (1980: 533) suggests Blavatsky's *Secret Doctrine* (1988 [1888]), in which there are references to the four bodies of man and the **Ray of Creation**, as a probable starting point for Gurdjieff's occult synthesis. Gurdjieff's pupils with some background in Theosophy would have recognised his cosmology and Laws of Three and Seven from their reading of *The Secret Doctrine*. Blavatsky's plan for the four volumes of *Secret Doctrine* is echoed by Gurdjieff's plan for his own texts. Gurdjieff's First Series, *Tales*, corresponds to volumes one and two of *Secret Doctrine*, which were to deal with the evolution of the cosmos and the evolution of man. Gurdjieff's Second Series, *Meetings*, corresponds to Blavatsky's third volume, which was to be about the lives of famous occultists. His Third Series, *Life*, corresponds to her fourth volume, which was to deal with practical occultism.

There is also a similarity between their stated aims. Blavatsky writes:

> until *the rubbish of the ages* is cleared away from the minds of the Theosophists [...] it is impossible that the more practical

teaching contained in the Third Volume should be understood.

(Blavatsky 1988 [1888]: vol.2, p.798; emphasis added)

Gurdjieff's aim for *Tales* was to destroy his reader's world-view, so that material in *Meetings* might be used to build a new world. He expresses this aim in a phrase, written as a quotation, almost identical to Blavatsky's: 'to corrode without mercy all *the rubbish accumulated during the ages* in human mentation' (*Tales*: 1184, emphasis added). Gurdjieff is also connected to Blavatsky through his choice of Beelzebub as the hero of *Tales*. Blavatsky entitled her magazine *Lucifer* (first published 15 September 1887) – Lucifer being the fallen angel whose myth is similar to Beelzebub's. In each case, the choice seems to be a continuation of the Romantic tradition of the anti-hero who represents aspects of the internalised myth of the Fall. Both Blavatsky and Gurdjieff actively invited disparagement as charlatan gurus.

See also: **hypnosis/hypnotism; occult/occult revival**

Further reading

On Theosophy, see Blavatsky (1988 [1888]); Ashish and Prem (1969); Ashish (1970); Carlson (1993); Washington (1993); Goodwyn (1994); Johnson (1994, 1995). For Annie Besant and Theosophy, see Wessinger (1988). For Theosophy, Hinduism and the Work, see Ginsburg (2001).

THINKING/THOUGHTS

Psychic power, of which will is a function (see **will/free will**), depends on a person's thinking centre, its functioning and content. In order to economise psychic power, we should often try to stop 'it' thinking. Whatever 'it' is thinking about is not valuable, and although it is difficult to stop 'it' thinking, it is possible (*Views*, 1923: 162; see **centres; intellectual/thinking centre, intelligence; reason**). Gurdjieff also uses the terms 'mentation', 'cognition' and 'pondering'.

THREE–STOREY FACTORY/DIGESTION OF THREE FOODS

The food diagrams (*Search*: 182–90) show how matter is transformed within the human body, which is defined as a factory having three storeys: the head, the chest, and the back and lower body. Gurdjieff describes three octaves that transform the three **foods**: the food we eat, **air** and **impressions**.

Each transformation takes the substance to a higher level of matter, through a process in which the three forces act in matter. The substance to be acted on is defined as 'oxygen', and conducts the passive force. When this is combined with a 'carbon', which conducts an active force, the result is 'new matter': a 'nitrogen' that conducts the neutralising force of this triad. When this substance is transformed further, a new triad begins: the 'nitrogen' substance becomes 'oxygen' and passive in relation to the next active 'carbon' (see Figure 28).

The first food octave starts with the note Do. This passive 'oxygen' is acted on by an active 'carbon' existing in the body, and results in the note Re. Re combines with a higher 'carbon' to produce Mi. In order for Mi to ascend to Fa, a shock is necessary; this is provided by the

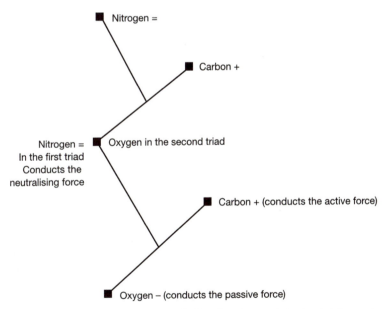

Figure 28   Three-Story Factory: Food: digestion, 'oxygen', 'carbon', 'nitrogen'

intake of air, which provides the Do of the air octave. The first food octave continues to Si 12 (see Figure 29). Si 12 is the finest energy in the physical body: it is the energy from which an astral body can be built (*Views*, 1924: 187).

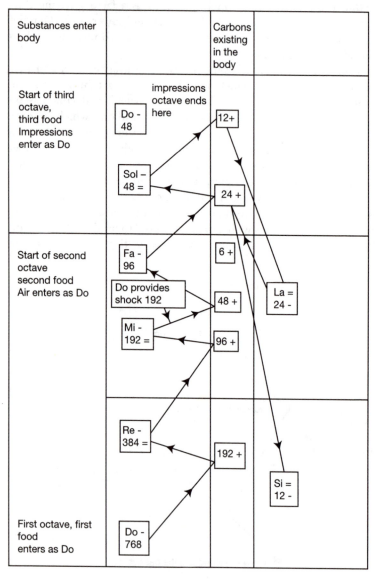

Figure 29 Three-Story Factory: digestion of first food

See Figure 30 for the development of the air octave and the beginning of the octave of impressions. Figure 31 shows how the stopped octaves of air and impressions are enabled to continue up to a certain point through the practice of **self-remembering**, the reception of impressions in a new way.

However, the food and impressions octaves might continue to develop further if they receive a second conscious shock. This is

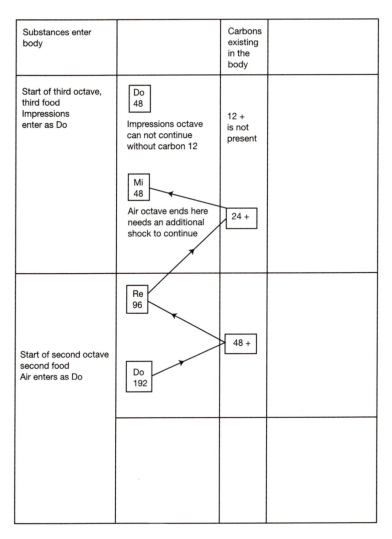

Figure 30   Three-Story Factory: digestion of air

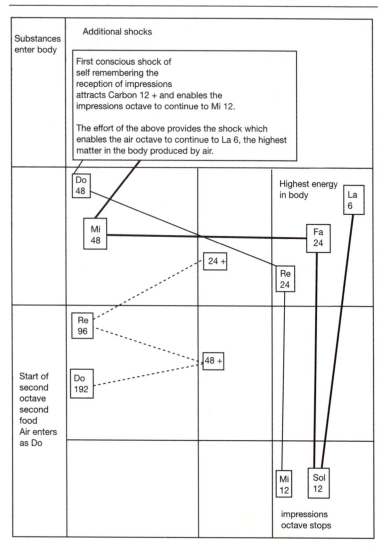

Figure 31 Three-Story Factory: digestion of impressions

connected with the emotions, the practice of not **considering**, not identifying and not expressing unpleasant emotions. Should the factory work with two conscious shocks, it would produce a quantity of fine matter that would change the character of the factory. The transformation of matter within the human body, thanks to the shocks it receives, is analogous to the transformation of matter in the three octaves of the **Ray of Creation**. The shocks can be equated with the intervals in the Ray of Creation (*Search*: 191).

The organism needs the coarse matters provided by the first and second foods, and this cannot be changed. However, the quality of impressions is not under cosmic law and can be improved, and this makes evolution possible. Man can feed on 'hydrogens' of impressions that are H 24, H 12, H 6 and even H 3. Such a man will not be the same as one who feeds on lower 'hydrogens' (*Search*: 321–2).

Just as the Ray of Creation, in relation to the table of hydrogens, shows in diagram form how the universe is created in descending triads from the finest matter to the coarsest, so the three-storey factory diagrams show the transformation of matter in ascending triads from the coarser to the finer matter (see also **alchemy; food; matter**).

Most of the energy produced by the three-storey factory is wasted on, among other things, muscular tension (*Search*: 350; also *Views*, 1914: 22–4, 1924: 201–2; see also **exercises**).

TIME/THE ETERNAL

Time was a subject of especial interest to Ouspensky, who brings together two pieces of information given by Gurdjieff: that time is breath, and that our sleeping and waking are the breath of organic life on earth. From these he constructed a table that shows the scale of time for an impression, a breath, a day and night, and a lifetime for eleven different cosmoses. He examines the time of breath as giving the sensation of the present, and from this deduces that a cosmos does not perceive itself in the same way as other cosmoses perceive it. The earth, for example, whose time of breath he calculated as eighty years, would experience itself in the form of a spiral formed of the eighty rotations round the sun that it would make during this time. Thus the earth would not experience itself in the way we experience it, as a sphere. He explored the relativity of time in different cosmoses and this enabled him to understand the functioning of the human body. If a relative concept of time is accepted, then what is an almost instantaneous time taken for a disease to infect an organism in our timescale becomes, for the infecting cosmos, a period equal to four centuries of our time. Ouspensky also constructed a table of the distance in kilometres travelled by light in each of the cosmoses, and related the different time in the cosmoses to time in the **centres**. He equated some of these ideas with **Gnostic** and Indian notions of cosmic time (e.g. the breath of Brahma, the days and nights of Brahma, and an age of Brahma). If the Brahma is equated with the Protocosmos, then the idea that Brahma 'breathes in and breathes out the universe' coincides with Ouspensky's Macrocosmos, our visible starry world. Ouspensky expressed time as the fourth dimension (see **dimensions**), in each moment of which there is a finite number of possibilities. However, each moment in time has an infinite existence in eternity (*Search*: 339–40, 329–34, 210–11). We can understand Ouspensky's theoretical extrapolations as tacitly accepted by Gurdjieff, who read the unpublished manuscript of *Search* and approved it.

In relation to life-span, Gurdjieff said that each centre has its allotted time to run, but that time exists only internally and is measured by associations. Life can be prolonged by spending the energy of the centres slowly and economically. 'Learn to think consciously. This produces economy in the expenditure of energy. Don't dream' (*Views*, 1924: 121–3).

Time is a central theme in Gurdjieff's writings. There are time anomalies in the narratives of his texts, each of which has differing time-spans: from the creation of the universe to 1921 in *Tales*; a period of about forty years in *Meetings*; and just over a decade in *Life*. The disjunction of sequential time is expressed most fully in *Life* (see **Life is Real Only Then, When 'I Am'**).

In the cosmology of *Tales*, the dichotomy of temporal and eternal is expressed in the **Ray of Creation** as a Fall. Time, referred to in *Tales* as the Heropass, is expelled from the Sun Absolute and, as in the Biblical creation when Adam and Eve are expelled from the Garden of Eden into a temporal world, the result is toil, suffering and death. Gurdjieff expresses his version of the relativity of time in Chapter 16 of *Tales*, where the beings in a drop of water experience their life-spans just as we do on Earth, although their lives in our experience last only a few seconds.

Thus we can see that in *Tales* time and the eternal are not expressed exclusively as separate concepts, but time is elided into the eternal (i.e. there may be extremely long life-spans, but these are not eternal). From man's perception, the higher the world, the longer the life-span. The quality of man's inner world also affects his life-span: this has diminished as the quality of his being has diminished. The Heropass alone has no source and, like divine love, blends with everything in the universe. Gurdjieff expresses an ambivalence towards time, which, although expressed as the 'disease of tomorrow' – is also that which will save man (*Tales*: 124, 362–3, 1118; see also **death**).

Gurdjieff's teaching and writings were influenced by contemporary interests in both pre-modern and post-modern concepts of time. Pre-modern concepts of time were explored and understood in relation to the change from lunar to solar calendars, and in the Greek Archaic epics (see **writings**). Modern concepts of time had been destroyed by Einstein's theory of relativity. Webb writes that Gurdjieff's teaching,

> having destroyed the Newtonian world of inherited conditioning, erected an astonishing Einsteinian universe where nothing was what it seemed, and where relationships of cause and effect were blurred or rearranged in new patterns.

(Webb 1980: 548)

See also: **astrology**

Further reading

Nicoll 1952; Ouspensky 1984 [1931].

TOAST OF/TO THE IDIOTS; THE SCIENCE OF IDIOTISM

In this ritual, introduced by Gurdjieff in 1922, toasts were drunk, usually in armagnac or vodka, to a hierarchy of 'idiots' ranging from 1, ordinary idiot, to 21, the Unique Idiot, which was God. Toasts were proposed and formally defined by a Director. The toasts most often given are: (1) ordinary, (2) super, (3) arch, (4) hopeless, (5) compassionate, (6) squirming, (7) square, (8) round, (9) zigzag, (10) enlightened, (11) doubting and (12) swaggering. The remaining ones are recalled as: (13) born, (14) patented, (15) psychopathic; these idiots may involve or evolve. (I have not found a definition for 16.) Idiots 17 to 21 reflect gradations of objective reason: no name is given for 17, 18 is the highest that can be reached, but can only be acquired after first descending to 1 (the ordinary idiot) and re-ascending; idiots 19 and 20 were for the sons of God. This ritual may derive from the still extant Georgian tradition (Moore 1991: 353–5). Bennett (1976 [1973]: 157) recalls Gurdjieff explaining that his 'Science of Idiotism' had come from a Sufi community (see **sufi/sufism**). However, Moore (1991: 355) doubts this, pointing out that alcohol is forbidden in Islam.

Bennett gives 'to be oneself' as an additional meaning of the word 'idiot'. Pupils had to choose their own category of idiot; the alcohol was given to strengthen the pupil's wish; a death and resurrection must be experienced in each stage in the change from one type of idiot to another. Bennett recalls the 'enlightened idiot' as being the one from which conscious descent must be made. He recalls Gurdjieff equating this with the saying of Jesus: 'Except ye become as little children, ye shall in no wise enter the kingdom of heaven' (Bennett 1976 [1973]: 158–9).

Taylor (1998: 170–71n.) recalls that usually seven or eight toasts were sufficient for a meal, and that the categories could vary. He understands 'idiot' as referring to:

> [the] particular 'idiosyncrasy' of a person, which holds him back from 'wholeness' of being and which chains him to mechanical behavior. [. . .] The number of toasts reflects the Platonic scale or chain of being between God and man, that is, the orbits of the seven visible planets and the musical proportions their distance from each other describes.

Taylor notes that Gurdjieff's meals, a combination of 'aristocratic material and philosophical orders', resemble Plato's *Symposium*, in which the form and use of the drinking cup is a metaphysical bond with the transcendent.

Nott defines Gurdjieff's term 'idiotism' as coming partly from the medieval English, in the sense of 'peculiar character or genius of a language, or a deviation from its strict syntactical rules.' He writes that according to Gurdjieff the Science of Idiotism was a mirror in which a man could see himself. He gives an account of how understanding his own 'idiot' showed him his **chief feature** (*Teachings*: 101–2, 217). Nott recounts the difference between a subjective and objective hopeless idiot. Those who work on themselves will have an honourable death, the others will 'perish like dogs' (*Journey*: 218).

The ritual toast of the idiots is one of Gurdjieff's teaching methods not continued by the Foundations.

Further reading

Zuber 1990 [1977]: 69–73.

TYPE

The science of types must be studied by meeting people. People of the same type will look alike, and have the same likes and dislikes. Although there are said to be twelve or more types, men usually meet only the six or seven fundamental types. The others are combinations of the fundamental types. To study types, one must know one's own type and be able to depart from it. Gurdjieff gave an exercise relating to types, in which pupils told their life stories in the group (*Search*: 246–7).

If men and women were to live in **essence**, they would find the right type, but wrong types come together because people live in personality and so the types/essences hate one another (*Search*: 254). People need to have near them a corresponding type of the opposite sex for mutual completion of their type. If sexual desire is gratified with someone of the wrong type, most of the typical manifestations of their individuality will gradually be lost (*Meetings*: 56; see also **gender**).

In relation to movements and breathing, Gurdjieff said that each type requires its own specific movement to induce a specific kind of breathing. Knowledge of the movements that cause a particular kind of breathing enables a man to control his organism, to set a centre in motion or to stop it (*Search*: 388).

Gurdjieff relates type with essence and astrological sign (refer to **astrology** and the **enneagram** of personality; *Search*: 366–7).

UNCONSCIOUS/UNCONSCIOUSNESS

Unconscious functioning can be understood as the state of 'sleep' or 'waking consciousness' in which man functions mechanically (see **machine/mechanicality**; **sleep**). See also the entry on **subconscious**, which is of a higher level than 'waking consciousness', and on **consciousness**, **conscience** and **psyche/psychology**.

Moore (1991: 59) equates Gurdjieff's notion of the unconscious mind, more or less, with the instinctive centre's functioning, with the cardio-vascular, respiratory, endocrinological, digestive, nervous and other autonomic systems.

Further reading

For a history of the unconscious that examines Janet, Freud, Adler and Jung against a socioeconomic background, see Ellenberger 1970; for Mesmer and the unconscious, see Crabtree 1993.

UNDERSTANDING

Understanding differs from knowledge. Understanding depends on the 'relationship of knowledge to being'. In order to understand more, we need growth of being rather than more knowledge. The intellectual centre may know something, but we will only understand it if we also feel and/or sense what is connected to this knowledge; that is, if two or three centres are connected. The difference between knowledge and understanding can be seen in the difference between knowing what to do and knowing how to do it. People believe that they have a common language, but apart from practical language this is untrue. In order to understand one another, we need the language of **relativity** (*Search*: 67–70).

See also: **allegory/analogy; Law of Duality/Two; symbols/symbolism**

UNDERSTANDING, LITERAL

Gurdjieff tells a pupil in 'Glimpses of Truth' that their talk will not be about the literal meaning of the saying 'as above, so below'. The pupil must 'never take anything literally' (*Views*, 1914: 14–5; 1924: 201, 260). When religious, alchemical or magical **symbols** are taken literally, they cause delusions (*Search*: 284).

Bennett (1976: 7–9) quotes Ouspensky as having written, around 1923, that Gurdjieff gave his pupils the beginning of ideas and waited to see what they made of them. If the pupil remembered the ideas literally, as Gurdjieff had given them, or if he thought that there was a secret, which he must find out, then he would lose the idea even in the form he had heard it. Ouspensky concluded that Gurdjieff's ideas were 'living': they never remained in their original form and would only grow if 'tended'.

We can see that if, for example, we take the **Ray of Creation** literally, then we find that there is a disparity between the involutionary and evolutionary processes. On the downward flow of the Ray of Creation, the suns and planets are created sequentially: i.e. our Sun remains a sun and, when the planets are created, the Sun continues to exist. However, in the evolutionary process, a planet becomes a sun. This suggests that there could be two sets of suns: the suns created during the involutionary process, which had not yet evolved, and the suns that are evolved planets. If, as Gurdjieff suggests, the Moon could evolve into a planet and subsequently into a sun, this suggests that all matter could be totally reabsorbed back into the **Absolute**. Thus any circular system of reciprocal maintenance could not function (see **law of reciprocal maintenance/reciprocal feeding; moon**).

A senior pupil of Gurdjieff's said that a paper had been found in which Gurdjieff refers to the 'Law of Nine', that perhaps this later became the Law of Seven; in any case, Gurdjieff wanted his pupils to be bewildered by what he said, so that they would continue to examine what they understood themselves and move on from there (Ravindra 1999: 47).

See also: **allegory/analogy; symbols/symbolism**

Further reading

For interpretation of texts, see Valdes 1991; for Biblical exegesis and hermeneutics, see LaCocque and Ricoeur 1999. See Thompson 1991 for an exploration of an open text.

UNITY

Gurdjieff applies the concept of unity to man and to the universe. Man is a multiplicity of small 'I's, but he can obtain inner unity through fusion brought about by **friction**. Man number five has obtained unity (*Search*: 32, 59–60, 71). In relation to the universe, the **Absolute** is the state of things when the 'All' constitutes one whole, infinite and indivisible. The idea of the unity of everything, of unity in diversity, is one of the central ideas of objective knowledge, which can only be understood by those with objective consciousness. For those with subjective consciousness, the world is split into 'millions of separate and unconnected phenomena' and cannot be expressed in ordinary language. This idea has therefore been expressed through **myth** and **symbols**. The symbol that unites all knowledge of the **Ray of Creation** is the **enneagram** (*Search*: 76, 278–9, 285).

Gurdjieff spoke to a pupil, by analogy (see **allegory/analogy**), of the overall unity of all that exists, about unity in multiplicity. 'Everything in the universe is one', the difference is only in scale; the same laws govern the great and the infinitely small (*Views*, 1914: 15–6).

Further reading

For the experience of the universe as one, which is central to mystical experience, see James 1985 [1929]; Ginsburg 2001.

VAMPIRISM

Vampirism is a science unknown to medicine. Gurdjieff suggests it can be practised consciously and unconsciously; as a result of vampirism the person being drained may grow paler or thinner. A certain vampirism occurs in the **group**, when they are all seated round a table: if members of the group holds hands with each other, there is a chain connecting everyone and Gurdjieff could drain 'the doctor until she dies of it' (*Voices*: 75–6).

Orage says that some people are vampires and will suck us dry, if we let them (*Teachings*: 143).

VIBRATIONS *see* **matter**

VIEWS FROM THE REAL WORLD: EARLY TALKS OF GURDJIEFF

Published in 1973, *Views* contains an account of a pupil's first meeting with Gurdjieff and thirty-nine talks given between 1917 and 1930. However, most of these talks were given in 1923 and 1924. They are ordered thematically rather than chronologically, and together give an overview of Work teaching. However, the talks (and the notes taken of them) were not always in English, so there is room for inaccuracy. (For an account of the compilation of *Views* by Jeanne de Salzmann, see Kherdian 1998: 192.)

Views shows that according to Gurdjieff's theory there are many ways to define a person and his functioning: through centres; centres and formatory apparatus; essence, personality and body; or mind and personality. His list of people's inabilities is also continually redefined, as are the starting points and directions for making efforts. However, each starting point from which the pupil might hope to overcome a disability leads on mainly to the experience and acknowledgement of further disabilities.

Man's helplessness is emphasised by the use of romantically dramatic language: 'abyss', 'quagmire of pseudo-knowledge', 'the dark labyrinths of human stupidity' and a green flowery meadow that hides a precipice all occur in a talk given in 1918.

Gurdjieff said that his teaching was not for everybody, and indeed the attraction for pupils of their uncompromisingly bleak power-lessness in the 'real world' needs to be understood in the context of the powerlessness experienced by them in the face of the Russian Revolution and World War I. Only those who are already despairing of themselves and of their contemporary 'world' are likely to accept this view of humanity (see the note on World War I in **faith**, and also **politics**).

Views gives a more direct recounting of Gurdjieff's talks than Ouspensky's accounts in *Search*. It sometimes has a warmer tone, and the later part of the book contains more optimistic views of the possibilities for waking up. However, much of *Views* is as Gnostically despairing of the state of man as is *Search* (see **difficulties**; **gnosticism**).

VOLUNTARY SUFFERING *see* **suffering/pleasure**

WAKING UP/AWAKENING

Organically, man can awaken; he sleeps because he is hypnotised (see **hypnosis/hypnotism**). At first a man must experience waking up in brief flashes, then more continuously when the full horror of his own mechanicality and nothingness gives him the courage to die to and give up all the small 'I's within him (see **'I'/identity**) that hinder his waking up (*Search*: 220).

In 1967 Tracol noted:

> Awakening is not the conquest of a state of higher consciousness. It is a movement, repeatedly attempted and repeatedly desired, a return to the consciousness of *what is*.
>
> (Tracol 1994: 112, emphasis in original)

Awakening requires a rupture in the thread of continuity, a change of levels, an **interval** between two completely different states (Tracol 1994: 113).

WAR

Gurdjieff arrived in pre-Revolutionary Moscow in 1912. Ouspensky notes that the start of World War I in 1914 acted for him as a reminder of the inevitability of death, and that the realisation that ordinary life would lead him nowhere showed him the necessity of intensifying his search. By 1915 the war was on Russian soil, and Ouspensky recognised that a previously 'hidden suicidal activity' of Russian life was becoming more visible. War is caused by **planetary influences**, resulting from two planets approaching too near each other and causing tensions. Though this lasts only a moment for the planets, on Earth people may slaughter each other for years. Because men are slaves inwardly and outwardly, they have no resistance to cosmic forces and cannot stop wars. If they awaken, men can stop wars, but to do this they need the help of a teacher and a group. Religions, such as Christianity, are no help at all, because men are not able to be Christians (*Search*: 3–4, 29, 24, 103–4, 143–4, 300; see also **law of solioonensius**).

Seen in these terms, the dangers and chaos of war in general, World War I, the Russian Revolution and the civil war that followed, provided an urgent impetus for learning to 'wake up' during the seven-year period in which Gurdjieff transmitted his teachings, lasting from 1914 until his arrival in Europe via Constantinople in 1921.

Although Gurdjieff said that the war prevented him from an early experiment with circulating his ideas in a written form (*Views*, 1914: 30), he also taught that, from the esoteric point of view, events that seemed to hinder the Work were actually helpful; that his ideas could only have been given during a time when the chaos of war distracted the majority, and only people who looked for these ideas could find them (*Search*: 342–3; see also **knowledge**).

In *Life*, Gurdjieff writes that his propensity for always placing himself wherever there were wars or revolution resulted from his wish to understand the significance and purpose of man's life. During his experience of wars, he had collected material that helped his **aim**, but the experience had also formed a second aim: to discover some means by which to prevent the human 'mass psychosis' that leads to war (*Life*: 26–8; see **politics, political ideology**).

> Only against the background of widespread belief in imminent social collapse can modernist activities be effectively grasped. The essence of Gurdjieff's message and the agitated reaction of Jean Toomer and Gurdjieff's many other disciples reveal a meaningful pattern in which we see people embracing ideas, methods, and solutions to problems that in retrospect may appear absurd. However, at the time these reactions

seemed to be appropriate to people engaged in a desperate search for some means of saving themselves and the world.

(Woodson 1999: 1)

See also: **writings**

WAYS/FOURTH WAY

The only possible ways in which man can evolve and achieve full development of his hidden possibilities, including immortality, are the three traditional ways of the fakir, the yogi and the monk, and Gurdjieff's way, which is a Fourth Way. Each of the traditional ways develops one aspect of a man, yet leaves the other aspects undeveloped. The fakir, for example, by imitating another fakir and enduring long and terrible suffering, may perfect his will to the point at which there is a possibility of acquiring a fourth body (see **bodies**), yet his emotional and intellectual functions remain undeveloped and, by this time, he is usually too old to begin new work on himself. The monk submits absolutely to his teacher in obedience, and his principal effort is to have faith in and to love and serve God. He struggles with his feelings until he develops unity and will over his emotions. However, his physical body and his mind remain undeveloped, and so he can not use what he has acquired without returning to the paths of the fakir and the yogi. The yogi begins his way with a teacher whom he imitates, like the fakir, and submits to, like the monk, but he gradually becomes his own teacher. He develops his mind and acquires knowledge; he may know everything, but can do nothing because he needs to develop his physical body and his emotions. These three ways must begin with a renunciation of everyday life, home, family and pleasures.

All of these ways are against nature, against God. They are opposed to everyday life, which even at its best, filled with scientific, philosophical, religious or social interests, can lead only to death. If a man is not in touch with a fakir or yogi school, then because the religions of the West have degenerated, and because spiritualist experiments and mystical and occult societies give no results, the only possibility for development is in a Fourth Way School.

This way, also against nature, is less well known than the other three, and a man must be able to find it. Even then a man's inner or outer conditions of life may prevent work. However, Gurdjieff also said that there is no requirement to renounce the usual conditions of life, because these conditions correspond to the man himself and allow the work to touch every side of his being at once. Thus the Fourth Way affects the physical body, the feelings and the mind simultaneously. There is a demand for understanding; the results of a man's work will be in proportion to the consciousness of the work. The Fourth Way has knowledge of exercises that make it possible to work on each part of a man's functioning in relation to the others. Work on the Fourth Way can be given to suit each individual who, when he attains will, can use it, because he has control over his physical, emotional and intellectual functions. Development on the Fourth Way begins with the first conscious shock. The Fourth Way is always temporary: it exists for a certain purpose, not that of teaching, and then it disappears. There are also artificial and wrong ways, but these produce only temporary or wrong results (*Search*: 47–51, 193, 312–13, 202; see also **evolution/involution**; **schools**; **'sly' man**; **stairway**).

The Hebraic, Egyptian and Persian teachings, of which we know only their theory, and the Hindu teaching, of which we know only the philosophy, make use of **symbols** to express the **unity** of diversity. These different ways, like the radii of a circle, get closer as they move towards the centre. Western European occultism and Theosophy also use symbols, but neither line of teaching possesses full knowledge and neither can lead to a practical result. The teaching that Gurdjieff expounds was unknown up to the present, and is self-supporting and independent of other teachings (*Search*: 285–6).

We might relate the temporary existence of Fourth Way Schools to the temporary need of the pupil for a teacher. Once the pupil no longer needs the teacher, the Fourth Way School would 'disappear' or cease to exist for him.

WILL/FREE WILL

By confining 'the manifestation of the laws of duality and trinity to the permanent line of struggle with himself', a man can introduce will, first into time, and second into eternity (*Search*: 180–1; see **time/the eternal**).

A sleeping person does not have enough will to control himself, but he has enough to obey a teacher. This is the only way for him to escape the Law of Fate (see **fate**). Abstaining from mechanical talking is a good exercise for developing will (*Search*: 165, 224; see also **stop exercise**).

Mechanical man does not have free will. What is termed 'will' in an ordinary person is just the result of desires. Only a man with a highly developed being, a **master** or real man, possesses will. To be effective, will has to be applied to all three centres simultaneously (*Views*, 1924: 71; 1922: 77). Ordinary man obeys orders from the mind, feelings or body; free will is the attribute of real man, of a master (*Search*: 246–7).

See also: **Absolute, the; carriage, horse, driver and master**

Further reading

Nietzsche 1998 [1886].

WOMEN *see* **gender;** for women pupils, see **Appendix 1; Appendix 2**.

WORK, LINES OF

A pupil may work on one or more lines of work. These are defined as work for himself, work for others in the Work, or work for the benefit of the Work itself. These lines can be controlled by a teacher for the pupil until the pupil is strong enough to withstand the **Laws of Accident** and **fate** (*Search*: 165).

See also: **work, to**

WORK, THE

The Work is the name by which Gurdjieff's teaching is most usually known and has its origins in **alchemy** where 'the Great Work' was that of transmuting base metals into gold. Gurdjieff refers to this process, in a psychological sense, as the transformation of man's inner substances. Gurdjieff's method of teaching, and thus the external form and focus of the Work, changed during his lifetime, although these teachings overlapped. In summary: the Work was focused during his time in Russia on cosmology; in the Caucasus and the Institute in France, the Work was focused on lectures, on manual labour, and on learning and giving public performances of sacred dancing/movements; this continued in France and the United States until around 1936; then, less publicly, in Paris until 1939 the Work was focused on writing and readings of his Three Series. In Paris during World War II, Gurdjieff was teaching French groups, readings and movements. After the war American and English pupils rejoined Gurdjieff in Paris and he made a final visit to the United States. For developments of the Work inside the **Foundations** since Gurdjieff's death, see **New Work** and **appendix 2**.

Since Gurdjieff's death, the Work has been adapted and/or appropriated by other teachers, some of whom acknowledge their debt to Gurdjieff and some of whom do not (see **appendix 2**). For a repudiation of three of these teachings, see Patterson (1998). However, a difficulty arises for anyone who makes suggestions of charlatanism and abuse of pupils against '*faux* Gurdjieffian' teachers: the same accusations might also be made against Gurdjieff (see Wellbeloved 1999).

Further reading

See the 'Works by Gurdjieff's pupils' section in the bibliography for accounts of Gurdjieff's teaching during these periods; for reports of group meetings in wartime Paris, see *Voices*.

WORK, TO

The phrase 'to work on oneself' includes within it many different activities. In general, it refers to the effort to awaken, to connect **centres**, in order to be able to observe the functioning of the **machine** and to remember the self, so that a process of change can begin through which man can become developed to his full potential (see also **self-observation**; **self-remembering**).

When a pupil begins to work, very little is asked of him; once he has made an effort, however, more and more effort will be demanded of him from then on. As the **Work** itself grows and changes, so a pupil must also grow, otherwise he will not remain useful (*Search*: 229–32; see **suffering/pleasure**; **super-efforts**; **teacher**). Elsewhere Gurdjieff says that in the beginning a great deal is demanded of the pupil, and later on less is demanded, for example in obedience to the teacher (*Search*: 240).

Gurdjieff outlines some of the difficulties for the pupil setting out on the 'journey' of the Work. First, the pupil should assess himself, his own nothingness. Are his desires 'madness'? A pupil should prepare for the worst, take with him everything he needs, he will not be able to return for things he has forgotten. If he wishes to return, his guide is not obliged to help him, and he may never be able to return (*Views*, 1918: 57–9; see also **difficulties**).

Work must be assessed by its quality, not its quantity. In order to be of value, work must include all three centres. Work takes place in daily life. A person may have abilities while in a monastery, but he needs to develop a **master** and this cannot be done 'in your room' (*Views*, 1923: 103–6, 1924: 147; see also **institutes**).

Pupils should make a programme for work and stick to it. They should not work for more than a third of their waking time, nor use the results of interior work for exterior work. Don't mix work and ordinary life (*Voices*: 275, 53, 116). Desire for the Work is not enough. The Work should be a need; the pupil must create a need. However, Gurdjieff also said that without a desire the pupil is wasting time: he must have a wish to change, though this is possible only by hard labour (*Voices*: 160, 274).

In 1978 Tracol said that:

> Gurdjieff's teaching is made for our own times. It speaks to men of our time. Gurdjieff's teaching is not apart from or in opposition to traditional teachings.

(Tracol 1994: 92)

The Fourth Way exists in Christianity, Hinduism, Islam and Taoism. Gurdjieff's Fourth Way does not contradict these, but cannot be mistaken for them (Tracol 1994: 93).

WORLD/S; ALL WORLDS

The world we live in is usually used in the singular, but we live in several worlds that are contained one within the other. The world that man is most immediately in relation to is the world of humanity, as part of organic life on Earth. The Planet Earth is the world for organic life, the world for the Earth is the planetary world, and the world for the planets is the Sun or the sphere of solar influence (i.e. the solar system). For the Sun, the world is the Milky Way, and a multitude of such worlds would be the world for the Milky Way. Philosophically 'we may say that "all worlds" must form for us some incomprehensible and unknown Whole or One.' This Whole or All may be called the **'Absolute'** or 'Independent'; it includes everything in itself, is not dependent on anything and is 'world' for 'all worlds' (*Search*: 76). The chain of worlds is expressed as the **Ray of Creation**; this is not 'the world' in totality, because the Absolute gives birth to what may be an infinite number of rays, and our Milky Way consists of many suns, each of which gives rise to a new ray.

- The Absolute
- All Worlds
- All Suns
- Our Sun
- The Planets
- The Earth
- The Moon

Man lives in and is influenced by all the above worlds (though not directly by the Absolute) and receives the strongest **influences** from the worlds nearest to him (*Search*: 80; see also *Views*, 1924: 65–8).

People live inside themselves, but to live only inside is not life. Life is when we examine ourselves and connect ourselves with the outside (*Views*, 1923: 268).

In *Life*, Gurdjieff writes that an ordinary man has two worlds, the inner and the outer, but, if he works on himself and 'becomes a candidate for another life', he may have three worlds. The other life is the real life referred to in his title *Life is Real Only Then, When 'I Am'*, and the third world is the 'real world' in which 'real life' is lived (*Life*: 169–70).

WRITINGS

Gurdjieff's mode of creating his texts comes somewhere between the oral and written traditions. There are various accounts of how *Tales* came into being through Gurdjieff's preliminary Armenian or Greek notes, his dictation (mostly in Russian) to a pupil acting as a secretary and, from there, via a number of different individuals and groups of translators and editors, to a written form, sometimes first in French and then in English (see de Hartmann 1992 [1964]; *Teachings*). Gurdjieff surrounded himself with pupils who had literary skills. Both *Tales* and *Meetings* owe a great deal to their editor, A.R. Orage (see **Appendix 1**; *Beelzebub's Tales to His Grandson*; *Meetings with Remarkable Men*; see also Taylor 1998, 2001).

Tales has now been published in a number of languages, but the English-language version, which was intended for the United States, was Gurdjieff's primary concern.

Tales was read aloud to groups and later modified by Gurdjieff, who would 'bury the dog deeper' if he felt his text had been too easy to grasp. Gurdjieff used strategies of paradox, humour, symbolism, inconsistency and deception within the narrative, all of which militated against a closed reading of his text. Readings were sometimes preceded by music, written by Gurdjieff in collaboration with Thomas de Hartmann (see **music; Appendix 1**). *Meetings* was read aloud by the Rope pupils (Patterson 1999: 91; see **Appendix 1**), and all Three Series were read aloud in Paris after World War II (Bennett 1980 [1949]). I have not seen any reference to *Herald* being read aloud to groups.

Gurdjieff was not isolated from the cultural mix of 1920s and 1930s Paris, in which occult and literary interests were intertwined. Gurdjieff's texts contain many occult references and are zodiacally structured. They may also be defined in relation to contemporary modernist literary interests, with their rejection of conventional literature, experimentation with punctuation, and Romantic interest in myth and the anti-hero.

Gurdjieff's writings also reflect the structuring of the Archaic epic. His syntax, which is complex and without punctuation, echoes the paratactic form of the **oral tradition** of his youth. (For modernism and parataxis, see Notopolous 1949; for structures and themes in Greek epic poetry, see Thalmann 1984; for Gurdjieff's use of formulaic epithets, compare Schein 1984.)

Theories about the Archaic epic (see Cornford in Harrison 1977 [1912]: 221–259) as a response to the changing world-view of time that had been brought about by the change from lunar calendar to solar calendar may have influenced Gurdjieff to write an epic that confronts a world-view of time. This had necessarily been changed by Einstein's redefinition of time in relation to matter. In this sense, Gurdjieff's epic 'destroys' or marks the closure of the 'Greek rational culture' that he scorned (see **time/the eternal**).

Ideas concerning the zodiacal structuring of myths became popular due to the publication of Frazer's *The Golden Bough: A Study in Magic and Religion* (1994 [1890–1915]), and were expressed by Theosophists (see Blavatsky 1988 [1888]: vol.2, p.353, who suggests a zodiacal structure for the Epic of Nimrod).

All of Gurdjieff's texts are structurally and thematically linked, and all refer to himself. He offers his own path as a teaching. However, the events he recounts have been shaped and mythologised, and so should not be taken literally (see **autobiographical writings**).

The four texts of Gurdjieff's writings, the Three Series of *All and Everything* and *Herald*, can be related to the Christian concept of the four last things: Death, Judgment, Heaven and Hell; the *Tales* can be related to Death, *Meetings* to Judgment, *Life* to Heaven and *Herald* to Hell (see **All And Everything**; **Herald Of Coming Good**; **Life Is Real Only Then, When 'I Am'**).

Webb (1976: 496–515) traces connections between occult writings and science fiction/fantasy texts between around 1900 and 1950. He points out that, while in fiction the reader knows he is reading fiction, occult texts are presented as reality, so the line between fact and fiction becomes blurred.

Further reading

For Archaic Greek epic, see Shein 1985, Thalmann 1984 and Reickl 1992; for parallels between Mesopotamian and Greek myths that throw light on *Tales*, see Penglase 1994. Compare Dostoyevsky, especially *Notes from the Underground* (1992 [1864]) and *The Brothers Karamazov* (1993 [1880]); Lautréamont's *Les Chants de Maldoror* (1970 [1869]), a cult text for the Surrealists; André Breton's *Nadja* (1999 [1928]) and *Anthology of Black Humor* (1997). For modernism, see Bradbury and McFarlane 1976: 96–102 and Nicholls 1995; for modernism and the occult, see Materer 1995 and Surrette 1993. Woodson 1999 looks at the influence of the Work and *Tales* on Toomer's group of writers in the Harlem Renaissance. For an example of occult fiction presented as fact, see the writings of Gurdjieff-influenced Carlos Castaneda; for the connection between Castaneda and the Work, see De Mille 1980.

ZODIAC

The symbolic diagram of the zodiac (see Figure 32) shows the Ecliptic; this is the yearly path of the sun as seen from an Earth-centred perspective. The 'path' is divided into twelve equal parts. These areas of the sky and their constellations are represented by the signs of the zodiac. The general map of the heavens can hold information about where the seven planets are at a specific moment in time. A diagram that represents this is a horoscope (see Figure 33). The practice of astrology is an interpretation of how this celestial map is related to terrestrial matters.

The zodiac is a 'moving diagram' and needs to be understood as being 'in motion', as does Gurdjieff's **enneagram**, which is itself a form of zodiac. The diagram of the zodiac can represent moments and cycles of time from seconds to thousands of years (see **time/the eternal** for discussion of a major theme in Gurdjieff's writings).

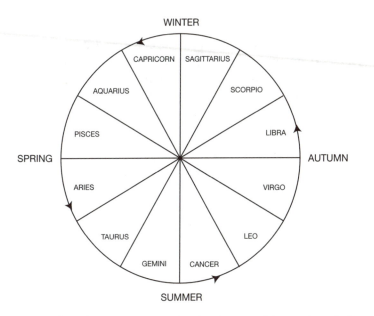

Figure 32 Zodiac: Horoscope as a map showing the path of the sun through the twelve months of the year

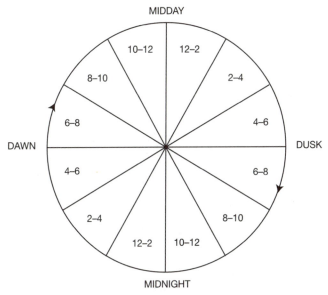

Figure 33 Zodiac: Horoscope as a map showing the path of the sun through the twenty-four hours of a day

Theosophical thinking about the zodiac considered that, while the clockwise motion of the sun through the zodiac represented the journey of ordinary man from life to death, the anti-clockwise journey is that of the disciple or initiate: one journey is 'in time' and the other goes 'against time' (see Figure 34; Bailey 1982 [1951]: 337–8).

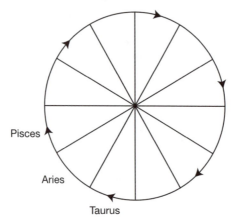

Movement through the zodiac in clockwise
direction from Aries to Taurus via Pisces

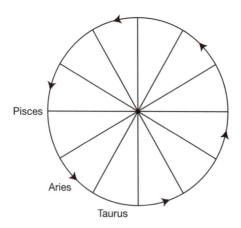

Movement through the zodiac anti-clockwise
from Aries to Pisces via Taurus

Figure 34 Zodiac: Time going in clockwise and anti-clockwise directions from data in Bailey 1983: 337 and 338

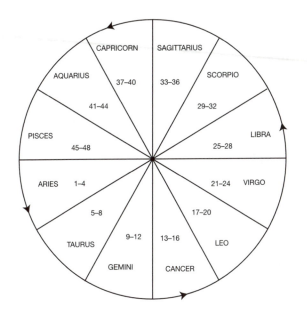

Figure 35 Zodiac: *Tales* chapters as zodiac moving forwards

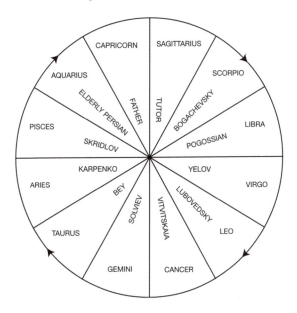

Figure 36 Zodiac: *Meetings* chapters as zodiac moving backwards

231

We might equate the two directions of the path through the zodiac to the involutionary and evolutionary directions in Gurdjieff's **Ray of Creation**.

Gurdjieff is employing a similar notion about the reversal of time in the zodiacal structures of his texts. *Tales*, a 'destructive' text, is structured as an involutionary zodiac, expressing the Fall, the continuing degeneration wrought by time; *Meetings*, the text that gives material for creating a new world, is evolutionary and goes backwards against the flow of time, while the narrative shows the **Seekers** intent on re-entering the past via ancient texts or schools of knowledge (see Figures 35 and 36; Wellbeloved 2001a).

See also: **astrology;** *Beelzebub's Tales to His Grandson; Meetings with Remarkable Men*

Further reading

For a Theosophical zodiac, see Leo 1989 [1913]. For myths in relation to the zodiac, see Lloyd-Jones 1978. For an account of the origins of the structure and functioning of the zodiac, see Campion 1994.

APPENDIX 1: BIOGRAPHICAL NOTES ON PUPILS

The biographical notes given below are on some of those who were taught by Gurdjieff and/or **P.D. Ouspensky, A.R. Orage** and **J.G. Bennett**, and who went on to become teachers and/or to write about the **Work**. In the first section are the early pupils who met Gurdjieff and formed his core group of pupils before he arrived in France. The second section contains notes on pupils who came to the Work after Gurdjieff established his **Institute** in France, often via Ouspensky, Orage or Bennett; the Rope Group of women pupils (see ROPE, THE), mostly writers; and the French pupils whom Gurdjieff taught during the years of World War II. Gurdjieff paid especial attention to pupils who had literary skills: Ouspensky in Russia, Orage in England, Toomer in America, and Jane Heap and the Rope Group in Paris. Each of these helped him significantly in the dissemination of his ideas: through teaching, through recording the teaching and/or through editing *Tales*. Pupils' own principal publications are listed in the bibliography.

1
Early pupils

Pyotr Demianovich Ouspensky (1878–1947) Ouspensky was born in Moscow. When he met Gurdjieff in 1915 he was already the successful author of *Tertium Organum* (1912) and a lecturer whose Theosophical interests and inner quest had led him to travels in India. He was a member, with his wife, of the earliest core group of pupils to whom Gurdjieff taught cosmological theory. Ouspensky began the process of separation from Gurdjieff in 1917 in Essentuki. He left Gurdjieff and began to teach in London in 1921; **A.R. Orage** was among his first pupils. Ouspensky decided that his split from Gurdjieff was final in

1924. He continued to teach in London, but he banned the mention of Gurdjieff's name. He published *A New Model of the Universe* in 1931, the year in which he made a last unexpected visit to Gurdjieff in France. This did not result in their reconciliation (see Moore 1991: 241). In 1935 Ouspensky acquired Lyne Place, Surrey, where pupils could take part in Work activities. In 1941, because of World War II, Ouspensky and his wife went to the United States where they led independent lives, each with their own groups of pupils. Ouspensky returned to London in 1946, leaving his pupils and wife in the United States. In September 1947 he told pupils that there was no 'System'. He died on 2 November. Ouspensky's pupils fractured into separate groups after his death, partly because they had been told there was no 'System', but also because Ouspensky had been certain that Gurdjieff's teaching was not complete: he had focused on the need to contact **schools**, and so his pupils continued to search for other teachers. Ouspensky's *In Search of the Miraculous* (1987 [1949]) had been approved by Gurdjieff as a true account of his teaching. It was published after the deaths of both men and has remained a key text in the **Work** (Rawlinson 1997: 293–6).

Sophie Grigorievna Ouspensky (1874–1963) Known to her pupils as Madame Ouspensky, she had a daughter from an earlier marriage when she met Gurdjieff in 1915 through Ouspensky. She stayed with Gurdjieff when Ouspensky went to London in 1921 and continued to live near him, visiting England occasionally from 1927 and moving there permanently in 1931. Ouspensky stayed mostly in London while Madame Ouspensky taught at Lyne Place in Surrey. In 1941 they went to the United States together, where she taught at Franklin Farms, Mendham, while Ouspensky stayed in New York. She remained in the United States when Ouspensky returned to England. After his death, she advised his pupils, and her own, to go to Gurdjieff in Paris. Because of the longstanding ban on the mention of Gurdjieff, pupils had not realised that he was still alive. Gurdjieff visited Madame Ouspensky on his last visit to the United States in the winter of 1948–9. Although she did not write about the Work herself, she supervised the publication of her husband's *The Fourth Way* (1957). She died in 1963. Both Lyne Place and Franklin Farms replicated aspects of Gurdjieff's Institute: they provided a place away from everyday life where Work could be carried out through physical activities under the supervision of the teacher. This model was adhered to by other pupils (see below) and still continues as the pattern for

Work. Madame Ouspensky had a reputation as a formidable teacher in her own right (see Rawlinson 1997: 296–8).

Thomas Alexandrovich de Hartmann (1886–1956)

Olga (Arkadievna de Schumacher) de Hartmann (1885–1979) Thomas de Hartmann married Olga, a singer, in 1906, the year his ballet *The Pink Flower* (Opus 6) was performed before Tsar Nicholas II. From 1908–11 de Hartmann studied conducting in Munich. He was a well-established composer in St Petersburg when he and his wife encountered Gurdjieff in December 1916. However, they abandoned their careers and travelled to France with Gurdjieff, staying with him until 1929 (see de Hartmann and de Hartmann 1992 [1964]). They were also part of the core group of Gurdjieff students at the Institute, where Olga became Gurdjieff's secretary and was much involved in the writing process of *Tales*. Gurdjieff and de Hartmann collaborated in the composition of **music**. Though separated from Gurdjieff after 1929, they remained faithful to his teaching and, after his death, moved to New York to support Madame Ouspensky at Franklin Farms. After Thomas died in 1956, Olga started the first Canadian group in Toronto, which later became the Gurdjieff Foundation of Canada. She died in 1979 (see Thomas C. Daly's Foreword to de Hartmann and de Hartmann 1992 [1964]: vii–xxi).

Jeanne (Allemand) de Salzmann (1889–1990) Born in Geneva, she trained as a dancer and met Gurdjieff in Tiflis in 1919. She was teaching Eurythmics and her pupils gave the first performance of Gurdjieff's sacred dances (see DANCE). She and her husband Alexandre de Salzmann, a theatre designer, travelled with Gurdjieff to France and lived at the Institute. Alexandre began to teach in Paris in 1931, gathering the first French group of Work pupils, which included the writer René Dumal. At his death in 1933, his wife took on his pupils. She moved to Sevres near Paris, where she taught her group. She sent pupils to Gurdjieff and began to take on the role of his deputy. During World War II, she was able to remain in contact with Gurdjieff, and after the war emerged as his principal pupil. At Gurdjieff's death in 1949, she was accepted as his 'successor' and began to set up a structure that would enable the Work to continue (see NEW WORK). Her son, Michel de Salzmann, took over the 'leadership' of the Work until his death in 2001 (Rawlinson 1997: 311–13; see also Ravindra 1999).

Olgivanna (Ivanova Lazovich) Lloyd Wright (1899–1985)   Olgivanna was born in Montenegro and grew up in Tiflis, Georgia. In 1915 she went to Moscow to study dramatic art. She married Vladimir Hinzenbergand there, but returned to Tiflis where her daughter Svetlana was born. In 1919 she met Gurdjieff, became a dancer in *Struggle of the Magicians*, and travelled with him to Constantinople. When Gurdjieff moved to Europe, Olgivanna separated from her husband, who went to the United States, and sent her daughter to live with her brother and sister-in-law in New York. In 1922 she became an administrator of Gurdjieff's Institute; she was one of his principal dancers and taught movements. On Gurdjieff's advice, she moved to the United States in 1925, where she married the architect Frank Lloyd Wright; they had one daughter: Iovanna. Wright established his Taliesin Fellowship in 1932, and from then until her death Olgivanna taught movements and other aspects of the Work. She and Iovanna, who had studied movements with Gurdjieff in 1948, gave a number of dance productions based on Gurdjieff's movements and cosmological teaching.

Jessmin Howarth

Rosemary (Lillard) Nott   They both met Gurdjieff in 1921, in Hellerau, near Dresden in Germany, where they were students of the Jaques-Dalcroze system of Eurythmics. Jessmin Howarth had been a choreographer at the Opera House in Paris. Both became lifelong students of Gurdjieff, and teachers of his movements and sacred dances (see Webb 1980: 187–8).

Pupils joining Gurdjieff after establishment of his Institute in France

Alfred Richard Orage (1873–1934)   Born in Yorkshire, A.R. Orage moved to Leeds where he joined the Fabian Society. In 1901 he founded the Leeds Art Club with Holbrook Jackson. In 1905 he became a member of the Theosophical Society and one of their lecturers. In 1906 and 1907 he published works on Nietzsche (see Steele 1990). He made an early childless marriage to Jean Walker, from whom he separated. In 1907 Orage and Jackson moved to London where they bought *The New Age*, a journal that reflected Orage's interests in Nietzsche and Socialist Politics, and was the first to introduce Freudian Theory to a general English readership. Partly funded, for a while, by G.B. Shaw, *The New Age* supported modernist writing and gained prestige in the literary and political worlds, publishing works by established authors (G.B. Shaw, Arnold Bennett, H.G. Wells) and by as yet unknowns (Katherine Mansfield, T.S. Eliot, Ezra Pound, Richard Aldington, T.E. Hulme). However, in 1921 Orage went to Ouspensky's lectures and, after Gurdjieff's London visit in 1922, became a pupil of Gurdjieff. He gave up the literary life in which he was well established to go and live at the Institute in France. In 1923 he was sent by Gurdjieff to New York, and on Gurdjieff's visit to the United States in 1924 was given the care of the New York branch of the Institute. Through his network of literary connections in both England and the United States, Orage brought much of the English-speaking literary world into contact with Gurdjieff. From 1924 (when Gurdjieff began to write) Orage was closely involved with the editing of *Tales*, and later *Meetings*: he is credited (*Meetings*: viii) with making the first English translation of the text. In 1927 he married Jessie Dwight. Throughout his time in New York Orage worked tirelessly to further Gurdjieff's cause, and through his pupils and **Toomer** provided much of the money needed to sustain the Institute. As a result of a combination of factors, Orage's stewardship of the Work in New York ended in 1931. He returned to England with his wife and young son, resuming the life of an editor, this time of the *New English Review*, and of political involvement, expressed through his interest in the Douglas System of Social Credit. In August 1934 he declined to become Gurdjieff's editor for the Third Series, and having given a talk on Social Credit for the BBC on 5 November, died the next morning (see Taylor 2001).

Orage's contribution to the Work, as editor and teacher, may have been underestimated because, until now, Gurdjieff's texts have not received as much attention as other aspects of his teaching, and also because Orage's own transmission of Gurdjieff's teaching, set out in Daly King's *The Oragean Version*, has not been published. This is in accordance with King's own wishes; however, many copies of it have been made and these are in circulation among Work pupils, so perhaps at some stage it will be officially published and become generally available (see Taylor 2000; Steele 1990; Welch 1952; Carswell 1978; Martin 1967; Hastings 1936).

Maurice Nicoll (1884–1953) Qualified as a physician in 1910, he became interested in psychology and studied with Jung at Zurich. Nicoll served in the Royal Army Medical Corps during World War I and in 1917 pioneered psychological treatment for shell-shocked soldiers. He met **Ouspensky** through **Orage** in 1921, but after meeting Gurdjieff went to live at the Institute with his family in November 1922. He left the Institute in October 1923, returning to London to practise psychiatry, and rejoined Ouspensky. From 1931, at Ouspensky's instigation, he began to teach his own group, and in 1939 retired from his medical practice and taught full-time. He recreated the work conditions of the Institute in several large Work houses. Nicoll remained independent of Gurdjieff, and neither he nor his pupils went to Gurdjieff in Paris after Ouspensky's death. Eventually many of his pupils, though not all, became part of the Gurdjieff Society in London (see **APPENDIX 2**). While remaining faithful to the Work, Nicoll made Gurdjieff's teaching his own – see the five volumes of his *Psychological Commentaries on the Teaching of Gurdjieff and Ouspensky* (1992 [1952–6]) and the bibliography for other publications (Rawlinson 1997: 298–301; Pogson 1987 [1961]).

John Godolphin Bennett (1897–1974) Although Bennett met **Ouspensky** and Gurdjieff in Constantinople in 1921, where, he recounts, he was serving in the British Army, he is placed in this section of pupils because he was not a member of Gurdjieff's early core group. He visited the Institute in 1922 and, although as a result of his work there he experienced cosmic timelessness and unusual flows of energy, he left the Institute and did not meet Gurdjieff again until after World War II. He returned to England and Ouspensky. In 1930 he started teaching a group of his own, but in 1945 was cut off by Ouspensky for giving public lectures; the two did not meet again. In 1946 he established a Work house: Coombe Springs, near London. He visited Gurdjieff in Paris in 1948 and 1949.

After Gurdjieff's death, Bennett agreed to the leadership of **Jeanne de Salzmann**, but became an independent teacher and had encounters with other spiritual teachers. These arose from travels in the Near East in 1953, from his introduction of Subud teaching to his pupils in 1957, and from his meetings in 1961 and 1963 with the Indian guru Shivapura Baba, who told Bennett that he would find God-realisation through Christ. As a result of this last encounter, Bennett was received into the Roman Catholic Church. In 1966 Bennett became involved with the Sufi Idries Shah, to whom he handed over his pupils and Coombe Springs. In 1971 Bennett established his International Academy for Continuous Education in Sherborne, Gloucestershire, England; he bought Claymont Court in West Virginia, United States, as a site for a Work house just before his death in 1974. Bennett published around thirty-five books related to the Work, including his four-volume *The Dramatic Universe* (1957–66) (see Rawlinson 1997: 183–6; G. Bennett 1990).

Jean Toomer (1894–1967)   Nathan Jean Toomer was born Nathan Pinchback Toomer in Washington, D.C. In 1920 he published short pieces under the name 'Jean Toomer' and in 1923 his lyrical novel *Cane* became the standard-bearer of what has been called 'the Harlem Renaissance'. In February 1924 he came under the influence of **A.R. Orage** and Gurdjieff in New York, spending the summer of 1924 at the Institute, though Gurdjieff's accident impeded personal contact with him. Back in New York, Toomer worked with Orage and organised a Gurdjieff group in Harlem in 1925 that included a talented group of black writers. In the summer of 1926 he worked closely with Gurdjieff and Orage on the translation of *Tales*. In the autumn he organised a group in Chicago that, with Orage's New York group, furnished the bulk of financial support for the Institute. In 1927 Gurdjieff trained Toomer to supervise American operations so as to free Orage to prepare *Tales* for publication. He returned to the Institute in the summer of 1929 and in summer 1931 established an imitation of Gurdjieff's Institute at Portage, Wisconsin, continuing this experiment in Carmel, California, in the spring of 1932. After Orage's death in 1934, Toomer broke off direct contact with Gurdjieff, though he continued the Work in Chicago and later in Pennsylvania. After Gurdjieff's death, under the influence of **Madame Ouspensky** and **John Bennett**, Toomer rejoined the Work, directing a group from 1954–7. He devoted his last years to recording his experiences with Gurdjieff (see Byrd 1990; Taylor 1998).

Rodney Collin (1909–56)   Born Rodney Collin-Smith and educated at the London School of Economics, he became a journalist, and married in 1930, the year in which he and his wife joined a **Nicoll** group. His contact with **Ouspensky** came through his visits to Lyne Place, and he was with the Ouspenskys in the United States during World War II. He had an intense attachment to Ouspensky and formed his own vision of Ouspensky's role in a cosmic drama. After Ouspensky's death, Collin had a series of revelations and experienced himself as being in touch with Ouspensky. He wrote about this in *The Theory of Eternal Life* (1950). In 1948 he went with some of Ouspensky's pupils to Mexico, founded a community at Tlalpam outside Mexico City, and held group meetings. Collin focused on the cosmic aspect of the Work. He incorporated **astrology** into Gurdjieff's cosmology via the notions of **types** and vibrations (see *The Theory of Celestial Influence,*

1954a) and his explorations of a planetary enneagram probably led to the development of the enneagram of personality (see ENNEAGRAM). His teaching also embraced the messages received from Ouspensky and Gurdjieff via a medium, Mema Dickens, the wife of one of his pupils. Collin was received into Roman Catholicism in Rome in 1954; he saw himself as an esoteric Christian, and thus his Christianity was not in conflict with the Work. He died in dramatic circumstances, falling from the bell-tower of Lima Cathedral. Through Collin, Work groups were established in Mexico, Peru, Uruguay and Argentina (see Rawlinson 1997: 306–8; Webb 1980; Collin-Smith 1988).

Robert de Ropp (1913–1987 or 1988)   Robert de Ropp gained a Ph.D. in plant physiology at the Royal College of Science in London. He met **Ouspensky** in 1936, but became especially attached to **Madame Ouspensky**, going to Lyne Place for Work weekends from 1936 until 1945, by which time the Ouspenskys were in the United States. De Ropp joined them in 1945, but became disillusioned about the Work. He met Gurdjieff during his final visit to New York. De Ropp became an independent teacher and set up a community in Santa Rosa, California, around 1967 (see de Ropp 1974, 1980; Rawlinson 1997).

Irmis Barret Popoff (1900–84)   Irmis Popoff was the daughter of a provincial Governor in Venezuela. She became one of the first pupils of **Ouspensky** in New York in 1941 and worked for some time as his secretary. After Ouspensky's return to London, she continued in the Work and through **Madame Ouspensky** she met Gurdjieff during his 1948–9 visit to New York. Thereafter she worked with Madame Ouspensky, **Willem Nyland**, Lord Pentland and **Jeanne de Salzmann**. She became involved in Mexican groups established by Christopher Freemantle and Venezuelan groups formed around Natalie de Salzmann. From 1965 she began to have groups herself and published *Gurdjieff: His Work on Myself... with Others... for the Work* in 1969. The following year she established the Pinnacle, a Work house in Seacliffe, Long Island, New York, and in 1978 published *The Enneagrama of a Man of Unity*. She continued to teach until her death in 1984.

Jane Heap (1883–1964)   Born in Kansas of an English father and a Norwegian/Lapp mother, Jane Heap (also known as 'jh') met **Margaret Anderson** in Chicago in 1910, becoming her partner and joint editor of *The Little Review*. Anderson and Heap moved in the same literary circles as **Orage**, who contacted them before coming to

New York in 1923. Once there, he introduced them to the Work and they introduced him to prospective pupils. In 1926 Heap led **groups** under Orage's guidance. In 1928 she arrived at the Institute, but Gurdjieff sent her to Paris to teach. The group she taught there included **Margaret Anderson**, **Georgette Leblanc**, **Solito Solano** and **Kathryn Hulme**; all them were writers and they went on to form the basis of Gurdjieff's Rope Group. In 1929 Heap and Anderson closed *The Little Review*, abandoning art for the Work. It was largely due to the charismatic Heap, whose group of artists had started in 1927, that Gurdjieff became well known among the expatriate American artists of the Left Bank. She, and then Gurdjieff, became part of Paris in the 1930s, much as Gurdjieff and the Institute had been part of Paris in the 1920s (Webb 1980: 431–2). In 1935 Gurdjieff sent Heap to London to teach. Nott (*Journey*: 78) writes that she had a strong masculine side and that she told him she 'was not really a woman'. Ouspensky refused to accept her in a group on account of this. Nott points out that Gurdjieff never turned away people who were 'attracted to their own sex'. Heap continued to teach separately in London, though she visited Gurdjieff occasionally; after the war, she and some of her pupils went to visit Gurdjieff in Paris. After Gurdjieff's death, she continued to teach and amalgamated her pupils with the Gurdjieff Society in London under the direction of Henriette Lannes. Though she did not write about the Work, some of her aphorisms are given in Anderson (1962) and her letters to Florence Reynolds have been published (Baggett 1999). See also the two publications about her published by the Two Rivers Press (see **Annie Lou Staveley**).

Annie Lou Staveley (1906–96)   Born in Washington, D.C., she married an English man and so went to live in London. They had a son, but the marriage was short-lived. However, she had already met **Ouspensky** in New York and thus was introduced to **Jane Heap**, who became her teacher in London. She visited Gurdjieff in Paris several times a year from 1946–9 (see *Memories of Gurdjieff*, 1978). Staveley went on to establish a Work community at Two Rivers Farm in Oregon around 1974, with a printing press that kept the original 1950 edition of *Tales* in print and published, among other books, John Lester's *Jane Heap Remembered: As Remembered by Some She Taught* (1988) and *The Notes of Jane Heap* (1994). Staveley visited New York each year to keep in touch with the Foundation and with **Jeanne de Salzmann**. I learned from one of her pupils that new receptive Work practices had been introduced to the community (see **New Work**) after one of these visits. However, she later returned to the former mode of teaching (see Staveley 1978; also Kherdian 1998).

Other pupils set up their own teaching centers along the lines of the Institute. (Information about **Louise March**, **Paul and Naomi Anderson** and **Willem Nyland**, all of whom began their own lineages in the teaching, comes from Speeth 1977: 101–4.)

Louise March   March studied at the **Institute** and was connected to the New York Foundation for many years. She set up the Rochester Folk Guild in 1957, and ten years later the East Hill Farm community of farmers and artisans.

Paul and Naomi Anderson   They were both pupils of **Orage** and Gurdjieff. Paul acted as Gurdjieff's secretary during his last visit to New York in 1948–9. Paul and Naomi were both involved with *Tales*, producing the first mimeographed copy of the English version which was published in 1930–1 to raise funds for Gurdjieff. They were members of the Foundation in New York, before leaving to set up the American Institute for Continuing Education (AICE) in the Berkshires.

Willem Nyland   A Dutch chemist and musician, Nyland studied with **Orage** and Gurdjieff and, having left the New York Foundation in the early 1960s, formed the Institute for Religious Development, consisting of several groups on the East and West Coasts, a community in Warwick, New York, and one in Sebastapol, California.

C.S. Nott (1887–1978)

Fritz Peters (1913–80)   Nott was a long-term pupil of Gurdjieff and friend of **Orage**, while Peters was the nephew of Margaret Anderson and Jane Heap's ward. They both told the story of their own experiences with Gurdjieff and the Work; their publications (which are valuable sources of information) are listed in the Bibliography.

The Rope Group

The composition of the Rope Group

The composition of the Rope Group is defined slightly differently by Moore (1991) and Patterson (1999). Moore writes that only **Kathryn**

Hulme, Louise Davidson and **Solito Solano**, who had their first group meeting with Gurdjieff in October 1935, can be described as members of the Rope. 'The Rope' is a term used by Hulme in the context of their inner-world journey, in the course of which, in order to climb, they needed to be roped together for safety. In June 1936, when **Margaret Anderson, Georgette Leblanc** and their friend and housekeeper Monique Serrure joined, Gurdjieff called the group as a whole 'Knachtschmidt and Company', but did not admit the second trio of pupils as deeply into his teaching as he did the Rope (Moore 1991: 260–5). Patterson, whose material about the group's direct encounters with Gurdjieff is edited from Solito Solano's diaries, which are held in the Library of Congress, writes that **Elizabeth Gordon** arrived as a member of the group in October 1935; that Alice Rohrer returned from the United States and arrived in the group in November 1935; and that Gurdjieff formed Solano, Gordon, Hulme and Rohrer into a mutually supportive group, mentioning the allegory of the rope and climbing on his birthday (13 January) in 1936. The group came to an end in 1939. In brief, this group of mostly lesbian pupils had close and intense, usually daily, contact with Gurdjieff, often during lunches or dinners held in restaurants or at his apartment. Occasionally they were joined by **Jane Heap**, and sometimes by other pupils or by the pupils' partners or friends: e.g. Janet Flanner (see SOLITO SOLANO) and her partner Noel Murphy, who sought Gurdjieff's medical advice. Margaret Anderson (1962: ix) defines their 'special Gurdjieff group' as including **Orage**, Heap, Solano, Hulme and later Caruso. Gurdjieff taught them through his ritual toast of the idiots, through reading his texts, through exercises and through the names of their 'inner animals' (see below). These names were not fixed: each one had seven aspects and could be transformed – i.e. Solito Solano's 'Kanari' might become a crow or a peacock (see Patterson 1999: 289–94). Although Gurdjieff teased and challenged the women, the account of their meetings transmits a sense of the fun and pleasure that they experienced, which is rare in accounts of the teaching. (Information about the Rope pupils comes from Patterson 1999 unless otherwise stated.)

Members of the Rope Group

The following are pupils who formed this group or were associated with it.

Solito Solano (1888–1975)   Born Sarah Wilkinson in Troy, New York, she changed her name to Solito Solano. After a rebellious youthful marriage and some time spent in New York as an aspiring actress, she moved to Boston as a newspaper reporter. By 1918 she was drama critic for the *New York Tribune* and met her partner Janet Flanner, with whom she travelled. In 1922 they arrived in Paris, where they lived together writing. In 1927 Solano met **Margaret Anderson**, who introduced her briefly to Gurdjieff. Solano became part of the **Jane Heap** group, but her interest in Gurdjieff only surfaced in 1934 after a painful separation from Anderson; in 1935 she met Gurdjieff again through **Kathryn Hulme**, and so became part of the Rope. Gurdjieff named Solano 'canary', 'Kanari', and it is Solano's diaries that provide most of the information we have about the group. In April 1939 the Rope lunches and meetings ended, and Solito accompanied Gurdjieff to New York as his secretary. After a brief return to France, she left for America with Janet Flanner in October 1939. She saw Gurdjieff on his last visit to New York in 1948–9, and in October of that year returned to Paris, arriving before Gurdjieff's death on 29 October. After his funeral, she returned to New Jersey to live with Elizabeth Jenks Clark ('Lib'), whom she had met in the American Women's Volunteer Services during World War II. She corresponded with other members of the Rope and edited all of Kathryn Hulme's writings. Lib and Solano settled in Orgeval, France, where Solano died in 1975.

Kathryn Hulme (1900–81) In 1922 Kathryn Hulme settled in New York. In 1925 she married Leonard D. Geldent, but met **Alice Rohrer**, who became her partner in 1927. Together they became members of Gurdjieff's group. Gurdjieff called Hulme 'crocodile', 'Krokodeel', saying that, though he did not want to eat a crocodile, it was a good animal to send on ahead to eat enemies. The interior animal of Krokodeel was defined as a baby two-and-a-half years old. Hulme revisited Gurdjieff after World War II in 1945, and in 1946 took her new partner, Marie Louise ('Malou') Habets, to meet him. (See *Undiscovered Country*, 1966, for an account of this meeting and of her years with Gurdjieff.) Hulme wrote an account of Habets' life in *The Nun's Story* (1956), which became a successful film four years later. In 1960 Hulme and Habets went to live in Hawaii. In 1971, at the request of Jeanne de Salzmann, Hulme wrote a film treatment of *Meetings*; it was not used, however. She died in Hawaii in 1981.

Alice Rohrer (Nickie, Wendy) (1885/90–1958) Alice Rohrer was a self-made, wealthy milliner from San Francisco, who met her partner **Kathryn Hulme** in 1927. They arrived in Paris in April 1931 and became interested in the **Work** via **Solito Solano**, who took them to meet **Jane Heap**. After a brief trip to America, Alice returned to France; she saw Gurdjieff in the Café de la Paix in Paris, and went over to speak to him. As result, she and Kathryn went to the **Institute** and stayed the night. They did not, however, regain contact with Gurdjieff until November 1935, when he was already teaching **Margaret Anderson**, **Solito Solano** and **Elizabeth Gordon**. Gurdjieff gave her the name 'boa constrictor' for her outer animal, but 'tapeworm' for her inner animal. In April 1937 Alice returned to America with Kathryn. In September, after an illness, she lost interest in the Work. By 1950 Alice had married Gusto; she died suddenly in 1958, after an evening spent with Kathryn Hulme and her partner Marie Louise ('Malou') Habets.

Elizabeth Gordon Referred to as Miss Gordon, she went to the Institute in 1922 and remained Gurdjieff's pupil from then on. She was a member of the Rope Group and its secretary. Gurdjieff gave her the role of 'Mother Superior'. During World War II she remained in Paris and attended Gurdjieff's group meetings. She was interned at some point during the war (perhaps 1943), and died while interned or shortly after her release.

Margaret Anderson (1886–1973) Margaret Anderson was born in Ohio. She moved to Chicago in order to pursue a career as a pianist, and earned money as a book reviewer. She became poetry editor of the literary review *The Dial*, where she learned how to publish a magazine. By 1913 she was book critic for the *Chicago Evening Post*. In 1914 she founded *The Little Review*, which she edited until 1916, when she met **Jane Heap** who became her partner and co-editor. The magazine published work by Yeats, Wyndham Lewis, T.S. Eliot and Ford Madox Ford; in 1920 they were prosecuted for publishing chapters of Joyce's *Ulysses*. The Dadaist Tzara, Breton and all the founding Surrealists were published in *The Little Review*. In 1924 Anderson, having learned about the Work through Orage in New York, left for France in order to visit Gurdjieff at the Institute. She sailed with **Georgette Leblanc** (with whom she had formed a new partnership), Monique Serrure and **Louise Davidson**, and was followed shortly after by Heap. Anderson and the others all arrived at the Institute just after Gurdjieff's car accident; on his recovery, he spent his time writing. Anderson was taught by Heap in the group she had formed in Paris (see **Heap**), until Heap went to London in 1935, and for four years from October 1935 Anderson was part of the group of women taught by Gurdjieff. He told her that her inner animal was a

Tibetan yak: her name in the group was 'Yakina'. In October 1937 she and Leblanc left Paris to live in Normandy. Leblanc died in 1941, and in 1942 Anderson sailed from Lisbon for New York. During the voyage she formed an enduring friendship with the widow of the opera singer Enrico Caruso, Dorothy Caruso (1893–1955), who became interested in Gurdjieff and his teaching. After the war, in the summer of 1948, they returned to France to see Gurdjieff and in December followed him back to New York. Anderson published *My Thirty Years War* (1930), *The Fiery Fountains* (1951), *The Unknowable Gurdjieff* (1962) and *The Strange Necessity* (1969). She died in Cannes in 1973. (See Drabble 1995: 728; Scott, Friedman and Breyer 1988; Anderson 1962; Caruso 1952; Patterson 1999.)

Georgette Leblanc (1869–1941) Georgette Leblanc was born in Rouen, France. In 1893 she was a singer in the Opéra Comique; in 1911 she acted in Maeterlinck's play *The Blue Bird* and she remained with him until 1919. Sometime in the early 1920s she met **Margaret Anderson** in the United States and they formed a partnership that lasted until Leblanc's death. Anderson interested Leblanc in Gurdjieff and in 1924 they travelled to the Institute, together with **Louise Davidson**, who was to act as Georgette's theatrical manager, and Monique Serrure, who was both friend and housekeeper, and who also stayed with Leblanc until her death. When the Institute closed in 1924, Anderson stayed in France with Leblanc and Serrure. She received notes from Solito Solano about her meetings with Gurdjieff, and in May 1936 became part of the group. Gurdjieff's work with her greatly improved her health: she became pain-free and full of energy. Her *Story of the Blue Bird* was published in 1939, and her experiences with Gurdjieff are recorded in her autobiography *La Machine à Courage: Souvenirs* (1947), translated into English in Anderson (1962: 136–56). She died in Le Cannet, France, in 1941.

Louise Davidson Louise Davidson was an actress and theatrical manager (see **GEORGETTE LEBLANC**). Gurdjieff's name for Louise was 'sardine', the sardine when it is out of water: gasping, quivering and flipping its tail. Later, he added 'wart', meaning carbuncle, and she became 'sardine-wart' (Patterson 1999: 92). Louise returned to the United States at the outbreak of World War II.

World War II Group in Paris

An account of some of Gurdjieff's wartime groups in Paris is given in *Voices*, although mostly pupils are identified by nicknames. Gurdjieff's group of French pupils included Henriette Lannes, Henri Tracol, Maurice Desselle and the movements teacher Marthe de Gaigneron, all of whom were involved with the **Gurdjieff Society** in London and with the **Foundations** (see APPENDIX 2. The writers René Zuber and René Dumal, the latter of whom was originally a pupil of Alexandre de Salzmann, are mentioned in *Voices*; Pauline de Gampierre is mentioned in Ravindra (1999). I have no information about the many other pupils who attended those meetings and who will have made their own significant contributions to the continuation of the **Work**.

APPENDIX 2: GURDJIEFF FOUN-DATIONS AND WORK-DERIVED GROUPS

A comprehensive list of all the Gurdjieff and Gurdjieff-derived teachings would require its own separate volume, or maybe several volumes. However, this appendix gives the names of some of the Gurdjieff Foundations that teach the **Work**, and examples of some of the groups that have assimilated Gurdjieff's teaching into new forms. Biographical notes on pupils with names in **bold** can be found in **Appendix 1**.

The Foundations

Gurdjieff's successor **Jeanne de Salzmann** remained the overall head of the Work groups from 1949 until her death in 1990. In England, these groups were formalised into the Gurdjieff Society in London, led by Henriette Lannes from 1950 until 1980. The Society brought together pupils who had been taught by Gurdjieff and those who had been pupils and teachers in **groups** with **Ouspensky**, **Nicoll** or **Heap**. In New York, the Work was led until 1931 by **A.R. Orage** as a branch of Gurdjieff's **Institute** in France. It became the New York Gurdjieff Foundation, and was led by Lord Pentland from 1953 to 1984. There are reported to be Gurdjieff Foundations in California, Chicago, Ohio, Los Angeles, Texas, Washington, Canada, Germany, Switzerland, Caracas and Sydney (see Patterson 1992; Kherdian 1998). There are Work groups that have been formed outside the umbrella of the Foundations by people who have attended one of the Foundations for a while and then left, but have nonetheless retained their Work interest and practice. There are also Work groups led by people who have never been members of a Foundation, but who have discovered Gurdjieff through reading.

We will take a brief look first at three examples of the formalised approaches resulting from contacts with Gurdjieff's teaching, through his pupils or his writings: **The School of Economic Science**, **The Fellowship of Friends/The Gurdjieff–Ouspensky Fourth Way Schools** and **The Emin**. We will then consider five teachers who have taken on aspects of Gurdjieff's trickster role: **Oscar Ichazo, Jan Cox, E.J. Gold, Idries Shah** and **Gary Chicoine**.

The School of Economic Science

The School of Economic Science was founded by Andrew MacLaren to arouse interest in land tax reform. His son Leon (Leonardo da Vinci), born around 1911, steered the School in a new direction. He met the **Work** after Ouspensky's death via Dr Francis Roles, Ouspensky's pupil and physician, who had founded The Society for the Study of Normal Man in 1951, also known as the Study Group. In 1959 Roles and MacLaren became pupils of Maharishi Mahesh Yogi, teacher of Transcendental Meditation or TM, but after a visit to India they transferred their allegiance to the teaching of Shankaracharya (Shantananda Saraswati). They returned to London and founded the School of Meditation, where methods of TM meditation were taught; they also introduced these techniques into The School of Economic Science. This became independent of other groups in about 1966, and teaches a mixture of Gurdjieff/Ouspensky Work with Hindu teachings (see Rawlinson 1997: 424–30, who cites Hounam and Hogg 1985 as his source; see also MacLaren 1997). Shaw (1994: 120–42) gives an account of his brief membership of the School, finding it a genteel teaching. He attended their Course in Philosophy, which has been advertised in London Underground stations for the last forty years. He disagrees with the views of journalists Hounam and Hogg (1985) who present the school in a bad light. They had suspicions about the School's financial prosperity (it owns a considerable amount of property) and its links to Liberal Party politicians. For an account of some of Ouspensky's pupils who became pupils of Maharishi Mahesh Yogi, see Collin-Smith 1988.

The Fellowship of Friends/Gurdjieff-Ouspensky Fourth Way Schools

The Fellowship of Friends (FOF) was founded by Robert Earl Burton in 1970. Their main teaching centre is the Apollo (formerly Renaissance) farming and wine-making community in the Sierra Nevada mountains of California. They list thirty major cities worldwide where they have teaching centres, known as the Gurdjieff–Ouspensky Fourth Way Schools. These are mostly in the United States and Europe, but also include Moscow, Tel Aviv and Tokyo. Jeanne Chapman writes in the introduction to Burton's *Self-*

Remembering (1995) that, while Gurdjieff specialised in physical training through his dances and Ouspensky specialised in intellectual discipline, Burton makes the Fourth Way his own through the education and discipline of pupils' emotions (see WAYS/FOURTH WAY), and that he has put **self-remembering** at the heart of his teaching. The main text is presented in a form that resembles a wisdom book, with short, usually bland paragraphs of wise remarks, sometimes in answer to brief questions. Burton's Fourth Way teaching includes ideas from the writings of Gurdjieff, **Ouspensky**, **Nicoll** and **Collin**. His own innovation is the use of playing cards to symbolise aspects of **centres**: e.g. the King of Diamonds represents the intellectual part of the **intellectual centre** (Burton 1995: 206). His practical innovation lies in his use of bookmarks: printed cards advertising the Gurdjieff–Ouspensky Schools that are inserted by his pupils into Work books in shops and libraries. Burton says that he did not hesitate to advertise the teaching via bookmarks that are an 'invitation to immortality' because Ouspensky met Gurdjieff through an advertisement in a newspaper (Burton 1995: 182). On one hand, Burton's teaching emphasises emotional development through an appreciation of 'C' **influences**, which are partly transmitted via the collections of antique paintings and furniture owned by Burton. On the other hand, his teaching provides an Ark against the coming destruction due to a 'Hydrogen War' or earthquake, and it teaches the way to immortality (see Burton 1995). Patterson (1998: 47–61, 116–17, 135–7) gives a case against Burton and the FOF, pointing out his deviation from Gurdjieff's teaching and recounting accusations of Burton's sexual and financial exploitation of his pupils that are derived from lawsuits against Burton by former pupils. He cites Seligman, 'Lawsuit Sheds Light...', *San Francisco Chronicle*, October 12, 1997. Patterson also mentions the physical brutalising of pupils by Burton's own teacher Alexander Francis Horn. Horn (who learned of the Fourth Way through his first wife, Carol, a student at one of the ten-month courses run by **J.G. Bennett**) taught via his Theatre of All Possibilities, which doubled as a Fourth Way School (Patterson 1998: 49; see also Horn 1987a and 1987b, which together contain seven plays). Horn writes about esoteric theatre in an introduction to his plays, which appears in both texts, that the plays 'embody many esoteric traditions', among which he includes the teachings of Gurdjieff, Ouspensky, Nicoll and Collin.

The Emin

William Shaw joined the Emin as one of the 'cults' he had decided to explore undercover in London in the mid-1990s. The Emin teaching was first presented to Shaw as The Eminent Theatre Journey. Raymond John Schertenleib, the founder of the Emin, gave his name as Raymond John Armin, and is also known as 'Leo'. Born around 1925, he grew up in London. He had been in India on National Service and become interested in Indian cosmology, making lone pilgrimages to sages in whatever time he was able to spend away from the army. Shaw recounts that Leo went bankrupt in Nottingham in 1965. The story of how the Emin was founded says that Leo's son met a woman carrying a book of Sufi tales and suggested she should meet his father. Thereafter, Leo began to be a guru to the woman and her friends. The Emin was founded in 1972, and Leo began an outpouring of mystical texts (Shaw 1994: 31). Leo's *The Night Watchman* was published in 1993 and contains autobiographical details about his life, which may be fact or fiction. Leo now lives in Florida and is distant from, but revered by, his followers. Shaw describes the Emin as having a mix of magical and esoteric ideas that, in my opinion, might have come from a variety of sources, including **Theosophy**. They have a specially adapted Tarot pack of cards, an interest in auras, and a theory that includes a Law of Two and a Law of Three (see Shaw 1994: 19–70; see also the Emin Home Page at *www.emin.org*). Although Shaw does not suggest any Emin connections to Gurdjieff teachings, I have included them here because of my own observations. In around 1996 in Kensington High Street in London I was handed a flyer about the Emin that advertised an exhibition and sale of Emin arts and crafts, being held that day at the nearby Commonwealth Institute. While I was there, they had a demonstration of dancing that was clearly derived from Gurdjieff's movements.

Trickster teachers

The following teachers – **Oscar Ichazo**, **Jan Cox**, **E.J. Gold**, **Idries Shah** and **Gary Chicoine** – were not taught by Gurdjieff or his pupils, but have taken up all or some of the following elements of Gurdjieff's teaching: the publication or oral dissemination of a mythologised early life-story that includes travels to the East and undisclosed centres of spiritual learning; cosmological and psychological theory similar to Gurdjieff's; the setting up of institutes, together with the role of 'trickster teacher', which incorporates telling 'lies' and giving 'shocks' to pupils through unpredictable behaviour, in ways that are similar to Blavatsky and Gurdjieff.

Oscar Ichazo (1931–)

The following facts about Ichazo's life are taken from Ichazo (1982) and Bleibtreu (1982), and from John Bleibtreu's introduction to Ichazo (1982) and his introductory remarks to a lecture given by Ichazo published in Bleibtreu (1982). Ichazo was born in Bolivia. In early childhood he had significant spiritual experiences. He was educated in La Paz, Bolivia, and in Lima, Peru, and at universities in La Paz. He studied law and became a journalist. At nineteen he was appointed Director of the Library of Congress in Bolivia, and also elected to Congress, though he took up neither the post nor his seat. At twenty-three he studied with a group of elderly mystics in Buenos Aires. Ichazo said the idea of these people coming together to share knowledge was 'originated somehow by Gurdjieff'. He then travelled to the Middle and Far East. He had an intuitive understanding of the enneagon or **enneagram**, which he 'found before reading Gurdjieff' (Bleibtreu 1982: 132, 144). He began to teach in 1956, and in 1968 founded the Institute of Gnosiology in Santiago, Chile. He moved to Arica and subsequently (with the Arica Institute) to New York. Bleibtreu gives the number of people who have been involved in Ichazo's work as 250,000. (See Moore 1992; Ichazo 1982; Bleibtreu 1982; Rawlinson, 1997: 331–33; Patterson, 1998: 21–46; 'The Arica Training' in Tart 1975; Lilly 1972.)

Jan Cox

Jan Cox, about whom there is a lack of biographical information, has published *The Dialogues of Gurdjieff: An Allegorical Work Adventure* (1979), which is described on his webpage as 'An astounding romp with the figure of "G" in post-war Paris as he leads a young American on adventures that redefine the concepts of reality, consciousness and human knowledge'. *The Death of Gurdjieff in the Foothills of Georgia: Secret Papers of an American Work Group* was published in 1981 and *And Kyroot Said* in 1981. The titles of these initial publications and the notes about them on Cox's webpage (*www.jancox.com*) indicate in provocative terms a kinship to, an appropriation of, or a reworking of Gurdjieff's teaching. The webpage (*Jan Cox's Industrial Strength Mysticism*) offers other publications, tapes and daily messages, and says that he has been teaching groups privately in Atlanta, Georgia, and throughout the United States for over thirty years. These talks are now available on Cable TV show *New Intelligence*. Rawlinson (1997: 220) notes that Cox uses a method akin to **E.J. Gold**, where 'the truth is wrapped up in such a way that it is the process of unwrapping it which actually reveals what it is'.

Eugene Jeffrey Gold (1941–)

E.J. Gold, known as 'EJ', has assumed the roles of 'Sufi' and 'Fourth Way' teacher via publications and teaching methodology that are directly and indirectly indebted to Gurdjieff's own publications and teaching methods. The name of Gold's institute, The Institute for the Development of the Harmonious Human Being (IDHHB), echoes Gurdjieff's Institute for the Harmonious Development of Man; his autobiographical publication *Autobiography of a Sufi* (1976/7) echoes Gurdjieff's autobiographical writing; and, like Gurdjieff, he sets himself up to be seen as a charlatan guru whose masks are easily seen through. In his *Secret Talks with Mr G* (1978), 'Mr G' is Gold rather than Gurdjieff, in spite of a photograph in which Gold impersonates Gurdjieff (see Rawlinson 1997: 271–3). A useful account of Gold's teaching methods can be found in Claudio Naranjo's apparently wry preface to Gold's *The Seven Bodies of Man* (1989). See *www.galax-yezine.org/bios/ejbio.html* for the Science Fiction Museum webpage that gives a biographical summary detailing E.J. Gold's publications, tapes and illustrations. E.J. Gold is the director of the Science Fiction Museum.

Idries Shah (1924–96)

Shah was born in Simla of an Indian father and Scottish mother. He came to England as a child. He published *Oriental Magic* (1956) and *Destination Mecca* (1956). In 1962 he convinced **J.G. Bennett** that he had been sent by Gurdjieff's secret Sufi Centre to complete Gurdjieff's teaching in the West. Bennett handed over his property and his pupils to Shah, who sold the house, Coombe Springs, and set up his own Sufi Centre in Tunbridge Wells, where he continued until his death in 1996 (see Rawlinson 1997: 524–7). Bennett's brother George gives the date of handing over the house as 1966 (see Shah 1970; G. Bennett 1990; see also Washington 1993).

Gary B. Chicoine (1942–)

In 1977, three years after the death of **J.G. Bennett**, Chicoine wrote to Bennett's pupils at Sherborne claiming to be a Sufi teacher named Risshi Dada Narayan. He arrived and took on the role of their teacher. He set up the Alexandria Foundation in 1981 and published his writings. In 1986 a number of pamphlets proclaimed him an avatar, explaining that, for this purpose, he had to appear as a charlatan. However, a month later he abandoned his role as avatar and disbanded the Foundation. He still teaches pupils in Scotland (see Rawlinson 1997: 203).

Websites

Searches on the Internet show how widely Gurdjieff's name has become known. As well as homepages for some of the teachings mentioned above, we can see how his teaching has become connected and mixed with others. One example is the Church of Conscious Harmony in Texas, which gives the two sources of their theology as the 'contemplative dimension of the Gospel' and 'the esoteric Christian tradition of transformative psychology known as "The Work", or "The Fourth Way" '. There are many other sites to explore. There are now probably more people involved in Gurdjieff's teaching outside the Foundations than within, and it seems likely that the teaching will continue to be mixed with others.

BIBLIOGRAPHY

In addition to sections on works by Gurdjieff and by his pupils, there is a general section that contains academic publications relating to Gurdjieff and a small selection of works relevant to Gurdjieff studies, in the fields of: the oral tradition, the Archaic epic, Sumerian, Greek, Turkic, the Romantic tradition, Nietzsche and Theosophy, and New Religious Movements, together with literary and analytical texts, modernist and Symbolist texts, with special reference to the literary worlds of Russia and Paris, psychology in the first quarter of the twentieth century and the occult background to Gurdjieff's teaching. The four sections are:

1   works by Gurdjieff
2   works by Gurdjieff's pupils (these are mainly autobiographical)
3   general
4   reference works

1
Works by Gurdjieff

G.I. Gurdjieff, *The Herald of Coming Good*. Edmunds, WA: Sure Fire Press, 1988; reprint 1st pub., Paris: privately published, 1933.
——, *All and Everything: Ten Books in Three Series*:

First Series: *An Objectively Impartial Criticism of the Life of Man or Beelzebub's Tales to His Grandson*. London: Routledge & Kegan Paul, 1950.
Second Series: *Meetings with Remarkable Men*. Trans. A. R. Orage, London: Picador, 1978; 1st pub., London: Routledge & Kegan Paul, 1963.
Third Series: *Life is Real Only Then, When 'I am'*. London: *Viking Arkana, 1991; 1st pub., New York: Duton* for Triangle Editions, 1975.

——, *Views from the Real World: Early Talks of Gurdjieff*. London: Routledge & Kegan Paul, 1976; 1st pub., 1973.
——, *Struggle of the Magicians*, Cape Town: Stourton Press, 1957.

2
Works by Gurdjieff's pupils

Anderson, M., *My Thirty Years War*. New York and London: Routledge & Kegan Paul, 1930.

——, *The Fiery Fountains*. London: Routledge & Kegan Paul, 1951.

——, *The Unknowable Gurdjieff*, London: Routledge & Kegan Paul, 1962.

——, *The Strange Necessity*. New York: Horizon Press, 1969.

Baggett, Holly (ed.), *I Know a Way: The Letters of Jane Heap and Florence Reynolds*. New York: New York University Press, 1999.

Bennett, J.G., *Idiots in Paris: Diaries of J.G. Bennett and Elizabeth Bennett*. Daglingworth: Coombe Springs Press, 1980; 1st pub., 1949.

——, *Witness: The Story of a Search*. London: Hodder & Stoughton, 1962.

——, *Gurdjieff: A Very Great Enigma*. Coombe Springs: Coombe Springs Press, 1963.

——, *Gurdjieff: Making a New World*. London: Turnstone, 1976; 1st pub., 1973.

——, *Enneagram Studies*. York Beach: Samuel Weiser, 1983; 1st pub., 1974.

——, *The Sevenfold Work*. Daglingworth: Coombe Springs Press, 1979; 1st pub., 1975.

——, *The Dramatic Universe*. Sherborne: Coombe Springs Press; vol.1: 1976, 1st pub. 1957; vol. 2: 1976, 1st pub. 1961; vol. 3: 1976, 1st pub. 1966; vol. 4: 1977, 1st pub. 1966.

Blake, A.G.E. (ed.) *John G. Bennett's Talks on Beelzebub's Tales*. Sherbourne: Coombe Springs Press, 1977.

Butkovsky-Hewitt, A., *With Gurdjieff in St Petersburg and Paris*. London: Routledge & Kegan Paul, 1978.

Caruso, D., *Dorothy Caruso: A Personal History*. New York: Heritage House, 1952.

de Hartmann, Thomas, *Musique pour les mouvements de G.I. Gurdjieff*. Paris: Janus, 1950.

de Hartmann, Thomas and de Hartmann, Olga, *Our Life with Mr Gurdjieff*. Revised and enlarged edn, London: Arkana, 1992; 1st pub., 1964.

de Ropp, Robert, *The Master Game: Pathways to Higher Consciousness Beyond the Drug Experience*. London: Pan, 1974.

de Salzmann, Michel, 'Gurdjieff, G.I.', *The Encyclopædia of Religion*, ed. Mircea Eliade *et al.*, 16 vols. New York: Macmillan, 1987.

Dukes, P., *The Unending Quest*. London: Cassell, 1950.

Heap, Jane, *The Notes of Jane Heap*, ed. Michael Currer-Briggs *et al.* Aurora: Two Rivers Press, 1994.

Hulme, K., *The Nun's Story*. Boston: Little Brown, 1956.

——, *Undiscovered Country: A Spiritual Adventure*. Boston and Toronto: Little Brown, 1966.

Leblanc, Georgette, *La Machine à Courage: Souvenirs*. Paris: J.B. Jarin, 1947.

Lester, John, *Jane Heap Remembered: As Remembered by Some She Taught*. Aurora: Two Rivers Press, 1988.

March, Louise, *The Gurdjieff Years: 1929–1949*. Walworth: Work Study Association, 1990.

Nicoll, Maurice, *Dream Psychology*. London: Henry Frowde/Hodder & Stoughton, 1920.

——, *The New Man: An Interpretation of Some Parables and Miracles of Christ*. Boulder and London: Shambhala, 1984; 1st pub., 1950.

——, *Living Time and the Integration of the Life*. London: Watkins, 1952.

——, *Psychological Commentaries on the Teaching of Gurdjieff and Ouspensky*, 5 vols. London: Vincent Stuart and New York: Weiser, 1952–6; repr. London and Boulder: Shambhala, 1992.

——, *The Mark: On Symbolism of Various Passages from the Bible*. London: Vincent Stuart, 1954.

Nott, C.S., *Journey Through This World*. London: Routledge & Kegan Paul, 1969.

——, *Teachings of Gurdjieff: A Pupil's Journal*. London: Arkana, 1990. 1st pub., London: Routledge & Kegan Paul 1961

Orage, A.R., *Nietzsche in Outline and Aphorism*. Edinburgh and London: T.N. Foulis, 1909.

——, *On Love: With Some Other Aphorisms and Essays*. London: Janus, 1957; repr. *On Love and Psychological Exercises*. York Beach: Samuel Weiser, 1998.

Ouspensky, P.D., *Tertium Organum: The Third Organ of Thought*, trans. Nicholas Bessaraboff and Claude Bragdon, Rochester: Manas Press, 1920.

——, *A New Model of the Universe*. London: Arkana, 1984; 1st pub., 1931.

——, *In Search of the Miraculous: Fragments of an Unknown Teaching*. London: Arkana, 1987; 1st pub., New York: Harcourt Brace and World, 1949.

——, *The Psychology of Man's Possible Evolution*. London: Hodder & Stoughton, 1951.

Peters, F., *Gurdjieff (Boyhood with Gurdjieff and Gurdjieff Remembered)*, London: Wildwood House, 1976; 1st pub., 1964, 1965.

——, *Balanced Man: A look at Gurdjieff fifty years later*. London: Wildwood House, 1978.

Popoff, Irmis B., *Gurdjieff: His Work on Myself... with Others... for the Work*. Wellingborough: The Aquarian Press, 1978; 1st pub., 1969.

——, *The Enneagrama of a Man of Unity*. Maine: Samuel Weiser, 1978.

Reyner, J.H., *Gurdjieff in Action*. London: Allen & Unwin, 1980.

——, *The Gurdjieff Inheritance*. Wellingborogh: Turnstone, 1984.

Staveley, A.L., *Memories of Gurdjieff*. Aurora: Two Rivers Press, 1978.

Taylor, Paul Beekman, *Shadows of Heaven: Gurdjieff and Toomer*. Maine: Samuel Weiser, 1998.

——, *Gurdjieff and Orage: Brothers in Elysium*. York Beach: Weiser Books, 2001.

Toomer, Margery Latimer and Jones, Robert B. (eds), *The Collected Poems of Jean Toomer*. Chapel Hill: University of North Carolina Press, 1988.

Toomer, Nathan Jean, *Cane*. New York: Boni & Liveright, 1922.

——, *Essentials*. Chicago: Lakeside Press, 1931; repr. with intro. by Rudolf Byrd, Athens: University of Georgia Press, 1993.

——, *The Wayward and the Seeking*, ed. Darwin T. Turner. Washington, D.C.: Howard University Press, 1980.

Tracol, Henri, *The Taste for the Things that are True: Essays and Talks by a Pupil of Gurdjieff*. Dorset: Element, 1994.

Walker, K., *A Study of Gurdjieff's Teaching*. London: Jonathan Cape, 1957.

Welch, Louise, *Orage with Gurdjieff in America*. Boston and London: Routledge & Kegan Paul, 1982.

Wolfe, Edwin, *Episodes with Gurdjieff*. San Fransisco: Far West Press, 1974.

Young, James Carruthers, 'An Experiment at Fontainebleau: a Personal Reminiscence', *The New Adelphi* (London) 1(1), September 1927: 26–40.

Zuber, René, *Who Are You, Monsieur Gurdjieff?*, trans. Jenny Koralek. London: Arkana, 1990; 1st pub. in French, 1977.

3
General

Almaas, A.N., *Facets of Unity: The Enneagram of Holy Ideas*. Berkeley: Diamond, 1998.

Amis, Robin, *A Different Christianity: Early Christian Esotericism and Modern Thought*. Albany: State University of New York Press, 1995.

Anonymous, *Meditations on the Tarot: A Journey into Christian Hermeticism*, trans. from the French by Robert A. Powell. Rockport and Dorset: Element, 1991.

Ashish, Sri Madhava, *Man, Son of Man*. London: Rider, 1970.

Ashish, Sri Madhava and Prem, Sri Krishna, *Man, the Measure of All Things: In the Stanzas of Dzyan*. London: Rider, 1969.

Bailey, Alice A., *A Treatise on the Seven Rays*, vol. 3, *Esoteric Astrology*. 5th edn (5 vols), London and New York: Lucis, 1982; 1st pub., 1951.

Barker, Eileen, *New Religious Movements: A Practical Introduction*. London: Her Majesty's Stationery Office, 1989.

Bely, Andrei (pseud Boris Nikolayevich, Bugayev), *Moscow, Petersburg*, 1st pub., Russia, 1916.

Bennett, George, *Needs of a New Age Community*, *www.bennettbooks.org/aboutJGB.html*, 1990.

Blake, Anthony G.E., *Intelligent Enneagram*, London: Shambhala, 1996.

Blavatsky, H.P., *The Secret Doctrine: The Synthesis of Science, Religion, and Philosophy*, 2 vols. London: Theosophical Publishing House, 1888; repr. Pasadena: Theosophical Press, 1988.

Bleibtreu, John (ed.), *Interviews with Oscar Ichazo*. New York: Arica Institute Press, 1982.

Bradbury, Malcolm and McFarlane, James (eds), *Modernism*. London: Pelican, 1976.

Breton, André, *Nadja*, trans. Richard Howard. London: Penguin, 1999; 1st pub., 1928.

—— (ed.), *Anthology of Black Humor*, trans. Mark Polizzotti. San Fransisco: City Lights, 1997.

Brook, Peter, *Threads of Time: A Memoir*. London: Methuen, 1988.

Brooks, Donald, *Number and Pattern in the Eighteenth Century*. London: Routledge & Kegan Paul, 1973.

Bucke, Richard, *Cosmic Consciousness: A Study of the Evolution of the Human Mind*. Philadelphia: Innes & Sons, 1901; repr. New York: Dutton, 1969.

Burton, Robert Earl, *Self-Remembering*. York Beach: Samuel Weiser, 1995.

Butler, Christopher, *Number Symbolism*. London: Routledge & Kegan Paul, 1970; 1st pub., 1964.

Buzzell, Keith A., *Man – A Three Brained Being*. Fryeburg: Wylanned Institute, 1996 (distributed Abintra, *abintramolalla.net*).

Byrd, Rudolph P., *Jean Toomer's Years with Gurdjieff: Portrait of an Artist 1923–1926*. Athens and London: University of Chicago Press, 1990.

Campbell, Bruce, *Ancient Wisdom Revealed: A History of the Theosophical Society*. Berkeley: University of California Press, 1980.

Campion, Nicholas, *The Great Year: Astrology, Millenarianism and History in the Western Tradition*. London: Arkana, 1994.

Carlson, Maria, *No Religion Higher Than Truth: A History of the Theosophical Movement in Russia, 1875–1922*. Princeton: Princeton University Press, 1993.

Clairborne, Robert, *The Roots of English: A Reader's Handbook of Word Origins*. New York: Random House, 1989.

Caracciolo, Peter L. (ed.), *The Arabian Nights in English Literature*. London: Macmillan, 1988.

Carswell, John, *Lives and Letters: A.R. Orage, Beatrice Hastings, Katherine Mansfield, John Middleton Murry, S.S. Koteliansky 1906–1957*. London and Boston: Faber & Faber, 1978.

Challenger, Anna, *An Introduction to Gurdjieff's Beelzebub: A Modern Sufi Teaching Tale*. Ph.D. thesis, Kent State University, 1990.

Collin, Rodney, *The Theory of Eternal Life*. Cape Town: Staunton Press, 1950.

——, *The Theory of Celestial Influence: Man, the Universe, and Cosmic Mystery*. London: Arkana 1993, 1st pub., London: Vincent Stuart, 1954a.

——, *The Christian Mystery*. Tlalpam: Ediciones Sol, 1954b.

——, *The Theory of Conscious Harmony: From Letters of Rodney Collin*. London: Vincent Stuart, 1958.

Collin-Smith, Janet (ed.), *The Mirror of Light: From the Notebooks of Rodney Collin*. London: Watkins Publishing House, 1959; repr. 1979.

Collin-Smith, Joyce, *Call No Man Master*. Bath: Gateway Books, 1988.

Cooper, Susan, *J.B. Priestley: Portrait of an Author*. London: Heinemann, 1970.

Cox, Jan, *The Death of Gurdjieff in the Foothills of Georgia: Secret Papers of an American Work Group*. Stone Mountain, 1981.

Crabtree, Adam, *From Mesmer to Freud: Magnetic Sleep and the Roots of Psychological Healing*. New Haven and London: Yale University Press, 1993.

Curry, Patrick, *A Confusion of Prophets: Victorian and Edwardian Astrology*. London: Collins & Brown, 1992.

De Mille, Richard (ed.), *The Don Juan Papers: Further Castaneda Controversies*. Santa Barbara: Ross-Erickson, 1980.

de Ropp, Robert, *Warrior's Way*. London: Allen & Unwin, 1980.

Dodd, C.H., *Parables of the Kingdom*. London: Nisbet, 1936.

Dostoyevsky, Fyodor, *Notes from the Underground*, trans. Constance Garnett. New York: Dover, 1992; 1st pub., 1864.

——, *The Brothers Karamazov*, trans. David McDuff. London: Penguin, 1993; 1st pub., 1880.

Durkheim, Emile, *The Elementary Forms of the Religious Life*, trans. Rodney Needham. Chicago: Chicago University Press, 1963.

Eade, J.C., *The Forgotten Sky*, Oxford: Clarendon Press, 1984.

Eliot, T.S., *The Wasteland*, New York: Boni & Liveright, 1922.

Ellenberger, Henri F., *The History of the Unconscious: The History and Evolution of Dynamic Psychiatry*. London: Allen Lane/Penguin Press, 1970.

Ellwood, Robert J., *Religions and Spiritual Groups in Modern America*. Englewood Cliffs: Prentice-Hall, 1973.

——, *Alternative Altars*. Chicago: University of Chicago Press, 1979.

Eliade, Mircea, *The Myth of the Eternal Return: or Cosmos and History*, trans. Willard R. Task. London: Arkana, 1989; 1st pub., 1954.

Erdener, Yildiray, *The Song Contests of Turkish Minstrels: Improvised Poetry Sung to TraditionalMusic*. New York and London: Garland, 1995.

Faivre, Antoine, *Access to Western Esotericism*. Albany: State University of New York Press, 1994.

Faivre, Antoine and Needleman, Jacob (eds), *Modern Esoteric Spirituality*. New York: Crossroads Press, 1992.

Fedorov, Nikolai Fedorovich, *What Was Man Created For? The Philosophy of the Common Task*, trans. and abridged Elisabeth Koutaisoff and Marilyn Minto. London: Honeyglen, 1990; 1st pub. 1906, 1913.

Foley, John Miles, *Immanent Art: From Structure to Meaning in Traditional Oral Epic*. Bloomington and Indianapolis: Indiana University Press, 1991.

Fowler, A., *Spencer and the Numbers of Time*. London: Routledge & Kegan Paul, 1964.

Frazer, James George, *The Golden Bough: A Study in Magic and Religion*, ed. Robert Frazer. London: Oxford University Press, 1994; 1st pub., 1890–1915.

Freud, Sigmund, *The Interpretation of Dreams*, trans. A.A. Brill. New York, 1913; 1st pub., 1900.

——, 'Moses and Monotheism: Three Essays', *The Origins of Religion*, vol. 13, ed. and trans. James Strachey. London: Penguin, 1990; 1st pub. in German, 1939.

Fremantle, Christopher, *On Attention*, ed. Lillian Firestone Boal. Denville: Inductions Press, 1993.

Frye, Northrop, *The Great Code: The Bible and Literature*. London: Arkana, 1983.

Gaskin, John (ed.), *The Epicurean Philosophers*, trans. C. Bailey, R.D. Hicks and J.C.A. Gaskin, London: Everyman, 1995.

George, James, *Asking for the Earth: Waking Up to the Spiritual/Ecological Crisis*, Shaftesbury: Element, 1995.

Gilbert, R.A., *Revelations of the Golden Dawn: The Rise and Fall of a Magical Order*. London: Quantum, 1997.

Ginsburg, Seymour B., *In Search of the Unitive Vision: Letters of Sri Madhava Ashish to an American Businessman, 1978–1997*. Boca Raton: New Paradigm Books, 2001.

Gold, E.J., *The Seven Bodies of Man*, preface by Claudio Naranja. Nevada City: Gateways, *c.*1989.

Goodwin, Barbara, *Using Political Ideas*. Chichester: John Wiley & Sons, 1991; 1st pub., 1982.

Goodwyn, Jocelyn, *The Theosophical Enlightenment*. New York: New York State University Press, 1994.

Hanegraf, Walter J., *New Age Religion and Western Culture: Esotericism in the Mirror of Secular Thought*. Utrecht: Utrecht University Press, 1995.

Harrison, Jane Ellen, *Themis: A Study of the Social Origins of Greek Religion*. London: Merlin Press, 1977; 1st pub., 1912.

Hastings, B., *The Old 'New Age': Orage and Others*. London: Blue Moon Press, 1936.

Heelas, Paul, *The New Age Movement: The Celebration of the Self and the Sacralization of Modernity*. Massachusetts: Blackwell, 1996.

Heidegger, Martin, *Being and Time*, trans. Joan Stambaugh. Albany: State University of New York Press, 1996; 1st pub., 1927.

Hinnells, John R. (ed.), *New Penguin Handbook of Living Religion*, 2nd edn. London: Penguin, 1998.

Hopper, V.F., *Medieval Number Symbolism: Its Sources, Meaning and Influence on Thought and Expression*. New York: Columbia University Press, 1938.

Horn, Alexander Francis, *In Search of the Solar Hero*. Dorset: Element, 1987a.

——, *Ponderings of a Citizen of the Milky Way*. Dorset: Element, 1987b.

Hounam, P. and Hogg, A., *Secret Cult*. Tring: Lion Books, 1985.

Husserl, Edmund, *The Idea of Phenomenology*, trans. Lee Hardy. Dordrecht and London: Kluwer Academic, 1999; 1st pub., 1910.

Ichazo, Oscar, *Between Metaphysical and Protoanalysis: A Theory for Analyzing the Human Psyche*. New York: Arica Institute Press, 1982.

James, William, *The Varieties of Religious Experience: A Study in Human Nature*. London: Collins, 1985; 1st pub., 1929.

Jastrow, Morris and Clay, Albert T., *An Old Babylonian Version of the Gilgamesh Epic*. New Haven: Yale University Press, 1920. Reprint 1980.

Johnson, K. Paul, *Madame Blavatsky: The 'Veiled Years' – New light from Gurdjieff or Sufism?* London: Theosophical History Centre, 1987.

——, *In Search of the Masters: Behind the Occult Myth*. South Boston: n.p., 1990.

——, *The Masters Revealed: Madame Blavatsky and the Myth of the Great White Lodge*. New York: State University of New York Press, 1994.

——, *Initiates of Theosophical Masters*. New York State: University of New York, 1995.

Jonas, H., *The Gnostic Religion*. Boston: Beacon Press, 1959.

Joyce, James, *Ulysses*, Shakespeare & Co Paris; 1922, part pub. 1919, 1920.

——, *Finnegans Wake*, London: Faber, New York: Viking, 1939.

Jung, Carl Gustav, *Psychology of the Unconscious*. London: Kegan Paul, 1916.

Kelsey, Morton T., *God, Dreams and Revelation: A Christian Interpretation of Dreams*. Minneapolis: Augsburg, 1991; 1st pub., 1973.

Kherdian, David, *On a Spaceship with Beelzebub: By a Grandson of Gurdjieff*. Rochester: Inner Traditions, 1998.

King, C. Daly, *The Butterfly: A Symbol of Conscious Evolution*. New York: Bridge Press, 1996; 1st pub., *Beyond Behaviorism: The Future of Psychology*, New York: Grant, 1927.

Kirk, G.S., *The Nature of Greek Myths*. London: Pelican, 1974.

Kierkegaard, Soren, *Point of View for My Work as an Author*, trans. Walter Lowrie. New York: Harper & Row, 1962; 1st pub. in English, 1939.

Krell, David Farrell (ed.), *'Being And Time' (1927) to 'The Task Of Thinking' (1964): Martin Heidegger*. London: Routledge, 1993.

—— (ed.), *Basic Writings*. New York: Harper & Row, 1997.

Kyle, Richard, *The New Age Movement in American Culture*. Lanhan, New York and London: University Press of America, 1995.

LaCocque, André and Ricoeur, Paul, *Thinking Biblically: Exegetical and Hermeneutical Studies*, trans. David Pellauer. Chicago and London: University of Chicago Press, 1999.

Lautréamont, Comte de (pseud. of Isidore Ducasse), *Maldoror*, trans. Alexis Lykiard. London: Allison & Busby, 1970; 1st pub., *Les Chants de Maldoror*, Paris: n.p., 1869.

Lefort, Rafael, *The Teachers of Gurdjieff*. London: Victor Gollancz, 1976; 1st pub., 1966.

Leo (pseud. of Raymond John Schertenleib, a.k.a. Raymond John Armin), *The Night Watchman*. London: Gemstone Press, 1993.

Leo, Alan (pseud. of Frederick William Allan), *Astrology for All*, 2nd edn, 7 vols. Vol. 7, London: *Modern Astrology*, 1913; repr. *Esoteric Astrology*. Vermont: Destiny, 1989.

Levine, Janet, *The Enneagram Intelligences: Understanding Personality for Effective Teaching and Learning*. Westport: Bergin & Garvey, 1999.

Lilly, John C., *The Centre of the Cyclone: An Autobiography of Inner Space*. New York: Bantam, 1972.

Lloyd-Jones, Hugh, *Myths of the Zodiac*. London: Duckworth, 1978.

Lovejoy, Arthur Ockenden, *The Great Chain of Being: A Study in the History of the Idea* (William James Lectures, Harvard University, 1933). Cambridge: Harvard University Press, 1936.

Luce, J.V., *The End of Atlantis*. Athens: Efstathiadis Group, 1982; 1st pub., 1969.

Macgregor, Mathers S.L. *et al.*, *Astral Projection, Ritual Magical Alchemy, Golden Dawn Material*, ed. Francis King *et al.*, additional material R.A. Gilbert. Wellingborough: Aquarian, 1987.

MacLaren, Leon, *The Nature of Society and Other Essays*. London: London School of Economic Science, 1997.

MacLean, Paul D., *The Triune Brain in Evolution*. New York: Plenum Press, 1990.

Martin, Wallace, *The New Age Under Orage: Chaptrs in English Cultural History*. Manchester, Manchester University Press, 1967.

Massey, G., *The Natural Genesis*. London: Williams & Norgate, 1883.

Materer, Timothy, *Modernist Alchemy: Poetry and the Occult*. Ithaca and London: Cornell University Press, 1995.

May, Robert M., *Cosmic Consciousness Revisited: The Modern Origins and Development of a Western Spiritual Psychology*. Rockport: Element, 1993.

McIntosh, Christopher, *Eliphas Levi and the French Occult Revival*. London: Rider, 1975.

Metz, Barbara and Burchill, John, *The Enneagram and Prayer*. Denville: Dimension, 1987.

Meyer, Marvin (trans.), *Gospel of Thomas*. San Francisco: Harper, 1992.

Miller, Timothy (ed.), *When Prophets Die: The Postcharismatic Fate of New Religious Movements*. New York: New York State University Press, 1991.

Moore, James, *Gurdjieff and Mansfield*. London: Routledge and Kegan Paul, 1980.

——, *Gurdjieff: The Anatomy of a Myth*. London: Element, 1991.

——, 'Neo-Sufism: The Case of Idries Shah', *Religion Today* 3(3), n.d.: 4–8.

——, 'The Enneagram: a Developmental Study', *Religion Today* 5(3), n.d.: 1–5.

——, 'New Lamps for Old: the Enneagram Debacle', *Religion Today* 8(1), 1992: 8–12.

——, 'Moveable Feasts: the Gurdjieff Work', *Religion Today* 9(2), 1994: 11–15.

Mouravieff, Boris, *Gnosis Book 1: The Exoteric Circle*, trans. S.A. Wissa, ed. Robin Amis. East Sussex: Agora (for Praxis Institute Press), 1989.

——, *Gnosis Book 2: The Mesoteric Circle*, trans. S.A. Wissa, Manek d'Oncieu and Robin Amis. Newbury, MA, and East Sussex: Praxis Institute Press, 1992.

——, *Gnosis Book 3: The Esoteric Circle*, trans. Manek d'Oncieu, E. Witkin and S. Witkin, ed. Robin Amis. Newbury, MA, and East Sussex: Praxis Institute Press, 1993.

Naranjo, Claudio, *The One Quest*. London: Wildwood House, 1974.

Needleman, Jacob, *The New Religions*. New York: Doubleday, 1970; rev. edn with new preface, New York: Dutton, 1977.

——, *The Indestructible Question: Essays on Nature, Spirit and the Human Paradox*. London: Arkana, 1994; 1st pub. in French, 1992.

Neumann, Erich, *The Great Mother: An Analysis of the Archetype*, trans. Ralph Manheim. Bollinger Series XLVII, Princeton: Princeton University Press, 1955.

Nicholls, Peter, *Modernisms: A Literary Guide*. Basingstoke: Macmillan, 1995.

Nietzsche, Friedrich, *Thus Spake Zarathustra*, trans. Thomas Common. Ware: Wordsworth Editions, 1997; written 1883–5.

——, *Beyond Good and Evil: Prelude to a Philosophy of the Future*, trans. and ed. Marion Faber. Oxford: Oxford University Press, 1998; 1st pub., 1886.

North, J.D., *Chaucer's Universe*. Oxford: Clarendon, 1988.

Notopolous, J.A.B., 'Parataxis in Homer: A New Approach to Homeric Literary Criticism', *The Proceedings and Transactions of the American Philological Association*, vol. LXXX. Pennsylvania and Oxford: Lancaster Press and Blackwell, 1949.

Nurbakhsh, Javad, *Dogs: From the Sufi Point of View*. London and New York: Khaniqahi-Nimatullahi, 1989.

Nyanaponika Thera, *The Heart of Buddhist Meditation*. London: Rider, 1983; 1st pub., 1962.

Ong, Walter J., *Orality and Literacy: The Technologizing of the Word*. London and New York: Methuen, 1982.

Osborn, Arthur (ed.), *The Teachings of Bhagavan Ramana Maharshi*. London: Rider, 1971; 1st pub., 1962.

Palmer, Helen, *The Enneagram: Understanding Yourself and the Others in Your Life*. New York: HarperCollins, 1995.

Patterson, William Patrick, *Eating the 'I': An Account of the Fourth Way – the Way of Transformation in Ordinary Life*. Fairfax: Arete Communications, 1992.

——, *Struggle of the Magicians: Why Uspenskii left Gurdjieff*. Fairfax: Arete Communications, 1996.

——, *Taking with the Left Hand: The Enneagram Craze, People of the Bookmark, and the Mouravieff 'Phenomenon'*. Fairfax: Arete Communications, 1998.

——, *Ladies of the Rope*. Fairfax: Arete Communications, 1999.

——, *Voices in the Dark*. Fairfax: Arete Communications, 2000.

Penglase, C., *Parallels and Influences in the Homeric Hymns of Hesiod: Greek Myth and Mesopotamia*. London: Routledge, 1994.

Perry, Whitnall N., *Gurdjieff in the Light of Tradition*. Middlesex: Perennial Books, 1978.

Pogson, Beryl, *Maurice Nicoll: A Portrait*. New York: Fourth Way Books, 1987; 1st pub., 1961.

Quirolo, Lynn, 'The Enneagram in the Gospel of St John', *Stopinder: A Gurdjieff Journal for Our Time* 6 (Fall 2001): 73–82.

Ramana Maharishi, *The Teachings of Bhagavan Ramana Maharishi*. ed. Arthur Osborn. London: Rider, 1971, 1st pub., 1962.

Raschke, Carl A., *The Interruption of Eternity: Modern Gnosticism and the Origins of the New Religious Consciousness*. Chicago: Nelson-Hall, 1980.

Ravindra, Ravi, *Heart Without Measure: Work with Madame de Salzmann*. Halifax: Shaila, 1999.

Rawlinson, Andrew, *The Book of Enlightened Masters*. Chicago: Open Court, 1997.

Reich, Wilhelm, *The Function of the Orgasm: Sex-Economic Problems of Biological Energy*, trans. Vincent R. Carfagno. London: Souvenir, 1983.

Reickl, Karl, *Turkic Oral Epic Poetry: Traditions, Forms, Poetic Structures*. New York and London: Garland, 1992.

Reyner, J.H., *Gurdjieff in Action*. London: George Allen & Unwin, 1980.

Riso, Don Richard, *Personality Types: Using the Enneagram for Self Discovery*. Boston: Houghton Mifflin, 1987; repr. 1995.

Roberts, Carl Bechofer, *In Deniken's Russia and the Caucasus, 1919–1920: Being the Record of a Journey to South Russia, the Crimea, Armenia, Georgia and Baku in 1919 and 1920*. London: Collins, 1921.

Rosenthal, Bernice Glatzer (ed.), *The Occult in Russian and Soviet Culture.* Ithaca and London: Cornell University Press, 1997.

Roszak, Theodore, *The Making of a Counter Culture.* New York: Doubleday, 1969.

——, *Unfinished Animal: The Aquarian Frontier and the Evolution of Consciousness.* New York: Harper and Row, 1975.

Rudhyar, Dane, *The Astrology of Personality: A Re-Formulation of Astrological Concepts and Ideals in Terms of Contemporary Psychology and Philosophy.* The Hague: Servire, 1963; 1st pub., Santa Fe: Aurora Press, 1936.

Rudolph, Kurt, *Gnosis: The Nature and History of an Ancient Religion,* trans. Robert McLaghlan Wilson. Edinburgh: T. & T. Clark, 1983; 1st pub. in German, 1977.

Russell, Bertrand, *History of Western Philosophy,* 2nd edn. London: Routledge, 1996; 1st pub., 1945.

Savary, Louis M. and Berne, Patricia H., *Kything: The Art of Spiritual Presence.* Mahwah: Paulist Press, 1988.

Schein, S.L., *The Mortal Hero: An Introduction to Homer's Iliad.* California: University of California Press, 1985.

Schumacher, E.F., *A Guide for the Perplexed.* New York: Harper and Row, 1978.

Scott, Thomas L., Friedman, Melvin J. and Breyer, Jackson R. (eds), *Pound/The Little Review: The letters of Ezra Pound to Margaret Anderson.* New York: New Directions, 1988.

Scullion, John, 'Gurdjieff, Astrology and Beelzebub's Tales: An Interview with Sophia Wellbeloved', *Stopinder: A Gurdjieff Journal for Our Time* 5 (Summer 2001): 45–64.

Seabrook, William, *Witchcraft: Its Power in the World Today.* New York: Harcourt Brace, 1940.

Sepharial (pseud. for Walter Gorn Old), *The New Manual of Astrology in Four Books: Treating of the Language of the Heavens, Reading of the Horoscope, the Measure of Time, and of Hindu Astrology.* London: W. Foulsham & Co., 1912; 1st pub., 1898.

Shah, Idries, *Destination Magic.* London: Rider, 1956.

——, *Special Properties in the Study of Sufi Ideas.* Tunbridge Wells: Society for the Understanding of the Foundation of Ideas, 1966.

——, *The Way of a Sufi.* New York: Dutton, 1970.

Shaw, William, *Spying in Guru Land.* London Fourth Estate, 1994.

Smith, Russell A., *Gurdjieff: Cosmic Secrets.* Sanger: The Dog, 1993.

Speeth, Kathleen Riordan, *The Gurdjieff Work.* London: Turnstone Press, 1977.

Steele, Tom, *Alfred Orage and the Leeds Art Club: 1893–1923.* Aldershot: Scolar, 1990.

Steiner, Rudolph, *The Sun Mystery in the Course of Human History: The Palladium,* trans. D.S. Osmond. London: Rudolph Steiner Publishing, 1955.

Surrette, Leon, *The Birth of Modernism: Ezra Pound, T.S. Eliot, W.B. Yeats, and the Occult.* Montreal, Kingston, London and Buffalo: McGill-Queens University Press, 1993.

Tarnas, Richard, *The Passion of the Western Mind: Understanding the Ideas that have Shaped our World View.* London: Pimlico, 1991.

Tart, Charles T. (ed.), *Transpersonal Psychologies.* New York: Harper and Row, 1975.

——, *Waking Up: Overcoming the Obstacles to Human Potential.* Boston: Shambhala, 1986.

Taylor, Gary, *Orage and the New Age.* Sheffield: Sheffield University Press, 2000.

Thalmann, William G., *Conventions of Form and Thought in Early Greek Epic Poetry.* London and Baltimore: Johns Hopkins University Press, 1984.

Thring, M.W., *Quotations from G.I. Gurdjieff's Teaching: A Personal Companion.* Wiltshire: Luzac Oriental, 1998.

Thompson, Diane Oenning, *The Brothers Karamazov and the Poetics of Memory.* Cambridge and New York: Cambridge University Press, 1991.

Thompson, William, J.G. *Bennett's Interpretations of the Teachings of G.I. Gurdjieff: A Study of Transmission in the Fourth Way.* Ph.D. thesis, Lancaster University, 1995.

Tigay, Jeffrey H., *The Evolution of the Gilgamesh Epic.* Philadelphia: University of Pennsylvania Press, 1982.

Valdes, M.J. (ed.), *A Ricoeur Reader: Reflection and Imagination.* London: Harvester Wheatsheaf, 1991.

Van der Waerden, Bartel, 'Babylonian Astronomy II: The Thirty-Six Stars', *Journal of Near Eastern Studies* 3(1), January 1949: 6–26.

Vivekananda, Swami, *The Yogas and Other Works*, ed. Swami Nikhilananda. New York: Ramakrishna-Vivekananda Centre, 1953.

Vollmar, Klausbernd, *The Secret of Enneagrams: Mapping the Personality.* Shaftesbury: Element, 1997.

Waldberg, Michel, *Gurdjieff: An Approach to His Ideas*, trans. Steve Cox. London: Arkana, 1989; 1st pub. in French, 1973.

Wallace Budge, E.A., *Osiris and the Egyptian Resurrection*, 2 vols. New York: Dover, 1973; 1st pub., 1911.

Walpola, Rahula, *What the Buddha Taught.* Bedford: Gordon Fraser Gallery, 1967.

Washington, Peter, *Madame Blavatsky's Baboon: Theosophy and the Emergence of the Western Guru.* London: Secker & Warburg, 1993.

Waterfield, Robin, *Rene Guenon and the Future of the West. The Life and Writings of a 20th-Century Metaphysician.* Place of publication unknown: Crucible, 1987.

Watson, John, *Behavior: An Introduction to Comparative Psychology.* New York: H. Holt, 1914.

Webb, James, *The Occult Underground.* London: Open Court, 1971a.

——, *The Flight from Reason.* London: Macdonald, 1971b.

——, *The Occult Establishment.* La Salle: Open Court, 1976.

——, *The Harmonious Circle: The Lives and Work of G.I. Gurdjieff, P.D. Ouspensky, and Their Followers.* London: Thames & Hudson, 1980.

Weigel, Valentin, *Astrology Theologized: The Spiritual Hermeneutics of Astrology and Holy Writ, Being a Treatise upon the Art of Ruling Them by the Law of Grace.* Cornhill: George Whittingdon, 1649; repr. (ed. Anna Kingsford) London: G. Ridway, 1886.

Welburn, Andrew, *Gnosis, the Mysteries and Christianity: An Anthology of Essene, Gnostic and Christian Writings.* Edinburgh: Floris, 1994.

—— (ed.), *Rudolph Steiner's Writings On Spiritual Initiation.* Edinburgh: Floris, 1997.

—— (ed.), *A Vision for the Millennium: Modern Spirituality and Cultural Renewal: An Introduction to the Work of Rudolf Steiner* (authorized trans. of previously pub. material). London: Rudolf Steiner Press, 1999.

Wellbeloved, Sophia, 'G.I. Gurdjieff: Some References to Love', *Journal of Contemporary Religion* 13(3), 1998: 321–2.

——, Review of Patterson 1998, *Journal of Contemporary Religion* 14(2), 1999: 324–6.

——, *Gurdjieff, Astrology and Beelzebub's Tales: An Analysis in Terms of Astrological Correspondences*. Aurora: Abintra, 2001a.

——, *Changes in G.I. Gurdjieff's Teaching 'The Work'*, paper delivered at the Cesnur/Inform Conference in London. *http://www.cesnur.org/2001/london/wellbeloved.htm*, 2001b.

Wessinger, Catherine Lowman, *Annie Besant and Progressive Messianism (1847–1933)*. Lewiston and Queenston: Edwin Mellen Press, 1988.

West, John Anthony, *The Case for Astrology*. London: Viking Arkana, 1991; 1st pub., 1970.

West, M.L. (ed. and trans.), *Theogony, and Works and Days: Hesiod*. Oxford: Oxford University Press, 1988.

Williams, Virginia Parrott, *Surrealism, Quantum Philosophy and World War I*. New York and London: Garland, 1987.

Wittgenstein, Ludwig, *Tractatus Logico-Philosophicus*, trans. C.K. Ogden. London: Routledge, 1995; 1st pub., Routledge & Kegan Paul, 1922.

Wood, Florence and Wood, Kenneth, *Homer's Secret Iliad: The Epic of the Night Sky Decoded*. London: John Murray, 1999.

Woodson, Jon, *To Make a New Race: Gurdjieff, Toomer, and the Harlem Renaissance*. Jackson: University of Mississippi Press, 1999.

Woronzoff, Alexander, *Andrej Belyj's 'Petersburg', James Joyce's 'Ulysses', and the Symbolist Movement*, American University Studies III, Comparative Literature vol. 1. Berne and Frankfurt: Peter Lang, 1982.

Yates, Frances, *Giordano Bruno and the Hermetic Tradition*. London: Routledge & Kegan Paul, 1964.

Yeats, William Butler, *A Vision*. Revsd edn., London: Macmillan 1937, 1st pub., privately 1925.

Young, George M., Jr, *Nikolai F. Fedorov: An Introduction*. Belmont: Norlaand, 1979.

Zablocki, Benjamin, *The Blacklisting of a Concept: The Strange History of the Brainwashing Conjecture in the Sociology of Religion*. *http://www.sevenbridgespress.com/nova/zablocki.html*, 1998.

Zablocki, Benjamin and Robbins, Thomas (eds), *Misunderstanding Cults: Searching for Objectivity in a Controversial Field*. Toronto: University of Toronto Press, 2001.

4
Reference works

Anonymous, *Guide and Index to Gurdjieff's 'All and Everything: Beelzebub's Tales to His Grandson'*. Toronto: Traditional Studies Press, 1973.

Cooper, J.C., *An Illustrated Encyclopaedia of Traditional Symbols*. London: Thames & Hudson, 1981.

Drabble, Margaret (ed.), *The Oxford Companion to English Literature*. 5th (rev.) edn, Oxford: Oxford University Press, 1995.

Driscoll, Walter T. (ed.), *Gurdjieff: An Annotated Bibliography*. New York: Garland, 1985.

Eliade, Mircea *et al.* (eds), *The Encyclopædia of Religion*, 16 vols. New York: Macmillan, 1987.

Gettings, Fred, *Arkana Dictionary of Astrology*. Revsd. ed., London: Arkana, 1990.

——, *The Secret Zodiac: The Hidden Art in Mediæval Astrology.* London and New York: RKP, 1987.

Glyn, D., *A Short History of Archæology.* London: Thames & Hudson, 1981.

Hastings, James *et al.* (eds), *The Encyclopedia of Religion and Ethics*, 12 vols. New York: Charles Scriber, 1921.

North, John, *The Fontana History of Astronomy and Cosmology.* London: Fontana, 1994.

NAME INDEX